I0138716

MARCION AND LUKE-ACTS

MARCION AND LUKE-ACTS

A Defining Struggle

JOSEPH B. TYSON

University of South Carolina Press

© 2006 University of South Carolina

Published by the University of South Carolina Press
Columbia, South Carolina 29208

www.sc.edu/uscpress

Manufactured in the United States of America

21 20 19 18 17 16 15 14   10 9 8 7 6 5 4 3 2

Library of Congress Cataloging-in-Publication Data
Tyson, Joseph B.
    Marcion and Luke Acts : a defining struggle / Joseph B. Tyson.
       p. cm.
    Includes bibliographical references and indexes.
    ISBN-13: 978-1-57003-650-7 (cloth : alk. paper)
    ISBN-10: 1-57003-650-0 (cloth : alk. paper)
       1. Bible. N.T. Luke—Criticism, interpretation, etc. 2. Bible. N.T.
    Acts—Criticism, interpretation, etc. 3. Marcion, of Sinope, 2nd cent.
    1. Title
    BS2589.T98 2006
    226.4'006—dc22
    2006012413

Dedicated to the memory of John Knox (1900–1990),
my esteemed teacher, whose ground-breaking work
inspired this study

CONTENTS

PREFACE

The present volume is intended to be a contribution to the reopening of issues revolving around the date and context of the composition of the Gospel of Luke and of the Acts of the Apostles. Debates about the dating of these New Testament texts flourished during the nineteenth and early twentieth centuries but subsided thereafter. Scholarship associated with the Tübingen School and Ferdinand Christian Baur favored a date for Acts in the mid-second century, but rival hypotheses led not only to the diminished influence of Baur and his associates but also to theories about Luke-Acts that tended toward an earlier date for their composition. For most of the twentieth century most critical scholars have agreed that these texts were written after the destruction of Jerusalem in 70 C.E. but before the end of the first century. At the same time there has been a long tradition among conservative scholars that favored an even earlier date for the composition of Luke-Acts, that is, between 60 and 70 C.E.

A study of major commentaries on Luke and Acts published during the last few decades shows that the consensus dating of these texts holds among most critical scholars and that there is little interest in either questioning or defending it, except among those who would favor a date in the sixties. Nevertheless the question has been reopened by scholars such as Richard I. Pervo, who vigorously argues that Acts was composed in the first quarter of the second century.[1]

The present work builds on that of Pervo but goes beyond it by exploring the probable context within which both canonical Luke and Acts were written. It proposes that both Acts and the final edition of the Gospel of Luke were published at the time when Marcion of Pontus was beginning to proclaim his version of the Christian gospel, that is, ca. 120–125 C.E. The author of these documents no doubt had a number of purposes in mind when he composed these texts but prominent among them was the intent to provide the church with certain writings that would serve in its fight against Marcionite Christianity. The emergence of Marcionite Christianity in Asia and Italy in the early second century presented a challenge to other Christians, a challenge that was partially met by the author of Luke-Acts. The controversy with Marcion was, in effect, a defining struggle, a struggle over the very meaning of the Christian message.

This book makes a cumulative argument in the sense that, after the first, each chapter depends on the preceding chapters to build the case. Chapter 1 focuses attention on the date of the Acts of the Apostles. It surveys the history of scholarship on the date of Acts, starting with Baur in the early nineteenth century, and shows that Acts has been dated from about 60 to 150 C.E., with three dates being most prominently featured: an early, an intermediate, and a late date. Arguments for and against each of these are examined, and particular attention is given to recent studies that favor a late date, that is, 120–125 C.E. I then ask: If we should accept a late date for Acts, what might have been the context within which it was composed? Subsequent chapters claim that a major part of the context was the emergence of Marcionite Christianity.

Chapter 2 is devoted to a study of Marcion and Marcionite Christianity. Attention is given to what can be known about Marcion's life, times, and teachings. A great deal of caution is necessary at this point since all of our information is ultimately based on the writings of his opponents, most notably Irenaeus, Tertullian, and Epiphanius, all of whom wrote long after the time of Marcion himself. Although these texts are not fully reliable in reporting Marcion's teachings, they nevertheless provide us with a set of theological propositions that have an impressive coherence. Marcion's theology apparently was based on his interpretation of the letters of Paul, and he stressed the dichotomy between a God of law and a God of mercy. Marcion saw a total separation between the gospel of Jesus and all that went before it, most importantly the Scriptures of the Hebrew Bible. The coming of Jesus, for him, was unanticipated, and the Hebrew prophets were totally irrelevant for the Christian gospel. The early Christian fathers also tell us that Marcion had a text of the letters of Paul, whom he regarded as the only apostle, and a text he called "the Gospel." The chapter considers certain attempts to reconstruct Marcion's gospel, most notably that of Adolf von Harnack.

Chapter 3 is a study of the composition of Acts. It shows the ways in which its author attempted to meet the Marcionite challenge. For one thing the author of Acts characterized Paul as being in line with the Jerusalem apostles rather than acting as the sole apostle that Marcion supposed. He stressed the parallelism of Peter and Paul and portrayed Paul as a loyal Jew and devout Pharisee. He included speeches of Paul that link Christian beliefs and practices with the Hebrew Bible. In opposition to Marcionite Christianity the author of Acts claims that the Jesus movement was prepared for by the Hebrew prophets, and he claims that it is the fulfillment of prophecy and the Bible. In the text of Acts the credible characters explain the emergence of Gentile Christianity not as evidence of some non-Jewish character within the gospel but as rooted in the Hebrew Scriptures. Much that we find in Acts is directed against the contentions of Marcion and his followers.

Chapter 4 is a study of the composition of canonical Luke. It contends that Marcion did not alter the church's edition of the Third Gospel, as the church fathers claimed, but that the canonical edition of Luke was the result of the redaction of an earlier text, a text probably also used by Marcion as the basis for his own gospel. The author of canonical Luke, who was also the author of Acts, made use of the earlier text and added substantial material drawn from his Sondergut. This material includes the preface and infancy narratives of Luke 1–2 and, probably, the postresurrection appearances of Jesus in Luke 24. In my judgment these and other materials were added ca. 120–25 C.E., especially to serve the church in answering the Marcionite challenge.

Chapter 5 is an attempt to assess the literary, theological, and historical achievements of the author of Acts and canonical Luke. The chapter concludes with an examination of the effect on Christian-Jewish relations of the defeat of Marcion.

Many readers will recognize that the views expressed here reflect those of John Knox in a monograph he published in 1942.[2] Professor Knox was one of my mentors in my days at Union Theological Seminary, and it is to his memory that this book is dedicated. In my judgment Knox's book has not received the attention it deserves. I hope that my contribution will lead to a more sustained discussion of his views. I would not expect all readers to agree with his (or my) contentions, but renewed debates over dates and contexts should lead to a better understanding of the history of early Christianity and of Luke-Acts in particular.

Although this book has been written as a contribution to critical scholarship, I have attempted to avoid technical terminology as much as possible. Two terms, however, may need some words of explanation. I have generally used the terms *proto-orthodox* and *proto-orthodoxy* to designate theological positions taken in the second century that ultimately became widely accepted as "orthodox" Christian viewpoints. Theologies varied considerably in the second century, and at the time it was unclear which would become victorious. It is only in hindsight that we can talk about an emerging "orthodoxy." Much the same may be said about the terms *heresy* and *heretic*. In hindsight Marcion may be regarded as a heretic and his theology as heretical, but in the early second century the situation was much less clear. In addition it is probable that the Marcionites thought of their opponents as "heretics." I have, therefore, avoided the use of the terms *orthodox* and *heretic* except when they are used in quotations and allusions by ancient writers or when their use by these writers is clear.

In chapter 1 I have incorporated revisions of some material that originally appeared in my articles "The Legacy of F. C. Baur and Recent Studies of Acts," *Forum* n.s. 4 (2001): 125–44, and "The Date of Acts: A Reconsideration," *Forum* n.s. 5 (2002): 33–51. The section entitled "Themes and Literary Patterns in Acts" in chapter 3 contains some material from my "Themes at the Crossroads: Acts 15 in its Lukan Setting," *Forum* n.s. 4 (2001): 105–24. All such material is used with permission.

In the case of books and articles not originally published in English, I have made use of published English translations when available. When such editions were not available, the quotations included here are my own translations. Unless otherwise noted Scripture quotations are from the New Revised Standard Version Bible (NRSV), copyright © 1989 by the National Council of the Churches of Christ in the USA. Used by permission. All rights reserved. Abbreviations of biblical, apocryphal, and pseudepigraphical books, ancient authors, and commonly used journals, reference works, and serials follow the guidelines of the Society of Biblical Literature.[3]

I developed the idea of this book and much of its contents as a member of the Acts Seminar sponsored by the Westar Institute, Santa Rosa, California. I am exceedingly grateful to my colleagues in this seminar for their willingness to read and respond to early versions of this material and to the late Robert W. Funk for providing a public forum for honest, critical, and encouraging discussion among able and respected scholars.

MARCION AND LUKE-ACTS

CHAPTER 1

The Date of Acts

In 1976 Bishop John A. T. Robinson noted that the task of determining the dates of New Testament documents was not one that seriously engaged many modern scholars. He wrote: "In fact ever since the form critics assumed the basic solutions of the source critics (particularly with regard to the synoptic problem) and the redaction critics assumed the work of the form critics, the chronology of the New Testament documents has scarcely been subjected to fresh examination. No one since Harnack has really gone back to look at it for its own sake or to examine the presuppositions on which the current consensus rests. It is only when one pauses to do this that one realizes how thin is the foundation for some of the textbook answers and how circular the arguments for many of the relative datings. Disturb the position of one major piece and the pattern starts disconcertingly to dissolve."[1]

Robinson accepted this tendency among New Testament critics as a challenge and proposed a new chronology with substantially earlier dates for almost all the New Testament documents than those generally in use by modern critics. He claimed that Acts was written between 57 and 62 C.E. More on Robinson's approach will follow. I want first to examine his contention that most of us who work on Acts (and the other New Testament texts) tend to avoid the problem of chronology and simply repeat the conclusions of our predecessors.

A perusal of some recent monographs and commentaries on Acts shows that, as Robinson claimed, the matter of dating is not a front-burner item, despite or perhaps because of the current consensus. This consensus favors what we shall call an intermediate date for Acts. Joseph Fitzmyer, in his Anchor Bible commentary on Acts, provides some reasons for an early and a late date for Acts, but then he opts for an intermediate date of ca. 80–85 C.E. He comments: "Many NT interpreters use the date A.D. 80–85 for the composition of Luke-Acts, and there is no good reason to oppose that date, even if there is no real proof for it."[2] He concludes the section on date and place of composition with the surprising comment: "In the long run, it is a matter of little concern when or where Luke-Acts was composed, since the interpretation of it, especially of Acts, depends little on its date or place of composition."[3] James D. G. Dunn devotes only a paragraph to the date of Acts in his contribution to the Narrative Commentaries series. He favors a date in the eighties, "in the middle of the second generation of Christianity."[4] F. Scott Spencer, in one paragraph, expresses his agreement with most scholars in dating Acts between 70 and 100 C.E.[5]

Ben Witherington III acknowledges most of the pertinent issues for the date of Acts and comments on each one, concluding that "all in all, the late 70s or early 80s seems most likely for the date when Acts was composed."[6] Jacob Jervell notes that Acts would have been written after Luke, which he dates about 70 C.E. On the terminus ad quem he says that "the ecclesiastical relations assumed by Luke, with a very strong Jewish Christianity, are no longer conceivable in the second century."[7] So Jervell goes for a time between 80 and 90 for Acts. In his commentary on Acts in the Sacra Pagina series, Luke Timothy Johnson has no information about the date of Acts but refers readers to his Sacra Pagina volume on Luke, where he notes the traditional assignments and the critical challenges, with little detail. But Johnson intends to retain the consensus critical view of the date of Acts along with the traditional attribution to Luke, a contemporary of Paul. He says that "nothing in the writing prohibits composition by a companion of Paul who was eyewitness to some events he narrates. If a thirty-year-old man joined Paul's circle around the year 50, he would still be only sixty in the year 80, young enough to do vigorous research, yet old enough and at sufficient distance to describe the time of beginnings with a certain nostalgia."[8] So Johnson falls in line with most modern critics in dating Acts 80–85 C.E. In his International Critical Commentary volume C. K. Barrett has a great deal of information that bears on the date of Acts, but he has surprisingly few explicit comments about it. He understands Acts as "the history of the church in a time of conflict written in a time of consensus."[9] But when was this? Barrett says, "So far it may seem probable (though anything but certain) that Acts was written in the late 80s or early 90s."[10]

Other scholars may be mentioned, but these citations are representative, and they show that Robinson is right: most scholars who follow the consensus dating of Acts provide little in the way of argument for their conclusions. They tend to repeat what has now become traditional in critical scholarship, while hedging their bets with a small dose of uncertainty. A factor that may partially account for the lack of attention to the question of dating is the decreased interest in historical questions on the part of New Testament scholars. Those who pursue literary and rhetorical approaches to the study of New Testament texts have little need for precise dating and may be satisfied with establishing the time of writing for a text such as Luke-Acts broadly, as in the Greco-Roman period.

The date of our texts is, however, a matter of fundamental importance for any kind of historical reconstruction of early Christianity. If one is interested in historical traditions that might be included in a text, the social context mirrored by the text, or the ideological history of early Christianity, then a high degree of confidence in the date of the document is indispensable.

The lack of discussion about the date of Acts in present-day scholarship contrasts with more volatile times when it was a topic of great importance among New Testament critics. The contemporary consensus dating is so dominant that many readers may not realize that other dates have been seriously entertained. The range of proposed dates runs from about 60 to 150 C.E., but within these extremes three nodal dates have been most often cited.[11] Clearly an early date of 60 or so, as proposed by Robinson, was assumed by most Christian leaders right up to modern times. An intermediate date of 80–90 is, as we have seen, the current consensus among critical scholars. A date in the first half of the second century was favored by the so-called Tübingen School. It will be useful to examine briefly the history of scholarship on the date of Acts and in the process become familiar with the issues that have been prominent in these discussions.

A Late Date

At the dawn of historical criticism Ferdinand Christian Baur, the founder of the Tübingen School, set forth a bold proposal that placed the composition of Acts in the second century. In Baur's judgment Acts played a crucial role in the history of early Christianity. He characterized early Christianity as a kind of battle between competing sides. On one side were the Jewish Christians, led by Peter, who saw in Jesus the hope for the fulfillment of Jewish expectations but in other respects held strictly to Torah. In early Jewish-Christian theology Gentiles would be able to join with the Jewish Christians only on condition that they accept the observance of Torah. Torah was to hold its position as the dominant and defining force for both Christian and non-Christian Jews. On the other side were the Gentile Christians, led by Paul. In this group faith in Jesus was the only condition for entry, and Torah was denounced as ineffective in addressing the problem of human guilt and justification.

Baur's fundamental views about the course of early Christian history are closely connected to his studies of the book of Acts.[12] A. J. Mattill, Jr., has shown how Baur was influenced by the work of Matthias Schneckenburger on Acts.[13] Baur considered the work of Schneckenburger, who had been his student, as a watershed in the history of New Testament scholarship. Schneckenburger had produced a detailed study of the extensive parallels in Acts between Peter and Paul. The two perform similar miracles, experience life-changing visions, deliver apologetic and evangelistic speeches, and undergo imprisonments followed by remarkable releases. In content some of the speeches of Peter sound like Paul as we know him from his letters. In his speech to the household of Cornelius, Peter states: "I truly understand that God shows no partiality, but in every nation anyone who fears him and does what is right is acceptable to him" (Acts 10:34–35). After Peter has reported to the other apostles in Jerusalem about his vision and experience with Cornelius, they all are led to say, "Then God has given even to the Gentiles the repentance that leads to life" (Acts 11:18). And in the meeting of the apostles, with Paul present, Peter affirms, "we believe that we will be saved through the grace of the Lord Jesus, just as they will" (Acts 15:11).

Contrariwise, the speeches of Paul, with one exception, do not sound like the Paul of the letters. The one exception is in Paul's speech at Pisidian Antioch, where he announces that forgiveness of sins is available through Jesus Christ and that "everyone who believes is set free from all those sins from which you could not be freed by the law of Moses" (Acts 13:39). Here the Paul of Acts sounds like the author of Romans and Galatians. Elsewhere in Acts, however, the themes of the Lukan Paul are fundamentally Jewish, more specifically Pharisaic. The Lukan Paul stresses monotheism, creation, and resurrection. Most importantly, there is a great deal of stress on his observance of Torah. In his apologetic speeches in Acts 21–26 Paul repeatedly denies that he has done anything contrary to the laws of Moses or the traditions of his people. Nor has he taught any contrary practices. Precisely to avoid suspicion that he has taught contrary practices Paul is counseled by James to pay the expenses of four men who had taken on Nazirite vows (Acts 21:17–26). Paul is quite willing to do this, and in his defensive speeches that follow his arrest he stresses his connection with Jews and identifies himself with the party of the Pharisees (Acts 23:6; 26:5). It is made clear in Paul's appearance before the Sanhedrin that belief in resurrection is distinctively Pharisaic and consequently fundamentally Jewish (Acts 23:8).

The parallels that Schneckenburger observed are of fundamental importance in any study of Acts, and we shall return to them in chapter 3, below. For Baur they meant that Peter is made to sound like Paul, and Paul like Peter, and this was an important clue for understanding the place of Acts in the history of early Christianity.[14] He claimed that Acts was a consensus document, intended to heal the breach between Jewish and Gentile Christianity. He described Acts as "the apologetic attempt of a Paulinist to introduce and thus to produce the mutual approach and uniting of the two opposing parties, so that Paul appears as Petrine as possible and Peter as Pauline as possible."[15] Acknowledging his debt to Schneckenburger, Baur concluded that in Acts the "chief tendency is to represent the difference between Peter and Paul as unessential and trifling."[16]

If it is correct to conclude that there was long-term conflict between Jewish (Petrine) Christians and Gentile (Pauline) Christians, as Baur attempted to show in a number of studies, it is plausible to understand the Acts of the Apostles as a consensus document. After all, Schneckenburger's study showed that Luke made every attempt to minimize the differences between Peter and Paul, to portray Paul as Petrine and Peter as Pauline. Why would a writer do this? Baur answered that a writer such as Luke would produce this kind of history as the first step toward reconciliation between the opposing parties. If there was to be any form of agreement between the two groups, argued Baur, that agreement would be considered as well-established if it "could be regarded as one which the two apostles had themselves contemplated, and could be traced to their mutual agreement. This is the point where the Acts of the Apostles not only finds its place as a literary product, but also plays its part as an independent factor of the history in the development of these relations."[17] And Baur asserted: "The Acts is thus the attempt at conciliation, the overture of peace, of a member of the Pauline party, who desired to purchase the recognition of Gentile Christianity on the part of the Jewish Christians by concessions made to Judaism by his side, and sought to influence both parties in this direction."[18]

Baur contended that hostility between the two Christian parties extended through the first century and into the second. Thus the conciliatory Acts could not have been written until well into the second century. Baur was, however, vague in terms of providing a specific date for the composition of Acts and of describing the context within which it was written. Actually the date of Acts favored by Baur and the Tübingen School depends on the dating of Matthew and Luke. Baur was specific about Matthew. In his analysis of the apocalyptic discourse in Matthew 24, Baur insisted that references in it most appropriately fit with the time of the second Jewish rebellion against Rome during the reign of Hadrian (117–138 C.E.). He specifically pointed to the warning about messianic claims in Matt 24:5 and false prophets in Matt 24:11, which he took to be references to Bar Kokhba, the leader of the Jewish rebellion, who was widely regarded as Messiah at the time of the rebellion. It is known that the famous Rabbi Akiba even accepted Bar Kokhba as Messiah. Baur also maintained that the reference to the "Abomination of Desolation standing on the holy place" (Matt 24:15) is more appropriate for the second rebellion than for the first. Hadrian planned to build a temple to Jupiter on the site of the Jewish temple in an act that could meaningfully be described as the "Abomination of Desolation" predicted by Daniel. Baur wrote: "How significant the expression used by the gospel, if the statue of the pagan God was constructed as a continuing monument on the very spot where the true God was worshipped!"[19] He concluded that Matthew's apocalyptic chapter was written while construction of the Aelia Capitolina was going on and that Matthew thought of this as constituting the tribulation that was thought to come just before the Parousia—that is, Matthew was written in the years 130–134 C.E.

For Baur, Matthew was the earliest of the gospels, and it was used by Luke in the composition of the Third Gospel. A later chapter will be the occasion for us to look in detail at Baur's treatment of Luke, but a few words are necessary here. Baur shared the general conviction that Marcion used a version of the Gospel of Luke as, along with letters of Paul, authoritative Scripture. He was equally convinced, however, that canonical Luke was an even later version of this gospel and that it was produced specifically as an anti-Marcionite text. So since Acts did not appear before canonical Luke, which followed Matthew, the date of Acts must be placed some time in the middle of the second century, ca. 140–150 C.E.

Even before Baur's death in 1860 there was a reaction against his reconstruction of early Christianity and his late dating of the New Testament documents. Albrecht Ritschl, who had previously been identified with the Tübingen School, published one of the earliest challenges to Baur.[20] Ritschl minimized the differences between Gentile and Jewish Christians that were so crucial in the Baurian reconstruction. Ritschl also altered his own views about the relationships of the Synoptic Gospels and accepted the newer solution that considered Mark, rather than Matthew, to be the earliest gospel. A few decades later this solution, to be known as the two-document hypothesis, came to be almost universally accepted as the solution to the Synoptic Problem, as it is today.[21]

Ritschl played a prominent role in the decline of the reconstruction of early Christianity that had been identified with the Tübingen School, but other scholars participated as well. As might be expected strong reaction against the Tübingen School came from conservative Christian scholars, who maintained an early date for the composition of Acts. But credit for showing the fallacy of dating Acts in the second century usually goes to J. B. Lightfoot of Durham.[22] Lightfoot did not focus attention specifically on the date of Acts but rather on the letters of Ignatius of Antioch. Baur had pronounced these letters to be late and spurious, but in 1885 Lightfoot demonstrated that they were genuine texts of the Trajanic period. Most important for purposes of dating Acts was Lightfoot's observation that in the Ignatian letters, as well as in *1 Clement,* there is seemingly no memory of contention between Peter and Paul or between parties led by them. On the contrary these late-first-century and early-second-century documents betray only a sense of harmony between the two apostles. So even if Baur was right about controversies between Peter and Paul, such controversies did not continue beyond the end of the first century. Lightfoot's work is often regarded as setting a terminus ad quem for Acts at the end of the first century, but we shall see that this view has been recently challenged.

An Intermediate Date

A decade or so after Lightfoot's studies appeared, Adolf von Harnack published his masterful survey of New Testament chronology.[23] Although modern scholars do not often refer to this study, it is plausible to contend that, with respect to the dating of Acts, it raised the issues that are still acknowledged, and, moreover, that some parts of Harnack's solution to the issues are still generally accepted. As we shall see, however, Harnack changed his mind after the publication of the *Chronologie,* so we must distinguish between the views of the early and the late Harnack.

Harnack's *Chronologie,* published in 1897, discusses the then-known Christian texts from Paul to Eusebius. The section on Acts begins with a dismissal of the early date proposed by conservative anti-Tübingen critics, such as Friedrich Blass. Harnack says that the early date is excluded by the concluding verses of Acts, which show how, by the power of the Holy Spirit, the apostles brought the gospel from Jerusalem to Rome and "have created an entry to the Gentile world, while the Jews, in mounting masses of sin, fade away."[24] He states that Luke is less interested in the life of Paul than in the course of the gospel and that this is shown in the concluding celebratory word of the book, "unhindered": in Rome Paul, even though he is under house arrest, experiences two years of "unhindered" preaching and teaching (Acts 28:30–31). Furthermore, says Harnack, it is not likely that, by the reference to the two-year period, the author intended to provide a signal about the date of his writing. If Acts had been written at or near the end of this two-year period of Paul's confinement in Rome, we would expect the author to have given us some clue about this somewhere in the book. If Paul had still been alive at the time of the composition of Acts, that fact would have played a role somewhere in the book and be mentioned clearly at the end.

In addition Harnack maintains that evidence in the Gospel of Luke shows conclusively that it and Acts were both written after 70 C.E., since "the Gospel of Luke assumes, as almost all scholars now agree, the destruction of Jerusalem."[25] In an accompanying note Harnack reminds the reader that even the prologue to Luke (Luke 1:1–4) suggests that it was written in the generation after the eyewitnesses, that is, the second generation after Jesus. Furthermore, says Harnack, "it is not conceivable that Acts was written in 70 or in the years immediately following."[26] If it had been, the destruction of Jerusalem would have played some role in the text, as it does in such writings as the Epistle of Barnabas. We might even be tempted to think of Acts as having been written before the destruction of Jerusalem, except that such a date is excluded by the gospel. And since the early date is excluded, we have to consider the terminus a quo for Acts at a time when memory of the destruction had begun to fade, that is, ca. 80 C.E.

Harnack establishes the terminus ad quem at ca. 93 C.E., before the last years of Domitian. He supplies two reasons for this date. First, the author of Acts displays no knowledge of the letters of Paul, while late-first-century and early-second-century authors—Clement, Barnabas, Ignatius, and Polycarp—used them intensively. Second, Harnack thinks that the attitude toward Rome that is represented in Acts is most appropriate before the last years of Domitian. He describes the Lukan attitude as "naïve," and he explains, "only so can we explain the author's natural ways of narration: sometimes the authority is friendly, sometimes hostile, sometimes indifferent."[27] Presumably, such a guileless kind of narration would not have been possible for a Christian writer during the last years of Domitian. Harnack concludes: "Consequently I regard the writing of the work between 80–93 as probable, and I see nothing which tells against this conception of the book, nothing which would naturally categorize it otherwise. It is far enough from the life of Paul, so that real differences of interest and conception, which distinguish the book from Christian interests and struggles of the previous 40–50 years, may be explained."[28] The dates that the early Harnack proposes here are within the range of the intermediate dates subscribed to by the majority of scholars today.

An Early Date

But Harnack had second and third thoughts about the date of Acts. He became progressively concerned about the lack in Acts of any mention of or allusion to the destruction of Jerusalem. This issue was rather easily resolved in the 1897 *Chronologie,* in which Harnack had said Acts must be dated far enough after 70 C.E. so that the destruction of Jerusalem would no longer have been uppermost in people's memories. He held to the post-70 date in his study *Luke the Physician* (originally published 1906).[29] But in *The Acts of the Apostles* (originally published 1908) Harnack presented several arguments in favor of a date "at the beginning of the seventh decade of the first century."[30] He observed: "How remarkable it is that a vivacious story-teller like St. Luke should remain so 'objective' that, simply because he is dealing with the times before A.D. 66, he gives no hint of the tremendous change that came with the year A.D. 70!"[31]

The later Harnack is even more concerned about the end of Acts. In the *Chronologie* he insisted that the ending of Acts prohibited an early date for the composition of the book, but now he looks upon the ending of the book as a problem for intermediate and late dating. Why, if Luke wrote Acts as late as 80–93 C.E., when the fate of Paul was certainly known, does he not include something about this in his book? Harnack says that this problem is resolved "in the simplest way if St. Luke wrote his work soon after the two years which St. Paul spent in Rome, and thus while the Apostle was still alive."[32] At the end of his discussion Harnack says that his remarks are intended to raise some doubts about the intermediate dating, not to solve the problem, and he concludes: "Therefore, for the present, we must be content to say: *St. Luke wrote at the time of Titus or in the earlier years of Domitian, but perhaps even so early as the beginning of the seventh decade of the first century.*"[33] In 1911 these tentative views gave way to more forthright expressions, and Harnack stated his conviction about an early date for Acts.[34] He explained his hesitancy in the earlier book: "But it was not want of courage that caused me to express myself so cautiously; I was not yet clear as to the weight to be ascribed to the opposing arguments, and I had not yet come to an assured opinion as to the date of the gospel of St. Mark."[35] He affirms that the best explanation of the end of Acts is that it was written shortly after the two-year period mentioned in Acts 28:30. Other explanations are possible, and he writes: "For many years I was content to soothe my intellectual conscience with such expedients; but in truth they altogether transgress against inward probability and all the psychological laws of historical composition. The more clearly we see that the trial of St. Paul, and above all his appeal to Caesar, is the chief subject of the last quarter of the Acts, the more hopeless does it appear that we can explain why the narrative breaks off as it does, otherwise than by assuming that the trial had actually not yet reached its close."[36] Then we have Harnack's forceful rejection of any intermediate or late date for Acts: "If St. Luke, in the year 80, 90, or 100, wrote thus he was not simply a blundering but an absolutely incomprehensible historian!"[37]

Harnack's public change of mind is truly striking. Not only did he move up the date of Acts by several decades, but he also interpreted Acts in a very different way. For the early Harnack the end of Acts prohibits an early date for the book; for the later Harnack the end of Acts requires an early date. Even the intent of the author is seen differently: no longer is the life of Paul seen to be of minimal importance for Luke; now it seems unthinkable for him to have omitted mention of Paul's fate if he knew it. For the early Harnack the lack of mention of the destruction of Jerusalem was evidence that it occurred long in the past; now it is evidence that the book was written prior to this tragic event.

It is difficult to avoid having two minds about Harnack's public change of mind. On the one side it is admirable in that he was confident enough to re-engage ideas thought to be settled and to expose his self-contradiction. On the other side one would have been better satisfied if Harnack had more seriously engaged his earlier work. In 1897 he said it was unthinkable that Acts could be dated "in 70 or in the years immediately following."[38] In 1911 such a conception is not only thinkable; it is requisite. Such an about-face requires more explanation than Harnack provided. In any event his work demonstrates that the ending of Acts was and is a perplexing problem not only for the matter of chronology but also for the interpretation of Acts generally, and we shall return to the matter presently.

The early date for Acts espoused by the late Harnack affirms the traditional inter-pretation. Since Harnack's time a number of conservative scholars have also affirmed this early date. We have already noted John A. T. Robinson's proposals on early dat-ing. Probably the most serious recent effort along these lines is that of Colin J. Hemer.[39] His study stresses the significance of the end of Acts. Hemer was impressed with the presence in Acts 27–28 of a large number of insignificant details, a feature that he called the "immediacy" factor. Hemer wrote: "One would expect a voyage-narrative to become reduced and schematized even in the mind of a participant when it had lain untapped for an extended time. An important factor in the study of detail in Acts is the marked variation in its presentation, in the varying extent to which it has been shaped by tradition or hearsay. We can find among the stones on a beach a significant mingling of those which have been wave-worn and smoothed with those which have been freshly broken from the primeval rock. That is an image apt to redaction-critical study; the rough pieces stand closest to the final state of the book, and have been least shaped."[40]

With this characterization of Paul's voyage to Rome in mind, Hemer tackles the problems connected with the abrupt ending of Acts. He lists a number of proposals that have been entertained in critical scholarship and shows their deficiencies. For example, it is sometimes suggested that Luke did not include Paul's ultimate fate in his book because his intended audience already knew what had happened to Paul. But Hemer objects that "if it is valid at all, it could be saying too much, for an audi-ence which knew the outcome presumably knew much of the situation which pro-duced that outcome, and the idea poses a larger query against the point of other facets of Luke's book."[41] Finally Hemer claims that Acts must have been written during the two-year period of Paul's confinement in Rome, that is, ca. 62 C.E., at a time when his release was expected. On the basis of Acts 28, Philippians, Philemon, and selec-tions from the Pastoral Epistles, Hemer then reconstructs the life of Paul after the Roman confinement: he was released, and he conducted further missionary work in the East, but he never made it to Spain as he had once intended. "The presumption, then, about the remaining course of Paul's life is that it consisted of further travels, apparently in line with his new plan to return to the East, followed by re-arrest and martyrdom in Rome at an uncertain date, either in the Neronian persecution of 64 or its aftermath, or possibly some time later."[42] Contrasts between the Pastorals and the generally acknowledged letters of Paul are explained by Paul's changed situation and new perspective. The omission in Acts of information about Paul's fate is explained by Luke's intention not to reveal Paul's whereabouts to his enemies.

As he readily admits, Hemer's position about the date of Acts rests on his speculative reconstruction of the life of Paul. Indeed, the reconstruction itself requires one to presuppose the historical accuracy of the Acts narrative, as well as the Pauline authorship of the Pastorals. Hemer's use of the "immediacy" factor, which is employed to support the historical accuracy of Acts, is interesting from a form-critical perspective, but it may more readily be explained as the author's efforts to produce a rhetorically effective narrative.[43] Despite these and other problems, Hemer should be credited with providing us with a serious treatment of many of the issues associated with the dating of Acts. Further, he has called attention to the ending of Acts as a significant factor for the dating problem.

A Late Date Reconsidered

This brief and selective summary of the history of scholarship on the date of Acts shows that, despite the present consensus on an intermediate date, other plausible dates have been seriously considered, and plausible arguments have been marshaled for them. Recent scholarship on a number of issues, some of which played roles in the history of scholarship, impels us to take another look at an alternative date that was once considered quite feasible but has not been seriously entertained for over a century, namely a second-century date for the composition of Acts. In what follows I intend to discuss the major issues under consideration and assess the impact of recent scholarship on the dating of Acts. Five major issues require attention: external references to Acts; the significance of the events of 70 C.E.; the bearing of the end of Acts; the possible influence of Josephus on the writing of Acts; and the use of Paul's letters by the author of Acts.

1. External References

We start with a significant but relatively uncontroversial issue. An external reference provides a definite terminus ad quem for a document. External references to Acts are relatively late and leave us with a wide range of possibilities for the date of its composition. Although there are some questions about the first clear allusion indicating knowledge of Acts, it is fair to say that no writer confirms its existence before the middle of the second century. Ernst Haenchen has compiled an impressive list of allusions to and citations of Acts.[44] Hans Conzelmann also discusses many of the relevant texts.[45] Both agree that, as Conzelmann says, "We possess definite evidence only from the second half of the second century."[46] Haenchen cites a number of early Christian writers, including 1 Clement, Ignatius, Barnabas, Polycarp, 2 Clement, and Papias, who include short phrases that are intriguingly similar to those in Acts, but he believes that none of them clearly shows that these authors were drawing on it. He believes, rather, that Justin Martyr was the first Christian writer to refer to Luke-Acts.[47] In contrast to the earlier writers, who displayed fragmentary similarities with Acts, Justin, in *1 Apology* 50:12, brings together a number of references that follow the order of the last chapters of Luke and the first chapter of Acts. About the Justin passage Haenchen writes: "This first quotes the substance of Luke 23.49a in recapitulating the story of the Passion, next makes clear use of Luke 24.24, 44f. as the account continues, and finally narrates the Ascension and the conferring of the Holy Spirit with a verbal echo of Acts 1.8."[48]

John T. Townsend notes this conclusion but expresses some reservations about Justin's knowledge of Luke-Acts. He calls attention to Justin's *Dialogue with Trypho* 105, in which Justin cites a saying of Jesus that appears only in Luke 23:46.[49] But Townsend insists that other explanations are likely, including the possibility that Justin took this text from Marcion's gospel.[50] And "since the saying ultimately comes from Ps 30:6 (LXX = RSV 31:5), the existence of this saying in oral tradition would not be hard to explain."[51] Townsend concludes that it is only after about 170 C.E. that we can talk about definite citations and allusions to Luke-Acts. Thus, as he states, "there is no conclusive evidence that Luke-Acts was written in the first century."[52]

The bearing of external evidence in the case of Acts is difficult to measure. It seems significant that allusions and quotations are missing before the third quarter of the second century, but this lack may be accounted for in other ways. For example, Haenchen claims that there was little interest in the story of the apostles until late in the second century.[53] This might mean that, although Acts was written in the first century, it had limited circulation and influence for several decades. Further, an argument for a late date of Acts that is built on the lack of early external references is essentially an argument from silence. After all, the extant literature that might contain references to Acts is not extensive. Thus the late date of references to Acts does not require a late date for its composition, but it does grant us permission for it if, on other grounds, such a date seems probable.

2. The Significance of 70 C.E.

A reference to a datable historical event provides a terminus a quo for the document that includes it. The fall of Jerusalem and the destruction of the Jewish temple by Roman troops under Titus in 70 C.E. were clearly landmark events in the history of the Jewish people. Presumably, they also had major significance for early Christians, but Acts makes no mention of them.

John A. T. Robinson calls attention to these events as pivotal issues for dating any New Testament document. He finds it inexplicable that any New Testament author who wrote after 70 C.E. would have failed to mention this series of events. He writes: "One of the oddest facts about the New Testament is what on any showing would appear to be the single most datable and climactic event of the period—the fall of Jerusalem in A.D. 70, and with it the collapse of institutional Judaism based on the temple—is never once mentioned as a past fact."[54] Robinson is, of course, aware that many scholars think that Luke 19:41–44 and 21:20–24 are actually prophecies after the fact and demonstrate convincingly that the author of Luke-Acts wrote after the

Roman conquest of Jerusalem. But Robinson contrasts these sayings with a passage in the *Sibylline Oracles,* which he takes to be an uncontested prophecy after the fact: "A leader of Rome will come to Syria who will burn the Temple of Jerusalem with fire, at the same time slaughter many men and destroy the great land of the Jews with its broad roads."[55] Robinson comments: "It is precisely such detail that one does not get in the New Testament."[56] His principle would seem to be: If a New Testament writer does not make explicit and precisely detailed reference to the fall of Jerusalem, it is reasonable to conclude that this author was writing before 70 C.E.

Some scholars who reject Robinson's principle nevertheless exhibit some perplexity about the lack of an explicit mention of the destruction of Jerusalem. Early in the twentieth century Hans Windisch, who accepted a post-70 C.E. date for Acts, wrote: "It seems strange at first, it must be confessed, that no reference is made in Acts to the destruction of Jerusalem and the attendant humiliation of the Jews, but the judgment which actually took place in the year 70 is adequately characterised in the Gospels and the disaster of the year 70 by no means resulted in breaking the pride and self-confidence of the Jews, least of all in the Diaspora."[57] Windisch means to refer to Luke 19:41–44 and 21:20–24, which most scholars take to be just the kinds of explicit detailed prophecies *ex eventu* that Robinson requires. Ben Witherington expresses the view of many scholars who agree with Windisch: "I am among those who think that the *way* the fall of Jerusalem is portrayed in Luke 21:20ff., and its difference from the account in Mark 13:14–23, suggests that Luke was likely writing after A.D. 70 with the benefit of hindsight."[58]

The question to be raised at this point is that of the validity of Robinson's principle. Is it reasonable for us to expect that an early Christian author would inevitably make explicit and precise reference to the fall of Jerusalem and the destruction of the Jewish temple in 70 C.E. if he or she wrote after these events took place? The way historical critics have usually assessed the significance of internal evidence does not support Robinson's principle. A different point is usually made: if an author makes an explicit and obvious reference to an event whose date we are able to determine by means of sources outside the text under investigation, it is reasonable to assume that the author in question wrote after this event occurred. In other words, if the author of Luke-Acts had made an explicit reference to the destruction of the temple, perhaps including some words about Titus, the Jewish defenders, and the fire that broke out, then we would assume that Luke-Acts, or at least a part of Luke-Acts, must have been written some time after the summer of 70 C.E. But, even if one should discount the force of the Lukan sayings of Jesus due to their imprecision, the lack of explicit reference to the events of 70 C.E. does not require the conclusion that our author wrote before the events took place. To say, as Robinson does, that an early Christian author such as Luke would have been obligated to make certain references is to impose our own expectations of what should have been important for such an author.

Robinson's principle also involves an assumption about the date and context of Acts that is not explicitly stated. He assumes that Luke-Acts was written either before 70 C.E. or in the immediate aftermath of these events and in a context in which they had a significant impact. One might grant that if Acts had been written within a decade after the fall of Jerusalem and in conversation with Palestinian or diaspora Jews, lack of explicit reference would be surprising. If, however, a second-century date or a non-Palestinian provenance for Acts is plausible, this lack is much less surprising. Indeed, the early Harnack thought that a date for the composition of Acts soon after 70 C.E. was excluded by the very fact that the fall of Jerusalem was not mentioned. He felt that the references in the Gospel of Luke, stated as predictions of Jesus, were sufficient to show that the author was aware of the events, and the lack of explicit reference in Acts was entirely appropriate in a text written several decades after the fall of Jerusalem.[59]

In my judgment also, the sayings of Jesus in Luke 19:41–44; 21:20–24 provide ample evidence that the author of our texts wrote after the events of 70 C.E. His failure to make explicit reference to them in Acts is no barrier to this conclusion; indeed, it is what we would expect if the composition of Acts is to be dated in the late first or in the second century. As the early Harnack observed, a second-century date for Acts makes Luke's failure to include an explicit reference to the fall of Jerusalem quite understandable.

3. The End of Acts

A similar issue cited by Robinson and several other scholars is the ending of Acts, which involves another missing element. Luke does not tell the reader what happened to Paul, and he concludes the book of Acts in a way that does not seem to resolve the story. In the final scene Paul is said to have resided in Rome for two years, teaching "with all boldness and without hindrance" (Acts 28:30–31). The struggles of Harnack with the dating of Acts, discussed above, illustrate some of the difficulties that the ending of Acts entails. Like Robinson later, Harnack was impressed with the lack of reference in Acts to the destruction of Jerusalem, but his major contention was that an early date resolves the problem of the end of Acts. He concluded that Acts was written shortly after the end of the two-year period mentioned in Acts 28:30. Harnack's struggles demonstrate that the ending of Acts was and is a perplexing problem not only for the matter of chronology but also for the interpretation of Acts generally.

Harnack's contentions about the ending of Acts have been addressed by scholars who date the book after 70 C.E. Most would agree that, although sufficient notice of the fate of Paul was given in Acts 20:25, Luke's major purpose was not to portray the life and death of Paul but to provide a basis for legitimating the Gentile mission.[60] Luke's main story in Acts was that of the progress of the gospel from Jerusalem to Rome.

The assumption that Harnack makes about the ending of Acts is similar to the principle that we have just examined about the relevance of the fall of Jerusalem. If Luke had referred explicitly to the outcome of Paul's trial, then we would of necessity conclude that he wrote after the trial took place. But his failure to make explicit reference to the outcome does not require us to infer a pre-outcome date for the book. This would be another case where we impose on the author of Acts our own assumptions about what he should have known, should have considered germane to his purposes in writing, and should have included. Modern readers may find the end of Acts unsatisfying, but that should have no influence on the dating of the text.[61] Harnack's and Robinson's objections aside, Luke's failure to include a specific notice of the fall of Jerusalem and of the death of Paul do not require an early date for Acts.

4. The Influence of Josephus

Clearly Luke makes significant use of the LXX in both the gospel and Acts. In addition it is often alleged that he made use of the writings of Josephus and the letters of Paul. The use of the LXX is not debatable, but the influence of Josephus and Paul has been and is subjected to considerable debate. Possible allusions to these writers affect our perception of the date of Acts in significant ways. If it can be shown that the writings of Josephus influenced the composition of our texts, a terminus a quo of 93–94 C.E. is thereby established, since Josephus completed the writing of the *Antiquities of the Jews* at that time. If it can be shown that the letters of Paul were known and used by Luke, we have essentially the same result. Since it is generally agreed that the letters of Paul were not collected and distributed widely until near the end of the first century, they would not have been available to Luke until that time. In this way use of Josephus and Paul in Acts would, for all practical purposes, exclude the possibility that Acts was written in the first century.

The influence of Josephus's writings on the composition of Acts has been widely debated. The most recent argument for the use of Josephus by Luke is by Richard I. Pervo, who not only presents his own views but also includes useful references to previous scholarship.[62] Pervo notes that Luke did not quote substantive bits of material from Josephus, nor did he imitate the Jewish historian's style. Rather Pervo deals with hitherto neglected indications of dependence. He observes that "Luke did not imitate the style of Josephus, nor did he take over passages with but slight adaptations. One must further note that Josephus would have served Luke as a source quite differently from Mark, Q, Paul, or even the LXX."[63]

In his own judgment Pervo's cornerstone argument supporting the influence of Josephus on Acts is one that is often used to prove just the opposite. This argument treats the speech of Gamaliel in Acts 5:36–37 and its connection with *Antiquities* 20:97–102. Gamaliel's reference to Theudas and Judas as Jewish revolutionaries is often taken to be a sure sign that Luke did not know Josephus, since the two are mentioned in an incorrect chronological order in Acts. But Pervo points out that Josephus, mindful of the correct chronological order, nevertheless wrote about them in reverse, that is, in the same order as that in Gamaliel's speech. Furthermore Josephus is the only source known to us about Theudas and *Antiquities* the only text other than Acts to characterize him as an insurrectionist. Pervo concludes that "since the order Theudas-Judas in the *Antiquities* stems from Josephus's own narrative purpose and arrangement, the most economical solution to the error of Acts 5 is to attribute it to Luke's use of Josephus."[64]

Analysis of these passages also calls attention to Josephus's understanding of the Roman census as a watershed event in Jewish history, and Pervo thinks this understanding must have influenced Luke in his writing of the infancy narratives of his gospel. The fact is that the two writers share more in common than a few fragmentary notices. Pervo writes: "If Luke had access to part or all of the *Antiquities,* this hypothesis could explain how he came upon the theme of the 'census,' and, more specifically, it would explain his association of this event with the name of the Roman legate Quirinius [Luke 2:2]. In two cases, the prominence given to the Roman census of 6 CE and the order Theudas-Judas, Luke happens to share with Josephus not simply historical *data* but the results of historical *interpretation.* In this case two is not a company; it is a crowd, too much of a good thing to refuse."[65]

Pervo notes a number of other probable correlations between Luke and Josephus, including the reference to Lysanias in Luke 3:1, the mistaking of Paul as "the Egyptian prophet" in Acts 21:38; the characterization of Pharisees as ἀκριβής in Acts 22:3; 26:5; and the reference to Drusilla as the wife of Felix in Acts 24:24. He admits that these cases, although intriguing, are not so strong as the Theudas-Judas reference, but they tend to support the conviction that Luke knew and used some parts of Josephus's *Antiquities,* especially the last several books. Pervo comments: "Nearly every item of 'modern' history to which Luke refers can be found in Josephus. That may not be remarkable. Yet when Luke calls Jewish parties philosophical 'sects,' when he views the Census of 6 CE as a watershed event, when he introduces such characters as Judas, Theudas, 'the Egyptian,' and *sicarii,* it is appropriate to introduce the adjective 'remarkable.'"[66]

Josephus himself dates the writing of the last several books of the *Antiquities* in 93/94 C.E. If the author of Acts knew and used these books, we have a firm terminus a quo: Acts could not have been written before 93/94 C.E. Thus Pervo concludes that the range of possible dates for the composition of Acts is 100–130 C.E., and the most likely date is between 110–120 C.E.

5. The Use of Paul's Letters

The use or nonuse of the letters of Paul in Acts is a more complex issue than that of the influence of Josephus. In the history of scholarship the neglect of the letters has often been cited as a factor that prohibits a late date for Acts. Since the author of Acts seems not to know of these letters and never even mentions the fact that Paul wrote letters, it does not seem likely that he could have written after the letters became widely known. So goes the argument, frequently used in support of an intermediate date for Acts. Edgar J. Goodspeed's work is usually cited as providing a definitive date for the collection of Paul's letters at about 90 C.E.[67] Thus many scholars make use of Luke's apparent neglect of the letters to support an intermediate date and to reject a second-century date for Acts. Witherington, for example, notes Luke's "apparent ignorance" of the major Pauline letters and asks: "How could this have happened if Acts was written at a time when Paul's letters were already at least partially collected and circulating as a revered corpus of early Christian writing (2 Pet. 3:15–16)?"[68] The centrality of Paul as a character in Acts seems to require the author's knowledge of him as the writer of at least some of the letters in the New Testament.

One might think that scholars who favor an early date for Acts would be troubled by the apparent neglect of the letters. It would seem that Luke, the companion of Paul, would have known that Paul wrote letters and would have been familiar with some of their contents. But scholars who lean toward a pre-70 date for Acts do not consider this neglect to be a serious impediment. Some are able to affirm a connection between Luke and Paul even if they must agree that Luke was not in possession of fundamental information about Paul's life.[69]

Despite the consensus view favoring an intermediate date for Acts, scholars who lean toward a second-century date have not been without explanations for the apparent neglect of Paul's letters. John Knox, who claimed that Acts is a post-Marcionite text, provides an intriguing explanation. He addresses the question in his contribution to the Festschrift for Paul Schubert published in 1966.[70] Here he confronts an apparent impasse. First he recognizes that Luke made no use of Paul's letters in Acts. Second he acknowledges that Luke must have been acquainted with at least some of the letters. Knox writes: "This impasse should lead us to examine the hidden major premise of both sides, namely: If Luke knew the letters of Paul, he must have used them. I believe we are forced by the literary evidence (or rather, by the lack of it), on the one hand, and by the a priori probabilities, on the other, to question this premise and to consider seriously the possibility that Luke knew, or at least knew of, letters of Paul—even *the* (collected) letters of Paul—and quite consciously and deliberately made little or no use of them."[71] Knox maintains that Acts was composed as a post-Marcionite and anti-Marcionite text and that one of the author's purposes was to disassociate Paul from Marcion.[72] He notes that any use of Paul's letters would have been counterproductive and would have seriously detracted from the image of Paul that the author wished to convey.

John C. O'Neill, who favored a date for Acts of ca. 130 C.E., somewhat before the time of Justin Martyr, is unable to accept Knox's solution. Indeed he finds it incredible that Luke would have ignored Paul's letters.[73] Instead he questions the accuracy of Goodspeed's dating of the Pauline collection. He notes that Polycarp, ca. 135, was the first to exhibit knowledge of the Pauline corpus, and he concludes that "the author of Luke-Acts could still have written in ignorance of Paul's letters between A.D. 115 and 130, the limiting dates which were suggested earlier."[74] He also reminds us that "Justin almost certainly wrote after the Pauline collection was published, and not only does he never quote Paul but he never even mentions him."[75]

Other studies, some quite recent, have questioned the very premise that leads to this difficulty and have provided grounds for believing that Luke both knew and made use of Paul's letters.[76] In 1938 Morton S. Enslin wrote that Luke "may not have had copies of them [Paul's letters], may not have had them open on his desk as he wrote, but that he had heard them, some at least, read in church services, and knew at least imperfectly their content appears to me inescapable."[77] In the same article Enslin wonders, "Is it simply coincidence that the missionary journeys of Paul as sketched in Acts carry him to precisely those communities to which we have Pauline letters?"[78] Enslin calls attention to a number of features in both Luke and Acts that support his conviction. Why, for example, does Luke include the curious statement that the risen Jesus appeared to Simon (Luke 24:34)? Enslin suggests that the reference reflects 1 Cor 15:5. Furthermore, he holds that the long period between the resurrection and the ascension in Acts 1:3 (which appears to be a revision of the pericope about the ascension in Luke 24:50–51) was probably suggested by Paul's catalogue of appearances in 1 Cor 15. Enslin also reckons with the longer text of Luke 22:19b–20, which if genuine may have made use of 1 Cor 11:23–25. But Enslin puts little weight on this since he regards it as a "non-Western interpolation."[79] He was convinced that Acts 15 and Galatians 2 relate the same conference, and he claims that the differences between the two accounts are due to Luke's "deliberate alteration."[80] Enslin observes that the Pauline letters offer little that Luke could have used in a narrative construction and that since one of Luke's main interests was in minimizing any conflict in the early church, use of Paul's letters would have been counterproductive.

Enslin reflected again on the relation between Luke and Paul in an article published in 1970.[81] Here he revisited many of the same issues he had raised in the 1938 article, but by this time Knox's article had appeared in the Schubert Festschrift. Enslin found himself in agreement with Knox in the contention that Luke's action in regard to the Pauline letters was deliberate.[82] He noted that Justin had neglected to mention Paul's letters in order to avoid "what might have become an awkward problem."[83] Enslin asked: "Is it possible that Luke is in essentially the same situation [as Justin], and that his reticence reflects to some degree his opposition to the Marcionite use of his hero's writings? I see no way of proving this, although it seems to me quite possible. The objection that this would require a second-century date for his writing—at least for Acts as we have it—seems to me of no consequence, for I fail to see anything in the writing which requires or even renders likely an earlier date."[84]

In response to Enslin's articles C. K. Barrett maintained that no adequate explanation can be found for Luke's having deliberately suppressed "all, or nearly all, trace of his knowledge" of the Pauline letters.[85] In an article published in *Expository Times* Barrett observes that there was much of a noncontroversial nature in Paul's letters that Luke could have used if he were acquainted with them. Barrett concludes that the explanations that Knox and Enslin had suggested are not persuasive.

In 1985 William O. Walker, Jr., followed Enslin's lead and added to the evidentiary basis for the contention that Luke both knew and used some of Paul's letters.[86]

He regards Acts 16:1–3 as "an altered version of Paul's reference to the question of the circumcision of Titus in Gal 2:3–5."[87] He agrees with Enslin that Acts 15 was a deliberate alteration of Galatians 2. Walker concludes that Luke wanted to rescue Paul from those who would misuse him to support their own points of views, and he mentions Gnostics and Marcionites. Walker's conclusion reminds one of the Tübingen position on the treatment of Peter and Paul in Acts: "Unable then, to deny or ignore the fact that Paul had preached justification through faith, the next best expedient for Luke was to attribute the doctrine (in muted form) initially and primarily to the one great rival of Paul for preeminence in the church, namely Peter, thus making it impossible to reject Paul because of his espousal of the doctrine without, at the same time, rejecting Peter for the same reason."[88]

The core of any argument about the relation of Paul and Luke is a comparison of Galatians 2 and Acts 15. Most scholars agree that the two reports concern the same conference, but they are more impressed with the differences than the similarities. These differences are familiar—in Galatians Paul goes to Jerusalem by revelation, taking along Barnabas and Titus; he presents his gospel privately to the acknowledged leaders; Titus, a Greek, was not compelled to be circumcised; false brothers were present; James, Cephas, and John acknowledged Paul and Barnabas as missionaries to Gentiles and commissioned them to remember the poor. In Acts the controversy begins when certain Judeans come to Antioch to demand that believers be circumcised and compelled to observe Torah; Paul, Barnabas, and others are sent to Jerusalem to meet with the apostles and elders; Pharisaic believers demand circumcision and obedience to Torah, but Peter speaks against it, and Paul and Barnabas tell about their experiences among the Gentiles; James speaks in agreement with Peter and recommends that Gentile believers be required to observe only the four items in the so-called apostolic decree.

Walker has recently subjected Acts 15 and Galatians 2 to a detailed analysis and comparison, and he is convinced that Luke made use of Paul's letter.[89] Walker stresses the remarkable ideational and verbal similarities between the speech of Peter in Acts 15:7–11 and Galatians 2, the entirety of which he takes to be Paul's account of the Jerusalem conference. Walker concludes that Luke almost certainly used Galatians as his source for the Jerusalem conference. He notes that in Acts Peter has taken over the role of Paul in proclaiming to Gentiles a gospel free of Torah.[90] Further, Walker lists ten ideational and verbal similarities between Acts 15 and Galatians 2 that, in his judgment, can best be explained by assuming that Luke used Paul's letter as a source:

Both refer to proclamation to Gentiles as **gospel** (Gal 2:7; Acts 15:7).
Both speak of a **division of responsibility** (Gal 2:7; Acts 15:7).
Both speak of **divine selection** of Paul and Peter (Gal 2:7–8; Acts 15:7).
Both speak of **divine impartiality** (Gal 2:6; Acts 15:9).
Both speak about the **reception of the Holy Spirit** (Gal 3:2–5; Acts 15:8).

Both refer to the **law as yoke** (Gal 5:1; Acts 15:10).
Both speak of the **inability to observe Torah** (Gal 2:14; Acts 15:10).
Both express the same view about **law and gospel** (Gal 2:16; Acts 15:10–11).
Both assert the importance of **faith** (Gal 2:16; Acts 15:9).
Both assert the importance of **grace** (Gal 2:9; 1:6, 15; Acts 15:11).[91]

Thus, Walker concludes: "In short, virtually every idea and much of the actual wording of Peter's speech in Acts 15:7–11 have parallels either in Paul's report regarding the Jerusalem Conference (Gal 2) or elsewhere in the Galatian letter. Indeed, the Acts passage is so remarkably similar to the material in Galatians as to suggest that the author of Acts almost certainly knew this letter and, indeed, used it as a source in constructing Peter's speech at the Jerusalem Conference."[92]

In a dissertation completed in 2002 Heikki Leppä focuses attention on a comparison of Acts and Galatians and claims that one of Luke's purposes was to subvert Paul's letter.[93] He analyzes a number of verbal similarities that indicate Luke's acquaintance with Galatians. For example, συμπαραλαμβάνω appears in Gal 2:1 and Acts 12:25; 15:37, 38. These are the only uses of this word in the New Testament. Leppä comments that it is "used only in connection with Paul and Barnabas taking (or not taking) a companion with them on a trip in the NT. These four usages do not seem to be just random isolated incidents."[94] Unusual combinations of words used in similar contexts are also important indications for Leppä. For example, ζηλωτὴς ὑπάρχων appears in Gal 1:14; Acts 22:3; 21:20. This is a very rare combination, appearing only in these three verses in known Greek literature from the third century B.C.E. to the third century C.E.[95] Acts 11:2–3 is especially important in bringing together three terms that also appear in the Pauline letters in a related context (see Gal 2:7,12): όι ἐκ περιτομῆς, ἀκροβυστία, and συνεσθίω. Leppä comments: "An unusual, in fact hapax legomenon, word in Luke does not alone prove literary dependence. But, he employs the expression όι ἐκ περιτομῆς and the rare verb συνεσθίω in the very same context. Three unusual words or expressions in a closely related context is stronger evidence. The probability that all these details are just random isolated incidents is quite small."[96]

It is the dense correspondence between Acts 15 and Galatians 2 that most impresses Leppä. He is, of course, quite aware of the differences between the two accounts, on which he comments: "What matters is not *how much* the two stories are different, but *how* they are different. In this case Luke's story is not only different, but also very much *opposite* to Paul's own accounts. Therefore the tension between the two sources does not prove that Luke was not aware of Galatians. No one can create a mirror image without knowing the original image."[97] Leppä claims that Luke had several controlling theological reasons for subverting Galatians. He wanted to stress the continuity of Judaism and Christianity, Paul's close relation to the other apostles, and the unity of the first believers. Paul's letter to the Galatians provides scant support for these convictions, and so Luke found it necessary to turn this letter "upside down."

Other scholars have weighed in on the issue of the use of Paul's letters in Acts. In 1987 Lars Aejmelaeus claimed that Paul's speech at Miletus (Acts 20:18–35) drew heavily on Paul's letters.[98] A year earlier Michael D. Goulder limited his comparisons mainly to those between the Gospel of Luke and two of Paul's letters, 1 Corinthians and 1 Thessalonians, and found numerous indications that Luke knew these letters.[99]

The most exhaustive and comprehensive argument for the use of Paul's letters in Acts is that of Pervo.[100] Pervo draws on the work of Enslin, Walker, Leppä, Aejmelaeus, and others to form a comprehensive argument for the use of Paul's letters in Acts and for their influence on the gospel. He notes that an acknowledgment that Luke used Paul's letters carries with it a great deal of pain for many scholars. He writes, "Especially painful for some has been the inevitable conclusion that, if Luke knew Pauline letters, he ignored them at some points and contradicted them at others. Why this experience should be more painful than it is with regard to the gospel of Mark—which Luke also ignored at some points and contradicted more than once—is not perfectly clear, but there can be no doubt that it has been a burden."[101]

Pervo cautions that scholarship on the Synoptic Problem is not an adequate guide in studying the relationship between Acts and the Pauline letters, even if certain broad observations are possible. One may say that since Luke omitted sections of Mark and altered others, we should expect much the same procedure in the case of his use of the Pauline letters. But linguistic analyses of Mark and Luke can show that entire pericopes are parallels, that within individual pericopes there is significant verbal agreement, and that there is often agreement in sequence in a string of pericopes. Studies of Acts and the Pauline letters are necessarily more subtle. They must focus on fragments and short phrases, rather than full sentences or paragraphs. Pervo calls attention to a number of unusual expressions that occur in similar contexts or treat similar situations. He is aware that no single pair of passages, taken by itself, can prove that Luke was acquainted with Paul's letters, but he is convinced that the presence of a significant number of apparent parallels constitutes a weighty cumulative argument.

Altogether Pervo treats some 86/87 places in Acts that exhibit traces of Pauline letters, including Romans, 1 Corinthians, 2 Corinthians, Galatians, Ephesians, Philippians, Colossians, and 1 Thessalonians. The presence of Ephesians and Colossians in this list is significant in showing that what was available to Luke was a collection of letters assumed to be by Paul. It means that Luke wrote after the publication of the deutero-Pauline letters and that, unlike modern scholars, he was unable to distinguish between authentic and inauthentic Pauline letters. This observation virtually excludes contentions that Luke may have known the real Paul. The Paul known to Luke was the Paul who had been filtered through the deutero-Pauline school.

Pervo makes no claim that all the citations he analyzes are of equal weight. Some he characterizes as small traces or random echoes. But some passages are weighty. He pays significant attention to a comparison of Acts 15 and Galatians 2. Here we meet, as he fully recognizes, some of the thorniest issues in all of New Testament scholarship.

Pervo, in agreement with Leppä and Walker, is convinced that Acts 15 was written with Galatians in mind; indeed the letter to the Galatians was Luke's chief source of information about this meeting of Paul and the Jerusalem leaders. Pervo calls attention to similar descriptions of the cause of conflict, the participants at the meeting, the sequence of events, and similar verbal expressions as evidence of literary dependence. He says that the best case for literary dependence of Acts 15 on Galatians 2 was made by Lightfoot, although Lightfoot did not come to this conclusion. It will be useful to have these comments by the bishop of Durham before us:

> The *geography* is the same. In both narratives the communications take place between Jerusalem and Antioch: in both the head-quarters of the false brethren are at the former place, their machinations are carried on in the latter: in both the Gentile Apostles go up to Jerusalem apparently from Antioch, and return thence to Antioch again. The *time* is the same, or at least not inconsistent
> The *persons* are the same: Paul and Barnabas appear as the representatives of the Gentile Churches, Cephas and James as the leaders of the Circumcision. The agitators are similarly described in the two accounts: in the Acts, as converted Pharisees, who had imported their dogmas into the Christian Church, in the Epistle, as false brethren who attempt to impose the bondage of the law on the Gentile converts. The two Apostles of the Gentiles are represented in both accounts as attended: "certain other Gentiles" (ἐξ αὐτῶν) are mentioned by St Luke; Titus, a Gentile, is named by St Paul. The *subject of dispute* is the same: the circumcision of the Gentile converts. The *character of the conference* is in general the same; the exemption of the Gentiles from the enactments of the law, and the recognition of the Apostolic commission of Paul and Barnabas by the leaders of the Jewish Church.[102]

Lightfoot was attempting to answer an old question: were Galatians and Acts describing the same conference? Pervo concurs with Lightfoot and most scholars today in affirming that the conference being described in the two accounts is the same. But Pervo is interested not only in these more general similarities but also in some of the small details. Drawing on Walker and Leppä, he considers, for example, the roles of Titus in Paul and Timothy in Acts. In Gal 2:3, Paul says that Titus, a Greek, was not compelled to be circumcised (although it is not clear whether he voluntarily accepted it). No mention is made in Acts of Titus, his presence at the conference, or his circumcision. But just after the narrative about the conference we read of Paul's circumcising Timothy, the son of a believing Jewish mother and a Greek father (Acts 16:1–3). Luke comments that Paul wanted Timothy to accompany him and that he had him circumcised because of the Jews in Lystra. The verb for accompanying (συμπαραλαμβάνω) had been noted by Leppä, and it attracts Pervo's attention as well. He writes: "Whereas Luke erases the uncircumcised Titus from the story while narrating the circumcision of Timothy, here he uses a verb [συμπαραλαμβάνω] associated with Titus in relation to another person. This unusual verb appears in Galatians and Acts in association with a cluster of ideas and motifs: Paul's associates, the Jerusalem Conference and its consequences, a collection, circumcision, and Paul's break with Barnabas."[103]

Pervo agrees with Walker's conclusions about the speech of Peter in Acts 15:7–11, but he adds an important qualification: "The Peter of Acts 15 conveys the ideas of Paul in Galatians, but he does so with the accents of Ephesians. In short, the speech of Peter in Acts 15:7–11 is a paraphrase of Galatians as Galatians could be understood in a later period. The speaker is a 'Deutero-Pauline Peter.'"[104] Pervo has in mind passages such as Eph 2:8, in which "salvation" is substituted for "justification," as used in the authentic Pauline letters. He notes further that Luke shares the Deutero-Pauline concern to flatten out differences between Peter and Paul.[105]

A major reason that earlier scholars did not conclude that Luke used Galatians in constructing his narrative about the apostolic council is not that they ignored the similarities but that they misperceived Luke's intent. In agreement with Leppä, Pervo maintains that one of Luke's purposes in Acts 15 was to subvert Galatians 2. He writes: "To put it rather sharply, in the matters of the dispute at Antioch Luke has turned Galatians 2 upside down. Galatians appears to be his major source, but what he claims is quite opposed to what Paul says in Galatians. In other words, Luke can sometimes transform Galatians as he sometimes rewrites Mark."[106]

Despite the present consensus about the nonuse of the Pauline letters in Acts, Enslin, Walker, Leppä, Pervo, and other scholars have succeeded in mounting a serious counterargument. In my judgment they have shown that there is now sufficient reason to question the usual scholarly conviction that Acts was written in ignorance of the Pauline letters. The nonuse of the Pauline letters in Acts can no longer be cited as an impediment to a second-century date for Acts.

Conclusion

The issues addressed here may suggest to some readers that the problem of dating Acts is imponderable, that it is impossible to determine even a probable date for its composition. Nevertheless, given the widest range of dates that is generally accepted, that is, 60–150 C.E., and the three nodal dates that we have examined in this chapter, that is, an early, an intermediate, and a late date, several observations are in order.

First, arguments for an early date, that is., 60–70 C.E., are flawed. Luke's failure to mention specifically the fall of Jerusalem and the death of Paul do not require us to conclude that he wrote before these events occurred. Moreover, the sayings of Jesus included in the Gospel of Luke show convincingly that its author was looking back on the events of 70 C.E. and hence was writing after they took place. The author of Acts was certainly aware of what had been written in Luke 19:41–44 and 21:20–24.

Second, arguments for an intermediate date, that is, 80–90 C.E., although favored by most scholars today, are built on an inadequate foundation. They rightly cite Luke's knowledge of the fall of Jerusalem, but they fail to recognize the affinities between Acts on the one side and Josephus and the letters of Paul on the other.

Third, arguments for a late date for Acts, that is, 100–150 C.E., recognize more of the relevant factors affecting its composition and present us with fewer problems than do the other nodal dates. The terminus a quo is determined by the influence of Josephus on Acts and the use of Paul's collected letters. The terminus ad quem is the appearance of citations of Acts in Justin and later writers. In the first half of the second century the death of Paul and the fall of Jerusalem are distant memories that do not require explicit reference.

An attempt to narrow this range of dates (100–150 C.E.) and find a more precise time for the composition of Acts depends on a number of factors. Foremost among them is the question of context. Within the limits set forth above, is it possible to determine a time that would provide the conditions in which a book such as Acts might appropriately see the light of day? Are there issues to which the author of this book is responding? The chapters that follow will attempt to show that the struggle of the church with Marcion and Marcionite Christianity provides the most likely context for the writing of Acts.

CHAPTER *2*

The Challenge of Marcion and Marcionite Christianity

Although proto-orthodox Christians faced challenges from many sources during the second century, none seemed as ominous as that posed by Marcion. To judge from the attention he generated among other early Christian writers, his theology must have been perceived as something threatening to the very heart of Christian belief. It is no exaggeration to say that in his day Marcion posed the questions that involved the very definition of what Christianity was all about. And yet, for many reasons, he remains for us a most elusive figure.

Any reconstruction of Marcion's life and thought faces obstacles that are well known among scholars of ancient history. Figures from a past so long ago are generally inaccessible to us, but this is especially so for those who left no writings and those whose writings are unavailable. We have several references to a text written by Marcion known as the *Antitheses* and alleged quotations from it, but the text as a whole is not extant.[1] We also know of the so-called Marcionite prologues, short Latin prefaces attached to the Pauline letters, but they appear to have been composed by later Marcionites. Even if our texts were more complete, we would face serious problems of interpretation, but in the present situation we have little to go on if we want to learn anything historically reliable. Moreover, we have very little information pertaining to Marcion that comes from a time contemporary with him. Almost everything we have about Marcion comes ultimately from the polemical attacks on him by heresiologists of the second through the fourth centuries, above all Irenaeus, ca. 185 C.E., and Tertullian, ca. 207 C.E.[2] Irenaeus's major work was a five-volume attack on various heresies, including the beliefs of Marcion and his followers. Although he draws on Irenaeus for much of his information about Marcion, Tertullian provides us with a fuller treatment, devoting the entirety of five books to him and his followers. These and a few other writers include references to and quotations from Marcion's writings, but no texts have survived apart from the citations and allusions by his opponents, and so his voice can no longer be heard in an unfiltered way.

Like polemical attacks in general, those directed against Marcion are incomplete and misleading. Tertullian devoted significant attention to Marcion. We have the five books he wrote, specifically entitled *Adversus Marcionem,* and he notes that this is the third edition of his work but the only one to survive.[3] Tertullian reveals his bias at the very beginning of book 1, when he describes Pontus, the home of Marcion: "There is sternness also in the climate—never broad daylight, the sun always niggardly, the only air they have is fog, the whole year is winter, every wind that blows is the north wind. Water becomes water only by heating: rivers are no rivers, only ice: mountains are piled high up with snow: all is torpid, everything stark. Savagery is there the only thing warm—such savagery as has provided the theatre with tales of Tauric sacrifices, Colchian love-affairs, and Caucasian crucifixions."[4] Can we really have confidence in a writer who begins in such a way? Tertullian continues: "Even so, the most barbarous and melancholy thing about Pontus is that Marcion was born there, more uncouth than a Scythian, more unsettled than a Wagon-dweller, more uncivilized than a Massagete, with more effrontery than an Amazon, darker than fog, colder than winter, more brittle than ice, more treacherous than the Danube, more precipitous than Caucasus."[5] Tertullian's contemporaries would probably not have been offended and may even have admired his style at this point, but it does not encourage modern readers who would prefer a less biased report about Marcion and his beliefs.

Faced with such obstacles in the ancient sources, it would appear to be impossible to learn anything reliable about Marcion himself. Reconstruction of the historical Marcion may prove even more elusive than reconstruction of the historical Jesus. It is, however, possible to acquaint ourselves with the challenge that Marcion presented to those Christians who opposed him. Despite their polemical attacks, there is no reason to think that Irenaeus and Tertullian were attempting to mislead their readers about their own conceptions of the dangers that Marcionite Christianity posed. They may not have gotten it right when it came to describing Marcion's life and teachings, but they would not have invented their perceptions of the threat he posed to proto-orthodox Christianity. So our hope is a relatively modest one: to gain some access to Marcionite Christianity as seen from the position of those who opposed it and to use this knowledge as a basis for a few limited inferences about Marcion's life and teachings.

Secondary scholarship on Marcion has not been lacking. That of Adolf von Harnack has become standard for scholars today. Although Harnack was aware of the difficulties in using ancient heresiological sources for reconstructing the life and teachings of Marcion, he devoted surprisingly little attention to the problems. Subsequent scholarship would have been greatly aided by a full discussion of the ways in which we might make use of writers such as Irenaeus and Tertullian, and ways in which these authors tend to mislead us. Further, as it has been abundantly noted, Harnack himself was not unbiased when it came to Marcion. He regarded him as a major reformer of the early church and the only early figure to approach an understanding of the letters of Paul. Comparisons with Luther sprinkle Harnack's study of Marcion. For example, Harnack comments on a hearing in which Marcion presented a challenge to the leaders of the church at Rome as follows: "It will always remain memorable that at the first Roman synod of which we know, there stood before the presbyters a man who expounded to them the difference between law and gospel and interpreted their Christianity as a Jewish kind. Who does not think here of Luther?!"[6]

Although Harnack's study is still regarded as indispensable for Marcionite scholarship, a number of more recent scholars have questioned one or more of its conclusions. Walter Bauer shows us a different way of perceiving the theological and ecclesiastical landscape in the second century as one of immense diversity among Christian groups.[7] John Knox's study, *Marcion and the New Testament,* which is fundamental to my own work, opened the question of the relation of Marcion to the Acts of the Apostles and challenged some of Harnack's conclusions about his relation to the Gospel of Luke as well.[8] R. Joseph Hoffmann developed grounds for an earlier dating of Marcion than Harnack had proposed and reinterpreted certain aspects of Marcion's thought as well.[9] Gerhard May and Katharina Greschat have edited a collection of essays on Marcion that came out of a recent conference held in Mainz.[10] May's introduction, entitled "Marcion ohne Harnack," reveals the intention to press research beyond that of the great Berlin scholar.[11] Rather than discussing the work of these scholars in detail here, I intend to draw on them at specific points in this chapter, when their contributions appear to be most relevant.

In what follows we will discuss first what the sources reveal biographically about Marcion. In this discussion we will be especially interested in determining when it was that Marcion's opponents first became aware of him. Following this, we will discuss what the sources, chiefly Irenaeus and Tertullian, tell us about Marcionite theology and practice. Here we will attempt to understand what theological assertions and ethical and liturgical practices most bothered Marcion's opponents. Finally, we will turn to two special issues: Marcion and Paul; and the Gospel of Marcion.

Marcion's Life and Times

The early sources agree that Marcion's home was in Pontus on the Black Sea, described with such animus by Tertullian. Tertullian refers to him as a ship-master.[12] Other sources report that his father was a bishop, who expelled him from the Christian community at Pontus, and that he seduced a virgin. Most modern scholars take this last charge as a metaphor for heresy (he seduced the virgin church), and the supposition that he was expelled from the church by his father seems equally dubious. In any event at some point Marcion left Pontus with letters of recommendation from fellow citizens and engaged in missionary work in Asia Minor. Irenaeus, Tertullian, and others connect Marcion with one Cerdo, but they disagree on who was the master, and who the disciple. Irenaeus says that Marcion amplified Cerdo's doctrines;[13] Tertullian says that Cerdo "gave shape to this [Marcion's] outrage."[14] At some time Marcion came to Rome, where he presented the church with a sizable donation. He seems to have been well regarded in the capital for a number of years. Tertullian notes that at one time Marcion held the same convictions as did the "orthodox" but later adopted "heretical" views.[15] After challenging the leaders of the church to agree that the gospel of Christ was totally new and could not be adjusted to the Hebrew Scriptures, Marcion was compelled to break with Rome. But his movement continued for a number of centuries, especially in the East.

Our earliest sources are inconsistent and hence confusing in reporting Marcion's dates. Some of the confusion results from the fact that the authors of these sources are driven by a concept that, drawing on Hoffmann, we may designate, the "genealogy of error."[16] The concept is that right belief must precede wrong belief, that "orthodoxy" precedes "heresy." Clement of Alexandria articulates this concept most clearly and nails down three periods—Jesus; apostles; heresy—with precision: "The teaching of the Lord at his advent, beginning with Augustus and Tiberius, was completed in the middle-times of Tiberius. And that of the Apostles, embracing the ministry of Paul, ends with Nero. It was later, in the times of Adrian the king, that those who invented the heresies arose; and they extended to the age of Antoninus the elder."[17] Clement would date the ministry of Jesus as concluding ca. 30 C.E., and the times of the apostles and Paul ca. 60. He would designate the age of heresy as ca. 117–161 C.E. Earlier writers, including Irenaeus and Tertullian, think in similar terms. Irenaeus describes a genealogy of heresy that begins with Simon Magus, regarded as the father of all heresies, and proceeds through Menander, Cerdo, and Marcion. Cerdo, says Irenaeus, came to Rome at the time of the ninth bishop, Hyginus (137–140 C.E.), and Marcion succeeded him at the time of the next bishop, Anicetus (154–166 C.E.).[18] But prior to all of them, writes Irenaeus, were the apostles, who passed on the traditions obtained originally from Jesus. Since these writers approach the times of Marcion with a "genealogy of error" theory in mind, they are compelled to discount any information that would suggest an early date for him and to locate his times as late as possible.

Tertullian establishes the time of Marcion by means of a calculation that he says is based on the claims of Marcion's own followers. The tradition on which he draws apparently says that the time between Jesus and Marcion was 115 years, 6 months. If the time of Jesus is set at the fifteenth year of Tiberius, as Marcion apparently maintained, the time span in question began in 29 C.E. and ended in 144 C.E. Tertullian, who had already determined that Marcion came to Rome during the time of Antoninus Pius, confidently concludes that the Marcionite heresy first came to light under this emperor, and he believes that the followers of Marcion agree. "The dates themselves put it beyond argument that that which first came to light under Antoninus did not come to light under Tiberius: that is, that the God of Antoninus' reign [138–161 C.E.] was not the God of the reign of Tiberius [14–37 C.E.], and therefore he who it is admitted was first reported to exist by Marcion, had not been revealed by Christ."[19]

Drawing on this reference in Tertullian, Harnack concludes that the year 144 C.E. must originally have referred to some important date in the history of the Marcionite church. He is precise in calculating the time period as extending to the second half of July 144, and he writes: "This can only be the year of Marcion's final break with the church and the founding of his own church on the basis of the new scriptural canon."[20] But it does not seem legitimate to take Tertullian's comments as if they were meant to supply accurate biographical information about Marcion. In line with the concept of the late development of heresy, Tertullian's purpose was to show that Marcion's teachings did not come to light before the time of Antoninus Pius and that Marcion was "an Antoninian heretic, impious under Pius."[21] Hoffmann is correct in observing that "Tertullian's calculation is not offered, therefore, in the interest of supplying biographical information, but rather in order to prove that Marcion's teaching did not arise before the middle decades of the second century. Obviously, however, if the Marcionites had accepted this reckoning, as Tertullian claims, there would be no need for such proof. The only possible conclusion is that the Marcionites *themselves* posited a much earlier date for the founding of their church and, accordingly, for the teaching of Marcion."[22]

Unfortunately we have no way to document Hoffmann's claim that the Marcionites had an earlier date for the founding of their church. There is, however, an intriguing reference just following the statement of Clement of Alexandria quoted above. Clement says that the heretics allege that "Valentinus was a hearer of Theudas. And he was the pupil of Paul. For Marcion, who arose in the same age with them, lived as an old man with the younger [heretics]."[23] The statement about Marcion clearly does not represent Clement's views. The claim must, however, have been known in the third century as an allegation voiced by Marcion's supporters. It is likely that it represents a Marcionite reaction against the proto-orthodox conception about the late appearance of heresy, and it inspires no greater confidence than do Tertullian's and Clement's calculations. It is worth noting, however, that Clement's only means to refute the Marcionite claim is to reassert his views about the priority of truth to error.

Even if it seems appropriate to be dubious about the claims of Marcion's followers, there are good reasons to believe that his dates were somewhat earlier than those posited by Irenaeus and Tertullian. References from the early Christian writers are inconsistent, confused, and biased. Hoffmann's comments are apt at this point: "Tertullian's elaborate calculation like Irenaeus' genealogy and Clement's ambiguous chronology must be seen in this light. It is an attempt to counteract the effects of a tradition according to which Marcionism had developed much earlier than in the times of Antoninus. But the attempt leads to no consensus. Certain they are that Marcion did not converse with apostles: but they are far from certain about the facts of his life. Did his heresy erupt under Hadrian (Clement) or under Antoninus (Tertullian)? Was he a member of the church at Rome under Telesforus and a heretic under Hyginus (Tertullian), or a follower of Cerdo under the reign of Anicetus (Irenaeus)?"[24]

Despite the confusion, several modern scholars have attempted to sort through these references and have become convinced that Marcion's ministry began in the early decades of the second century. Harnack thought that Marcion must have been born ca. 85 C.E. and that he arrived in Rome ca. 138 and was excommunicated from there in 144. Harnack assumed that Marcion had an extensive ministry in the East prior to 138.[25] Knox generally accepts Harnack's dates but suggests that Marcion's ministry probably began in 120 or even 110 C.E.[26] Hoffmann, who doubts that Marcion ever really came to Rome, suggests that he was contemporary with Polycarp, that he was born ca. 70 C.E. and preached in Asia from 110 to 150.[27] Readers who wish to follow the intricacies of these analyses in detail should consult these important studies. In what follows, I do not intend to duplicate previous scholarly arguments but to call attention to some of the main references to be considered in any attempt to determine the times of Marcion.

Writing about 150 C.E., Justin Martyr is the first Christian author to refer to Marcion by name. He knows that Marcion teaches about two Gods and demotes the Creator-God to a lesser position. He expresses no knowledge relating specifically to Marcion's activity in Rome or about his excommunication from the church there, but what is striking is his sense of surprise that Marcion is still teaching. Justin first comments on the appearance of Simon of Samaria, generally regarded as the first of the heretics. He notes that Simon came to Rome during the reign of Claudius; he tells of his disciple Menander and then turns to Marcion. Justin writes: "Then there is a certain Marcion of Pontus, who is still teaching his converts that there is another God greater than the Fashioner. By the help of the demons he has made many in every race of men to blaspheme and to deny God the Maker of the universe, professing that there is another who is greater and has done greater things than he."[28]

Justin repeats these points later in the same document.[29] Hoffmann regards these references as the starting point for any attempt to date Marcion. They tell us that (a) Marcion has been successful in his preaching; (b) he has presented his views to a diverse audience; (c) he is still active. Hoffmann stresses the last of these points, calling attention to the phrase Justin used here: "Moreover, the phrase *kai nun eti* ['even until now'] suggests a longer period of heretical activity than is allowed for by the usual theory that Marcion became an influential teacher only after he reached the west. Inasmuch as Justin had sojourned in Samaria and Ephesus before coming to Rome, he was obviously in a position to know the extent of marcionite influence in the east."[30] It is not possible to press Justin's chronology, but it is notable that, despite the known tendency to view heresy as arising late, he begins his list of heretics in the time of Claudius (41–54 C.E.). Simon, he says, came to Rome during Claudius's reign, and Menander was his disciple. Justin does not specifically connect Marcion with Menander, but neither does he suggest a long period of time between them.[31] In any event his comments reveal his view that, before the middle of the second century, Marcion had had a successful tour of preaching, with converts from many nations and diverse cultures. We do not learn from Justin when he thought this ministry began, but his surprise that Marcion was then still active implies that he thought of him as at least a mature man, perhaps an old man, and that he understood him to be a well-known personage outside Rome. Justin's comments would not be inconsistent with a Marcionite ministry in the East that began in 120 or even 110 C.E.

Although Justin was the first to mention Marcion by name, it is likely that earlier Christian writers knew something of his movement. It has long been thought that there is an explicit reference to Marcion's *Antitheses* in 1 Tim 6:20. Here the author of the epistle (late first or early second century C.E.) warns Timothy to beware of the "Antitheses of falsely called Gnosis (ἀντιθέσεις τῆς ψευδωνύμου γνώσεως)."[32] Later writers explain that Marcion's *Antitheses* consisted of a comparison of law and gospel. Hoffmann sees some indications that the author of *1 Clement* was aware of Marcionite teachings, but he concludes that they "do not add up to the existence of a Marcionite 'error' as early as ce 98."[33] Hoffmann is, however, persuaded that something quite similar to Marcionite teaching was known by Ignatius, who wrote about 117 C.E. He has in mind Ignatius's suspicions about literal interpretations of the Hebrew Scriptures, and his defense of monotheism, both of which may well have been reactions to Marcionism.[34] The case for Ignatius is plausible, but an even stronger case can be made for Polycarp of Smyrna.

The key statement in Polycarp's letter to the Philippians is the following: "'For everyone who does not confess that Jesus Christ has come in the flesh is an antiChrist'; and whosoever does not confess the testimony of the Cross is of the devil: and whosoever perverts the oracles of the Lord for his own lusts, and says that there is neither resurrection nor judgment,—this man is the first-born of Satan."[35] In 1921 Harnack expressed doubts about the genuineness of this verse, because he knew that Polycarp wrote ca. 117 C.E. and that Marcion could not have been this early.[36] But in 1936 P. N. Harrison showed that the Polycarp letter was the result of the conflation of two previous letters and that the first twelve chapters dated from 132–133 C.E.[37] Only chapters 13 and perhaps 14 were written ca. 117 as a kind of covering letter for the transmission of Ignatius's seven letters. Thus the statement quoted above comes from the later letter of Polycarp, written after 130 C.E., and it may indeed refer to Marcion.

Harnack had also noted that the viewpoints condemned by Polycarp in Phil. 7:1 do not point specifically to Marcion.[38] Many groups were docetic, and the other charges are somewhat nebulous. But a key is the statement that "this man is the firstborn of Satan." Irenaeus knew that Polycarp had used this phrase and was certain that he used it to condemn Marcion.[39] But Irenaeus gave the use of the phrase a different setting. He placed its use in Rome at a later time and made it part of a brief dialogue between Marcion and Polycarp: "And Polycarp himself replied to Marcion, who met him on one occasion, and said, 'Dost thou know me?' 'I do know thee, the first-born of Satan.'"[40] Irenaeus thought that both Marcion and Polycarp came to Rome during the time of Bishop Anicetus (154–166 C.E.). It seems that Irenaeus located the meeting of Polycarp with Marcion at the time when the former met with Anicetus, that is, ca. 155 C.E. Hoffmann rightly observes that "the sentence which he [Irenaeus] attributes to Polycarp first appears in that writer's letter to the Philippians, dating in part from around C.E. 130. That Polycarp used the same words in rebuking Marcion at Rome in the reign of Anicetus a generation later (155) may reasonably be doubted, inasmuch as the choice of Rome as the scene of the encounter between the two rivals is probably to be explained on theological grounds: As the See associated with the two great Apostles, Rome represents the locus of the *traditio veritatis.*"[41]

These important testimonies from Justin and Polycarp, as well as inferences to be drawn from the Pastoral Epistles and Ignatius, give strong support for earlier dates for Marcion. From Justin we learn that Marcion had had an extensive ministry in the East prior to 150 C.E., and from Polycarp we can conclude that his teachings were known in the East by 130 C.E. Indications from Ignatius and the Pastorals suggest even earlier dates. We probably will not be far off if we conclude that Marcion's views were known, at least in part and in some locations, as early as 115–120 C.E.

Marcionite Theology and Practices

Limited as we are by the lack of unbiased sources dealing with Marcion, we must focus here on the ways in which his theology and practices were perceived by his opponents. Having said this, it is yet significant that we are able to form an impression of Marcion's theology that is remarkably coherent.

Harnack asserts that the gospel of Christ constituted the origin and the totality of Marcion's religious life. In Harnack's words, Marcion "felt in the gospel the whole force and power of the 'Numinous,' to use [Rudolf] Otto's expression."[42] He notes the force expressed in what appears to be the opening of Marcion's *Antitheses:* "O wonder beyond wonders, rapture, power, and amazement is it, that one can say nothing at all about the gospel, nor even conceive of it, nor compare it with anything."[43] Harnack stresses Marcion's reading of the Pauline epistles as his "point of departure." "The point of departure for Marcion's criticism of the tradition cannot be mistaken. It was provided in the Pauline contrast of law and gospel, on the one side malicious, petty, and cruel punitive correctness, and on the other side merciful love."[44] This observation is confirmed by Marcion's collection of the Pauline letters, headed by Galatians. Irenaeus and Tertullian both cite this connection. The latter writes, "The separation of Law and Gospel is the primary and principal exploit [*opus*] of Marcion. His disciples cannot deny this, which stands at the head of their document, that document by which they are inducted into and confirmed in this heresy."[45]

Paul's writings about the justification of sinners through Jesus Christ must indeed have had a powerful effect on Marcion's religious life. He found that the characteristics attributed to the divine in the Hebrew Scriptures were at fundamental odds with those associated with the divine in the letters of Paul. For him there was an irresolvable contrast between a God who enacted laws and judged humans in accordance with their obedience or disobedience of them and a God who justified sinners. He was also struck with the contrast between the teachings of Jesus and those of the Hebrew Scriptures, and he could not become convinced that Jesus and Paul meant to signify the same deity who was known through the Hebrew Scriptures. These convictions evidently formed the center of Marcion's faith and led him to challenge much that was taken for granted by other Christians. Marcion's core convictions, which were clearly rooted in the Pauline epistles, led him to the further conviction that the God who was revealed by Jesus was totally unknown before the time when Jesus appeared. What Jesus revealed and Paul taught was fundamentally new, unexpected, and unanticipated. At one point, Marcion went before the leaders of the church at Rome to ask for their understanding of two passages in a text that must have been generally known:[46]

> He also told them a parable: "No one tears a piece from a new garment and sews it on an old garment; otherwise the new will be torn, and the piece from the new will not match the old. And no one puts new wine into old wineskins; otherwise the new wine will burst the skins and will be spilled, and the skins will be destroyed." (Luke 5:36–37)
> No good tree bears bad fruit, nor again does a bad tree bear good fruit. (Luke 6:43)[47]

Marcion understood these sayings as declarations by Jesus that what he revealed was new and, hence, incompatible with what had gone before. The good he equated with the new; the bad with the old. It was apparently these contentions that led the Roman leaders to break off relations with Marcion and his followers.

Our ancient sources agree that Marcion made a total separation between the religion that Jesus and Paul espoused and that of the Hebrew Scriptures. The God of Jesus was totally unknown before Jesus appeared.[48] The God who ruled prior to 29 C.E. knew nothing of Jesus or of the second God.[49] The revelation of the God of Jesus occurred when Jesus first appeared, and Marcion was willing to date it with precision—in the fifteenth year of Tiberius, emperor of Rome. This is the first verse of Marcion's gospel, a verse that also appears in Luke 3:1. If he knew the verse in the Lukan form, he would have been impressed with the evangelist's own precision at this point—"In the fifteenth year of the rule of Tiberius Caesar, while Pontius Pilate was ruler of Judea, Herod tetrarch of Galilee, Philip, his brother, tetrarch of the country of Ituraea and Trachonitis, and Lysanias tetrarch of Abilene, in the time of the high priests Annas and Caiaphas, God's word came to John, the son of Zechariah, in the desert" (Luke 3:1–2). He might well have observed that Luke found it extremely important to call attention to this very important date. But Marcion would not have been able to use the Lukan phraseology in this form, since it refers to the appearance of John the Baptist rather than to Jesus. The Marcionite form combined Luke 3:1a with 4:31 and evidently ran: "In the fifteenth year of the rule of Tiberius Caesar in the times of Pilate, Jesus Christ came down to Capernaum, a city of Galilee, and he was teaching them in the synagogue."

Consonant with his conviction that the God of Jesus had been totally unknown before the fifteenth year of Tiberius, Marcion concluded that there could be no connection between Jesus and the Hebrew Scriptures. Irenaeus scored Marcion for excluding the Hebrew patriarchs—Abel, Enoch, Noah, Abraham—from salvation.[50] But it was the separation of the prophets from Jesus that seemed most unsettling for

Marcion's opponents.[51] As Harnack, in expressing Marcion's views, put it: "Christ is all in all and hence also the founder and the perfecter of faith. Before him were only false prophets, and after him there is no need of any further revelation but only of a restorative reformation."[52] Evidently Marcion stressed a nonallegorical, nonfigurative interpretation of the prophets and, indeed, of the entire Hebrew Scriptures. Tertullian condemned him for this because it meant that he was in agreement with Jews, who likewise denied that the prophets predicted the coming of Jesus.[53] Marcion's insistence on literal interpretation is especially stressed in a reference by Tertullian to Isa 7:14; 8:4: "Appeal next, as your custom is, to this description of Christ which Isaiah makes, and assert your claim that it in no point agrees. In the first place, you allege, Isaiah's Christ will have to be named Emmanuel, and afterwards to take up the strength of Damascus and the spoils of Samaria against the king of the Assyrians: and yet he who has come was neither known by any name of that kind, nor has ever performed any warlike act."[54]

But Marcion evidently believed in the authority of the Hebrew Scriptures and accepted Isaiah and the other prophets as trustworthy predictors of the future. It follows that the future one predicted by these prophets was not Jesus and that such a one has not yet come. That coming is still to be anticipated as a future event, as Jews believe.[55] If Tertullian is right, the distinction between the two Christs was, in part, relative to the extent of their functions: "Neither for that matter can you establish that suggestion of yours, with a view to distinguishing between two Christs, as that the Judaic Christ was intended by the Creator for the regathering out of dispersion of the people [of Israel] and no others, whereas your Christ has been advanced by the supremely good god for the deliverance of the whole human race."[56]

If Christ is all in all, and if Jesus revealed a hitherto unknown God, it follows that the God of Israel is not to be the object of Christian worship. The qualities of this God are at odds with those of the father of Jesus Christ. But Marcion nevertheless accepted the Hebrew Bible as the book to be identified with this God, in a sense, the book that revealed this God. In this sense it is a trustworthy Scripture, accurately describing the Creator-God, giving a truthful account of history, and containing yet to be fulfilled prophecies. Harnack calls attention to the fact that "Marcion remained true to the Jewish-Christian tradition in identifying the creator of the world and the God of the Jews."[57] But Marcion was pointed in his criticism of this God. A Creator-God was no more acceptable to Marcion than to the Gnostics, although he was not interested in describing the creative activity in their terms. For him neither the creation stories of Genesis nor the Torah as a whole was to be challenged on the grounds of their accuracy but rather in terms of the God portrayed in them. Despite his animus against him, Tertullian is probably correct in claiming that Marcion had deep suspicions about the God of the Hebrew Scriptures. This God enacted the *lex talionis,* which allowed for physical retaliation that for Marcion was deeply objectionable.[58] This God is inconsistent: "he forbids labour on sabbath days, and yet at the storming of the city of Jericho he commands the ark to be carried round during eight days which include the sabbath."[59] This God was inconsistent on the matter of sacrifices.[60] This God was either capricious or lacking in foresight, since he sometimes approved a person and later disapproved him;[61] or God repents a previous action, as in the case of Saul (1 Sam 15:11) or Jonah (Jonah 3:10; 4:2).[62] This God seems not to be omniscient, unaware of the whereabouts of Adam in the Garden of Eden (Gen 3:9, 11) or of Cain's murder of Abel (Gen 4:9–10).[63]

Marcion's alleged ditheism receives significant attention from his opponents. Irenaeus argues that reason alone shows that the Creator is God and that there is only one God.[64] So Marcion is to be condemned for ditheism, which, in Irenaeus's view, results in atheism. "Marcion, therefore, himself, by dividing God into two, maintaining one to be good and the other judicial, does in fact, on both sides, put an end to deity. For he that is the judicial one, if he be not good, is not God, because he from whom goodness is absent is no God at all; and again, he who is good, if he has no judicial power, suffers the same [loss] as the former, by being deprived of his character of deity."[65] Tertullian likewise condemns Marcion for belief in two Gods,[66] but then goes in the opposite direction from Irenaeus and stretches the number of Marcionite deities from two to nine.[67]

The heresiologists were convinced that the qualities of the two Gods are justice and love, and that for Marcion these were mutually exclusive. The God of Israel is shown in the Hebrew Scriptures to be a God of unmitigated justice, promulgating laws and judging without a sense of mercy or compassion. The God of Jesus, on the contrary, transcends any sense of human justice and approaches humankind as unknown and alien. Further, since the God of Israel is associated with the created order, this God is also associated with matter. This God is to be characterized as one whose concerns are material. Harnack lists the following characteristics of Marcion's Creator-God: *"his ignorance of the existence of the other God; his profane revealedness; the identity of his nature with the nature of the world* (even though it is the higher), *and the base and contemptible method of procreation which he has arranged or which he at least tolerates."*[68]

It would follow that the God of Jesus is pure spirit, and the Son of God cannot truly participate in matter. Tertullian is certain that Marcion is to be counted among the Docetists.[69] If the God of Jesus Christ is not the Creator-God and not in any way associated with anything material, as Marcion claimed, the Son of God could not be a material being. Thus he only appeared to come in the flesh. He was not truly born.[70] Tertullian ridicules Marcion's view that birth is vile and beneath the dignity of God by observing that Jesus' death on the cross, which Marcion apparently accepted, was far viler. He asserts that "nativity cannot be more undignified than death, or infancy than a cross, or [human] flesh than condemnation. If Christ did in very truth suffer those things, it was a lesser thing to be born."[71] We should assume from what Tertullian says that, according to Marcion, Jesus truly suffered on the cross, but his Christology is by no means clear. Consistent with the view that human procreation is vile and objectionable, Marcion's gospel lacked birth and infancy narratives. But substantial portions of the crucifixion stories were included.

It may be an understatement to say that Marcion's Christology is unclear. Markus Vinzent, in an analysis of the end of Marcion's gospel, concludes that the nature of Christ can best be described as a "pneumatic corporeality." He writes: "Marcion held firmly to the belief that Christ was a spirit, a spiritual nature without bones (therefore he also eliminated ψηλαφήσατέ με καὶ before ἴδετε [Luke 24:39]), but he also stressed that Christ did not appear without a body. So from Tertullian and other opponents it is clear how Luke 24:37ff. serves as a central reference for Marcion's differentiating between the pneumatic corporeality, which Christ possesses and which is the soul of the believers, and the material body, which comes from the Demiurge and is therefore doomed."[72] Vinzent concludes that the lack of an ascension story in his gospel is consistent with Marcion's views generally. There is no hint of an ascension in Paul, and such a physical, locatable story would conflict with the understanding of Christ as a spiritual reality.

The practices of the Marcionites were, so far as we can determine them, consistent with the theological views discussed above. If the Creator-God, associated with the material order, is the inferior God from whom Jesus seeks to liberate humanity, it follows that those who are so liberated will avoid the material world as far as possible. Sexual acts and birth are regarded as contemptible and to be avoided. So the followers of Marcion do not marry, and the unmarried, divorced, and widowed are expected to remain celibate.[73] In regard to the liturgical use of food and dietary practices, we are told that Marcionites used milk and honey at baptisms, used water instead of wine at the Eucharist, and generally ate fish instead of meat.

But in a recent article Alistair Steward-Sykes reminds us that our sources for this information come from a time about two centuries after the time of Marcion and his original followers.[74] He claims that in the second century Marcionite liturgical and eating habits would not have varied significantly from those of other Christian groups. In the fourth century, however, such practices were regarded as heretical. Steward-Sykes writes: "In a second century context there was no difference between Marcionite and catholic sacred meals; both avoided meat, both employed bread and water, both employed wine, both knew the use of a variety of foods. . . . However, by the time of Epiphanius the boundary around the eucharist had shifted from participation to presence and the use of water in sacred meals had become the mark of a heretic, for bread and wine were now the unique media of sacred eating and the use of water something to be observed as unusual. . . . At the same time the old Christian avoidance of meat had, by the fourth century, become the mark of a heretic, and principled vegetarianism thus forbidden to the clergy. By this time, therefore, the Marcionites stood condemned on grounds of heteropraxy when, liturgically at least, they were guilty of no more than anachronism."[75]

These comments should remind us that most of our sources are not contemporary with Marcion himself and must be used with a great deal of caution. Two special features of Marcion's theology and religious practice remain to be considered, namely, his understanding of Paul and the Pauline epistles, and the gospel that Marcion regarded as authoritative for Christians.

Marcion and Paul

Paul's epistles unquestionably had a powerful influence on the development of Marcionite theology. Marcion's core ideas, examined above, reveal that the man from Pontus must have spent long periods of time poring over these letters. The inclusion of ten Pauline letters, headed by Galatians, in the Marcionite canon, simply underscores the significance the letters must have held for this early Christian leader. Harnack regarded Marcion as the first to grasp the significance of Paul for Christian faith, and he ranks him as one of three leaders of ancient Christianity. "No other religious personality in antiquity after Paul and before Augustine can rival him in significance."[76]

But to observe that the letters of Paul served as basic inspiration for Marcion does not tell the whole story, since the texts of the letters in the Marcionite collection sometimes varied from those used by proto-orthodox Christians. In some cases the Marcionite texts may be more original than those used by his opponents; but in other cases it is evident that Marcion edited the texts he received. In this respect, of course, Marcion is not unlike his opponents, since standard texts were unknown in the second century. As Knox observed, "it is unquestionably true that Marcion edited his text (who didn't, as a matter of fact?)."[77] In many cases his alterations are relatively insignificant, but some of the larger omissions appear to have been made in order to bring the Pauline letters into line with Marcion's theology. This, of course, would not be the way Marcion himself would say it, but in order to understand his approach we need to call attention to the main points that guided Marcion's interpretation of Paul.

It is no accident that the letter to the Galatians stands at the head of Marcion's collection of Pauline letters, and it is here that we find keys to his interpretation of Paul. At the very beginning of this letter we have a vigorous defense of Paul's apostleship: "Paul an apostle—sent neither by human commission nor from human authorities, but through Jesus Christ and God the Father, who raised him from the dead" (Gal 1:1). Here Paul strongly denies any association with other leaders and affirms his own independence. He repudiates the suggestion that his apostleship was based on a commission from other authorities. Then Paul expresses amazement that his converts in Galatia have turned to embrace teachings other than his. He employs exceedingly strong language to condemn these teachings. Such teachings cannot constitute another gospel, because there is only one gospel, and any who present their teachings as another gospel are anathema: "But even if we or an angel from heaven should proclaim to you a gospel contrary to what we proclaimed to you, let that one be accursed!" (Gal 1:8). Paul asserts that his gospel was revealed to him, that it was not of human origin (Gal 1:9).

In Galatians 2 Paul tells of his meeting with Jerusalem leaders. He claims that these leaders did not require the circumcision of the Greek Titus, but he notes that "false brothers" were secretly brought in to this private meeting as spies on the freedom he and his followers enjoyed. He insists, however, that he did not submit to the leaders or the "false brothers" (Gal 2:5).[78] The meeting ended amicably with a jurisdictional division of responsibilities: Cephas, James, and John were to work among the circumcised; Paul among the Gentiles (Gal 2:9b). But, says Paul, when Cephas came to Antioch, more problems ensued. Paul accused Cephas of acting dishonorably by succumbing to the pressure of "people from James" (τινας ἀπὸ ᾽Ιακώβου, Gal 2:12) and withdrawing from table fellowship with Gentile believers. He accused not only Cephas, but also Barnabas and the other Jews with them, of hypocrisy, and he found it necessary to remind Cephas of the gospel: "Yet we know that a person is justified not by the works of the law but through faith in Jesus Christ. And we have come to believe in Christ Jesus, so that we might be justified by faith in Christ, and not by doing the works of the law, because no one will be justified by the works of the law" (Gal 2:16).

Marcion apparently read Galatians 1–2 as fundamental to an understanding of Paul. He must have discovered here several keys that opened the doors to an understanding of the importance of the other letters and their bearing on the history of earliest Christianity. To begin with, Marcion was convinced that Paul not only claimed to be the only apostle of Jesus Christ, but that he was in fact what he claimed to be. He was appointed directly by Jesus Christ, and so his is the only gospel, revealed to him from heaven. And yet Paul was opposed by others who claimed to be apostles and denied the title to him. These were the Judaizers, who hounded Paul wherever he went and attempted to impose the Jewish law on Paul's converts. The incident at Antioch is an example of their efforts to undermine Paul's gospel, for here the representatives of James came from Jerusalem to bring pressure even on Peter to withdraw from eating with Gentiles. Although it dates from a time later than Marcion himself, the Marcionite prologue to Galatians states clearly the principles that guided his reading of this text: "Galatians are Greeks. These accepted the word of truth first from the Apostle, but after his departure were tempted by false Apostles to turn to the law and circumcision. These the Apostle recalls to the faith of the truth, writing to them from Ephesus."[79] The distinction here between the apostle and false apostles must go back to Marcion himself. He concluded that, shortly after Paul's divine appointment as apostle, others, notably James and Peter, began to oppose his preaching and induce his converts to depart from the true gospel and embrace Judaism. Harnack observed that Marcion "concludes from the Pauline epistles that the entire apostolic age had been moved exclusively by *one* major topic, that of the struggle of the Judaistic Christians against the true (i.e., the Pauline) gospel."[80] Indeed, all the Marcionite prologues provide evidence for this assertion. Marcion, Harnack said, "concluded that a large number of unauthorized and unnamed Judaizers had appropriated unto themselves the office of apostle in the church and had staged a propaganda campaign which had met with the greatest success in the entire empire, and in fact must have begun its unwholesome activity immediately after the resurrection."[81] This group certainly included James and Peter.

In Marcion's view these false apostles had also interpolated sections into Paul's own letters that attempted to compromise his preaching. In some of these sections Paul appears to draw on the Hebrew Bible as a text inspired by the God of Jesus or to make use of it as predictive of the revelation from Jesus. Some of these sections suggest that the God of creation and the God of Jesus Christ are the same (see, for example, Rom 1:19–21). Some associate Paul closely with the people of Israel (Rom 11:1). Some speak of affirming the validity of the law (Rom 3:31) or claim that justification by faith is possible apart from Christ (Rom 4:1–25) or that the covenant with the people of Israel endures permanently (Rom 11:29). Marcion was convinced that such features as these could not have come from the pen of the apostle who received his gospel from heaven. Thus he regarded these and other such sections as interpolations added by the false apostles, who desired to bring Christians back into the Jewish fold. Marcion was convinced that he had a duty to purge Paul's letters of these sections, so that readers would not be misled by them.[82]

The major elements in Marcion's understanding of Paul are clear: the affirmation that Paul was the only apostle; that his gospel was the only true gospel; that this gospel entailed a total renunciation of Torah and of the Scriptures associated with it; that false apostles, including James and Peter, attempted to undermine Paul's ministry and to re-Judaize Christian teachings; that these false teachers interpolated non-Pauline sections into Paul's letters; that when the interpolations are removed the letters of Paul consistently teach that the rule of law has been superseded through Jesus Christ, by whom human beings are justified by grace. Thus the purged letters of Paul, along with the gospel (on which see below), constitute sacred and authoritative literature for Marcionite Christians.

Marcion's Gospel

In reading Galatians Marcion must have been struck by the ways in which Paul called attention to "the gospel," and "the gospel I proclaimed." Paul's emphatic denial that there was "another gospel" (Gal 1:7–8) would have been understood as an unequivocal and authoritative claim. If Marcion understood the word "εὐαγγέλιον" in two senses, as signifying not only the message that Paul preached but also a book that contained the message, he would regard that book as having authority equal to that of Paul's letters.

Marcion's opponents are unanimous in saying that he and his followers had a canon that included the Pauline letters and a book that they called the "Gospel." Tertullian looks upon this title as a weakness, noting that the "orthodox" church has gospels that were written by named individuals but that Marcion's gospel lacked an author's name.[83] But Tertullian, along with Irenaeus, Epiphanius, and other opponents, was convinced that Marcion's gospel was a corruption of the church's Gospel of Luke. Irenaeus especially excoriates Marcion's treatment of the Gospel of Luke, which he describes as a mutilation. "Besides all this, he [Marcion] mutilated the Gospel according to Luke, discarding all that is written about the birth of the Lord, and discarding also many of the Lord's discourses containing teaching in which it is most clearly written that the Lord confessed His Father as the Maker of the universe."[84] Tertullian likewise claims that Marcion "mutilated" (*caederet*) the Gospel of Luke, which he chose from among the four gospels.[85]

Despite the claims of Marcion's opponents, there are grounds to doubt their understanding of the relation of Marcion's gospel to canonical Luke. Irenaeus and Tertullian were writing at the end of the second and beginning of the third centuries; Epiphanius lived during the fourth century. The ecclesiastical situation for all these writers was very different from that in Marcion's time. With Irenaeus we witness a growing sense that the church needs a definite measure of truth. This measure, it was thought, could be found in a canon, a list of authoritative and sacred books. Irenaeus himself was convinced that such stability was essential to the church's life, and his famous proclamation about the number of gospels reflects this conviction: "It is not possible that the Gospels can be either more or fewer in number than they are. For, since there are four zones of the world in which we live, and four principal winds, while the Church is scattered throughout all the world and the 'pillar and ground' of the Church is the Gospel and the spirit of life; it is fitting that she should have four pillars, breathing out immortality on every side, and vivifying men afresh."[86] Clearly Irenaeus has Marcion in mind when making this statement. His defense of four gospels means that the canon of the church is in line with the very structure of the world. It forms part of Irenaeus's concept of the church, which not only has the apostolic books but also has bishops who stand in a line of succession from the apostles and a creed which excludes beliefs such as those of Marcion.

But Irenaeus knew his own times better than he knew those of formative Marcionism. Indeed it is the challenge of Marcionism and other heresies that led Irenaeus to his convictions about the need for a definite church structure and canon. But Marcion himself must have lived at a more fluid time. Walter Bauer has convincingly shown that the early part of the second century was a time of great diversity in terms of Christian thought and practice. He observed that heterodoxy probably preceded orthodoxy in many locations and that, particularly in the East, Marcionism, or something closely resembling it, was the original form of Christianity.[87] Imposing late-second-century mores on an early-second-century figure leads to great misunderstanding. Thus to say that Marcion was faced with an authoritative canon of four gospels, selected one of the four, excised large chunks of material from it, and elevated it to a level above the others, in full consciousness of having chosen a practice opposed to the worldwide church, is anachronistic and misleading.[88]

Although we should doubt the claims of Marcion's opponents at this point, it is not clear how we should understand what he actually did. It is plausible to think that he chose one gospel out of several known to him, but in that event we should think of less formal collections of gospels and of books in various editions, with unstable texts. It might seem obvious that he would have chosen Luke as the gospel thought to have been written by the person most closely identified with Paul. But it is not clear that this identification was widely known early in the second century. After all, evidence for the conviction that the Gospel of Luke was written by a companion of Paul was not available before the publication of Acts, and it was Irenaeus who first made the connection, at least in writing that has survived.[89] So it does not seem likely that Marcion chose a gospel thought to have been written by a companion of Paul because he was impressed with the close relationship between the two. It seems more likely that the book that became Marcion's gospel had originally been a local Pontic text, probably the only gospel known in that region. The evidence for local texts at this time is strong, and the use of one gospel in a specific church is manifest.[90] But since there is significant overlap between the Gospel of Marcion and the canonical Gospel of Luke, it is not surprising that his opponents, speaking from within a very different context from his, would accuse him of mutilating the latter text.

The relationship of Marcion's gospel to canonical Luke will be treated more extensively in chapter 4, below. Here my major interest is in inquiring about the character and contents of Marcion's gospel. What did this text look like to those who wrote about it? Of course any attempt to describe this text is speculative, since the document itself is no longer extant and our only references to it are from Marcion's opponents. Tertullian devotes the entirety of book four of his *Adversus Marcionem* to an analysis of Marcion's gospel in comparison with canonical Luke. Epiphanius has some 78 short scholia, devoted to specific verses in Marcion's gospel. Is it possible to use these references to reconstruct Marcion's gospel?

Harnack's reconstruction is far and away the most frequently cited attempt.[91] He observed that Tertullian generally limited himself to short references and often omitted almost all verbal information, but he nevertheless treated his texts conscientiously. Epiphanius is also useful at those points at which his version of Marcion's text may be compared with that of Tertullian. Since Tertullian treated canonical Luke as a base and compared Marcion's gospel with it, his order in *Adversus Marcionem* 4 is that of canonical Luke, and Harnack follows this order.[92] Marcion's opponents did not accuse him of adding material to canonical Luke, but rather of omitting sections and altering the wording in some passages.[93] This should mean that the Gospel of Marcion would have contained a great deal of the same material we would find in canonical Luke, and this is the case in Harnack's reconstruction. Knox has provided us with a handy list of the pericopes that, according to Harnack, were almost certainly included in Marcion's gospel.[94] By Knox's count there were at least 682 verses in the Gospel of Marcion that are also included in canonical Luke, which in modern texts has 1,150 verses. This means that the two gospels would have overlapped about 60 percent of the time. Knox counts some 184 additional verses as uncertain, that is, they are unattested by the early witnesses. If these verses were also included in the Gospel of Marcion, that would mean that the two gospels overlapped about 75 percent of the time. It should be kept in mind that this is a listing only of the major pericopes without reference to the wording in individual verses, which in some cases may have varied significantly.

Harnack's reconstruction, of course, also noted the significant differences between the Gospel of Marcion and canonical Luke. By any measure, the most significant difference is to be found at the beginning of the two gospels. Marcion's gospel has nothing comparable to narratives in Luke 1–2 and very little from Luke 3:1–4:15. Only Luke 3:1a shows up in both gospels, and this verse forms the beginning of Marcion's. Not only is this a significant bulk of material; its inclusion or omission also makes a significant difference in the way the gospels will be read. In addition Harnack's Marcion lacks a number of pericopes that are contained in canonical Luke, including, for example, the parable of the prodigal son (Luke 15:11–32) and the narrative of Jesus' entry into Jerusalem, his weeping over Jerusalem, and the cleansing of the temple (Luke 19:29–46).

Harnack's reconstruction is rightly regarded as maximalist, and as such it has been frequently criticized. Some critics call attention to his own less-than-critical acceptance of Tertullian's attack on Marcion. Others think that his reconstruction was colored by his belief that Marcion used canonical Luke as his source text, as the early opponents had claimed. Perhaps the most acute recent critique is that of David S. Williams.[95] In fact Williams's criticisms raise doubts about the very possibility of reconstructing Marcion's gospel. Williams lists six problems that meet any modern scholar who attempts such a reconstruction. They are worth repeating here:

(1) Our major witnesses, Tertullian and Epiphanius, write in different languages, the former in Latin and the latter in Greek. Williams observes: "This creates a problem when comparing Tertullian's wording for a given passage with the Greek of Epiphanius and Luke."[96]

(2) Our two major witnesses are inconsistent in the "type and extent of the attestation they provide."[97] Tertullian rarely mentions what he thinks may be missing in Marcion's gospel, and since he passes over such material it is "difficult to tell whether such silence indicates that Tertullian simply had nothing to say concerning the passage, or whether it implies that the passage was actually missing from Marcion's Gospel."[98] Epiphanius, however, is specific about what he thinks Marcion left out but not about the actual wording of what he retained.

(3) In Tertullian's text quotations sometimes appear in different forms. "That is, on occasion Tertullian repeats all *or* part of a quotation he has already given from Marcion's gospel, but with different wording."[99] Williams acknowledges that the problem is compounded by the fact that Tertullian's is an ancient text that has also undergone changes in the process of transmission.

(4) "Tertullian varies between giving direct quotations, indirect quotations, and mere allusions. . . . In regard to allusions, the references are so vague that the wording of Marcion's text cannot be restored at all."[100]

(5) "Several times Tertullian charges Marcion with omitting material which does not appear in Luke at all."[101] The most notable illustration is Marcion's alleged omission of Matt 5:17, a charge which Tertullian makes three times over.

(6) "Marcion's text seems to have undergone widespread changes after the time of Marcion himself."[102] The result is that Tertullian and Epiphanius sometimes disagree on what was in and what was out of Marcion's gospel.

In view of these problems Williams proposes limiting the data to what he calls "explicit correlated readings," that is, direct quotations cited both by Tertullian and Epiphanius with a high degree of verbal agreement. Williams finds only twenty-three such readings, which he includes in an appendix to his article. Clearly this is a minimalist reconstruction of Marcion's gospel, and as such it fails to provide any sense of what that gospel may have looked like. Williams probably does not mean to suggest that these twenty-three citations (actually consisting of twenty-six verses) constitute the entirety of Marcion's gospel, but we gain no sense of what else might have been included. Indeed Williams's purpose seems to be to show that canonical Luke was not the basis for Marcion's gospel, a conclusion that I accept and to which I shall return in chapter 4. Williams's appendix may be useful as a kind of check list, but it cannot be regarded as an adequate reconstruction of Marcion's gospel.

Williams has, nevertheless, raised valid and serious questions about the process of reconstructing Marcion's gospel. Indeed his conclusion might well have been that such a reconstruction is impossible. On close examination, however, it turns out that the issues he raises relate more to the possible wording of Marcion's gospel than to the inclusion or exclusion of large sections. His proposals of "explicit correlated readings" may be of genuine help in nailing down the actual wording of a very few verses in the Gospel of Marcion, but we can gain a sense of what that gospel looked like only from a survey of some of the pericopes it probably contained.

Marcion's opponents were convinced that the text in question was a gospel, and that must mean that, in some sense, it resembled the gospels they knew. They further thought it was similar to canonical Luke. Although there is reason to doubt their charge that Marcion "mutilated" Luke, we nevertheless must acknowledge their perception that there is some resemblance between the two texts. For this to be the case Marcion's gospel must have resembled other known gospels in containing discourse and narrative material, and it must have contained some material that is found only in canonical Luke. Further, although Marcion's opponents call attention to what they regard as significant variations between canonical Luke and Marcion, their comments nevertheless require us to understand that these variations were embedded in larger pericopes.

For example, Tertullian and Epiphanius both refer to a verbal variation in Marcion's gospel as compared with Luke 5:14, one of Williams's "explicit correlated readings." Both quote the verse, and Epiphanius explicitly notes the difference: "'Go shew thyself unto the priest, and offer for the cleansing, according as Moses commanded—that this may be a testimony unto you [pl.],' instead of the Savior's 'for a testimony unto them.'"[103] It would be legitimate to conclude that this is the form of the quotation in Marcion's gospel. It would also be legitimate to conclude that the quotation appeared within a pericope about the healing of a leper, something like Luke 5:12–16. Luke 18:18–19 is another of Williams's readings. Tertullian quotes from it the verse *"Good Teacher, what shall I do to obtain possession of eternal life?"*[104] Epiphanius: "'One said unto him, Good master, what shall I do to inherit eternal life? He replied, Call not thou me good. One is good, God.' Marcion added, 'the Father,' and instead of 'Thou knowest the commandments,' says, 'I know the commandments.'"[105] The entire discussion requires the conclusion that Marcion's gospel contained something like the whole pericope that now appears in Luke 18:18–23.

Other examples could be examined, but the principle is the same: if Marcion's opponents refer to a sentence that is included in his gospel, with or without variations, it is reasonable to conclude that the pericope which surrounds the sentence in Luke, or something very much like it, also appeared in Marcion's gospel. Williams's issues make us rightly dubious about determining the wording of Marcion's gospel, but we can be reasonably confident about the inclusion or exclusion of the larger discourses and narratives. The obvious result should be that the Gospel of Marcion would look very much like canonical Luke, only shorter.

Harnack himself was not unaware of the kinds of difficulties that later critics have elaborated, and he understood the task of reconstruction to be one of making tentative suggestions. Critiques by Williams and others remind us that an examination of Harnack's suggestions about the actual wording of individual verses requires special caution. Each case should be questioned, and the basis of his suggested wording reexamined. Even with these reservations Harnack's reconstruction, in terms of its basic contents, is useful in giving us an impression of what Marcion's gospel must have looked like to those who first knew it.

In what follows I intend to make a few comments about the probable contents of the Gospel of Marcion. The information available to us does not allow us either to devise an outline of this gospel or to determine its contents exhaustively, but the observations that follow should result in providing some impression of its contents. In this section I will cite Marcion's gospel as "Gos. Mar.," but references to chapter and verse will necessarily be from canonical Luke. Thus the citation Gos. Mar. 4:31 refers to a verse in the Gospel of Marcion that also appears in canonical Luke 4:31.

The most nearly certain observation to be made about the Gospel of Marcion is that it lacks an account of Jesus' birth and infancy. It begins with the setting of time at 3:1a, but then it skips immediately to the narrative of an exorcism by Jesus in Capernaum, starting at Gos. Mar. 4:31.[106] The beginning ("In the fifteenth year of the rule of Tiberius Caesar") focuses attention on the date of the first appearance of Jesus and hence the time of the revelation of the God of grace. There are no predictions of the birth of Jesus or John, nothing of the parents, nothing of the circumstances of the births, no circumcision or presentation in the temple, no infancy narratives, and nothing of the twelve-year-old Jesus in the temple. Lacking is any account of the preaching or the imprisonment of John the Baptist; the narrative of Jesus' baptism by John, the temptation of Jesus, and the genealogies are all missing.

We can understand why Marcion would have omitted this material if it was known to him. In his theology conception and birth were among the most despicable instances of the Creator-God's rule, and doubtless Marcion could not imagine that Jesus was subject to them. In addition the omission of narratives that appear in the early chapters of canonical Luke serves to distance Jesus from any kind of Jewish heritage. There is no mention of any relationship to John the Baptist or his father, Zechariah, a priest of the temple; Jesus' mother does not undergo a postnatal cleansing, and Jesus is not circumcised. No genealogy connects him with Jewish ancestors or with parents of any kind. There is no anticipation of his appearance; he is not subject to being baptized, and he undergoes no temptations. These omissions, if it is right to regard them as such, are consonant with what we know of Marcion's theology, which would separate Jesus as much as possible from the Creator-God and his chosen people and would demonstrate the newness of his revelation.[107] The suddenness of Jesus' unannounced and unanticipated appearance heightens the drama at the beginning of the Gospel of Marcion. The lack of a birth and infancy account stresses the uniqueness of Jesus, who appears in the world without human connection or local habitation.[108]

We are told that Marcion rejected any belief that would associate Jesus with the Christ expected by the Jewish people, and some significant pericopes in the Gospel of Marcion may be understood to support this view. In Gos. Mar. 7:18–23 there are allusions to the story that John the Baptist sent to ask if Jesus is "the coming one." We are apparently to think that John is asking if Jesus is the Christ as traditionally expected, and it is significant that he receives no direct answer. Rather, Jesus says, "Whoever is not repelled by me is blessed" (Gos. Mar. 7:23). Epiphanius claims that Marcion altered the saying so that it referred to John the Baptist.[109] But the meaning is not clear, as Harnack said.[110] It is better to interpret it as Jesus' reply to John, in which he rejects the kinds of expectations that John's question implies. It is not an affirmation that Jesus is the Christ of Jewish expectation, and as such it conforms to Marcion's rejection of any belief that would associate Jesus with the Christ expected by the Jewish people. In addition there appears to be a specific rejection of the role of the Jewish Christ in Gos. Mar. 20:41–44. Apparently the Gospel of Marcion lacked the reference to Psalm 110 that we find in canonical Luke 20:42–43, and so read something like, "Why do you think the Christ is the son of David? David calls him Lord."[111] If David calls this figure "Lord," he cannot be his son. The conclusion must be that Jesus is not the Christ as expected by those who picture him as son of David.

Marcion's distancing of Jesus from Torah and the Hebrew Scriptures is prominently treated by his opponents, and it would be surprising not to find traces of this theme in the Gospel of Marcion. A well-attested verbal difference between the

Gospel of Marcion and canonical Luke is in Gos. Mar. 16:17. Marcion's gospel apparently read: "But it is easier for heaven and earth to go away than for one of my words to fall."[112] In canonical Luke at this point we have: "It is easier for heaven and earth to go away, than for one stroke of the Torah to fall" (Luke 16:17). Later, however, canonical Luke and Marcion seem to agree on wording that supports Marcion's reading: "Heaven and earth will pass away, but my word remains forever" (Gos. Mar. 21:33 = Luke 21:33: "Heaven and earth will pass away, but my words will not pass away"). For Marcion it is Jesus' words that are eternal; canonical Luke has two sayings, one supporting the eternality of Torah and one in agreement with Marcion.

Although Marcion's gospel does not affirm the permanence of Torah, this apparently does not mean that he regarded Torah or the Hebrew Scriptures as without value. A saying that meets the criteria of Williams's "explicit correlated readings" is Gos. Mar. 5:14. Here Jesus tells a healed leper to "show yourself to the priest and make an offering for your healing, as Moses commanded, for testimony to you." As we observed above, Epiphanius claims that the correct reading is "testimony to them."[113]

The relation of Jesus to the disciples comes in for particular attention, both in Marcion's gospel and canonical Luke. There is a good deal of attention paid especially to Peter's misunderstandings and failures. Jesus does not accept his confession, "You are the Christ" (Gos. Mar. 9:20), seemingly because the term would involve an understanding of Jesus as fulfilling Jewish messianic expectations. In the transfiguration story Peter's suggestion to build three tents—for Moses, Elijah, and Jesus—is said to come from his ignorance, as is also the case in canonical Luke (Gos. Mar. 9:33; cf. Luke 9:33). Peter's suggestion would seem to imply a close relationship of the three, which Marcion would certainly deny. Despite an expression of bravado by Peter, Jesus predicts his denial (alluded to in Gos. Mar. 22:33–34). But it is curiously unclear whether or not Marcion's gospel included the story of Peter's denial that appears in Luke 22:55–62.[114] If Marcion had known the story, it would have served as a perfect illustration of Peter's defection.

The narrative that describes the postresurrection appearances of Jesus is especially obscure in the Gospel of Marcion. Harnack made an impressive attempt to reconstruct Gos. Mar. 24, which, despite the reservations that we explored above, is worth an examination.[115] Such an examination exhibits the difficulties inherent in the task of understanding the Gospel of Marcion. Harnack quotes the passages that he thinks were almost certainly included in the Gospel of Marcion; he notes those verses that are unattested and those almost certainly omitted by Marcion.

Williams includes three readings from Luke 24 among his "explicit correlated readings:" Gos. Mar. 24:6, 7—referring to Jesus' predictions of suffering; Gos. Mar. 24:25—Jesus' rebuke to those who had not heeded his words (in Luke 24:25 the rebuke is for not heeding the words of the prophets); and Gos. Mar. 24:38, 39—Jesus' invitation to see his hands and feet. In Harnack's reconstruction significant sections of canonical Luke do not appear. There seems to be no reference to a stone that had been rolled away to unseal the tomb (Luke 24:2). The names of the women who first discovered the tomb to be empty are not provided (Luke 24:10). We are not told that Peter paid a visit to the tomb and left there perplexed (Luke 24:12). There are only fragmentary allusions to the Emmaus incident (Luke 24:13–35). Jesus does not discuss the Hebrew Scriptures, nor does he claim that the prophets pointed to his appearance (Luke 24:27, 44–46). There is no hint of an ascension (Luke 24:50–53).

The distancing of Jesus from the Hebrew Scriptures, a characteristic Marcionite theme, is clearly observable here. Instead of drawing attention to prophetic predictions of Jesus, Gos. Mar. 24 subtly avoids any connections between the prophets and Jesus. In Luke 24:25 the disciples on the way to Emmaus are rebuked for not believing the messages of the Hebrew prophets. But in Gos. Mar. 24:25 the rebuke is for not believing Jesus' words. Moreover, this rebuke comes in response to Cleopas's plaintive expression of hope that Jesus would be the one to redeem Israel (Gos. Mar. 24:21). Jesus, unrecognized by the travelers at this point, rejects this expectation and scolds them for their unbelief. He is not the one who fulfills Jewish messianic expectation.

The distancing of Jesus from the prophets, the Scriptures, and Jewish messianic expectations in Gos. Mar. 24 is closely connected with the treatment of the disciples in this chapter. It is not the disciples who discover Jesus' tomb to be empty on Easter morning. That honor belongs to others, presumably women (cf. Gos. Mar. 23:55–56), whose names are not given (cf. Luke 24:10). They report their discovery to the remaining disciples, who refuse to believe them. Following this in canonical Luke we have a curious verse about Peter running to the tomb but leaving without learning what had happened (Luke 24:12). Knox lists this verse as among those almost certainly included in the Gospel of Marcion, but Tertullian did not explicitly mention it, and neither did Harnack, who must have doubted its authenticity in canonical Luke. It is difficult to understand the reasons for including this verse, but even if it had been a part of the Gospel of Marcion, it would do little more than underscore Peter's lack of understanding (he "got up and ran to the tomb, bent over, and saw the linen cloths. And he returned by himself, wondering at what happened").[116]

In Harnack's reconstruction it is difficult to understand the course of the narrative after Gos. Mar. 24:13. Since there are no certainly included passages that describe the incident at Emmaus or separate this episode from the postresurrection appearance of Jesus at Jerusalem, we are left with the impression that the Gospel of Marcion had only one such appearance. It is not clearly locatable; the circumstances are fuzzy, and the participants are, for the most part, unnamed. Other than that of Jesus, which is not certainly attested, the only name that appears in the entire chapter is that of Cleopas, a name otherwise unattested either in the Gospel of Marcion or canonical Luke. Cleopas does not appear to be one of the remaining eleven, who are mentioned as unbelievers in Gos. Mar. 24:9, 11. But there are other unnamed disciples, who finally recognize the risen Jesus in what must have been conceived of as a Eucharistic meal of bread and fish. The narrative as reconstructed is confusing, but it is notable that the name of Peter never appears, and there is not even an allusion to a Petrine appearance as there is in canonical Luke 24:34. Apparently we are to think of him, and probably the other disciples as well, as being excluded from experiencing a postresurrection appearance of Jesus.

At the end of the Gospel of Marcion Peter and the other disciples are not privileged to be among those who discover the empty tomb or who experience the postresurrection appearance of Jesus, and they reject the reports brought to them. Marcion's gospel appears to be unrelenting in portraying those chosen by Jesus as blind to his purposes and failing to understand his teachings. In the end the Twelve almost disappear from the narrative; they have become false apostles. One who wanted to correct this impression would have to write something like the Acts of the Apostles and canonical Luke.

One additional observation about the Marcionite resurrection narrative needs to be made. Tertullian was perplexed about a verse in it, since it included words that would confirm belief in a physical resurrection of Jesus, and Tertullian knew that Marcion rejected this belief. In Gos. Mar. 24:39, the risen Jesus, in Harnack's reconstruction, says, "Look at my hands and my feet, because it is I. A ghost does not have bones as you see that I have." Tertullian writes: "Now here Marcion, on purpose I believe, has abstained from crossing out of his gospel certain matters opposed to him, hoping that in view of these which he might have crossed out and has not, he may be thought not to have crossed out those which he has crossed out, or even to have crossed them out with good reason. But he is only sparing to statements which he proceeds to overturn by strange interpretation no less than by deletion. He will have it then that [the words] *A spirit hath not bones as ye see me having,* were so spoken as to be referred to the spirit, 'as ye see me having,' meaning, not having bones, even as a spirit has not."[117] Tertullian's perplexity serves to confirm the contents of the Gospel of Marcion at this point. We may be reasonably certain that the gospel contained this verse, as Williams also maintained.

By way of summary, two themes are most prominent in Gos. Mar. 24. First, Peter is excluded from any participation in the postresurrection narrative, and the others are treated as unbelievers. Second, no connection is made between the resurrection of Jesus and the words of the prophets.

In the preceding discussion not only of the resurrection narratives but also of other passages included or omitted in the Gospel of Marcion, its relationship to canonical Luke remains an open question, which will be explored more thoroughly in chapter 4, below. Further, it is not suggested that the reading offered here is the only possible reading of Marcion's gospel. Any reading is plagued by the uncertainties of the text. But given the information available to us, this seems to be a plausible way to read this gospel as supporting many Marcionite convictions. The most certain observation we can make about the Gospel of Marcion is that it lacked all of what we find in Luke 1–2 and 3:1b–4:15. It is less certain but probable that it contained the pericopes discussed above that would underscore Marcion's views on the uniqueness of Jesus and his nonfulfillment of Jewish messianic expectations, as well as his views on Torah and the Hebrew Scriptures and the role of the disciples. The Gospel of Marcion must have contained some reference to the resurrection of Jesus, but most of what we now have in Luke 24 was not a part of it. We shall return to Marcion's gospel in chapter 4, below, in the attempt to gain a better grasp of its relationship to canonical Luke and hence its place in the history of Christian literature.

Marcion's Challenge

Marcion presented a formidable challenge to those who opposed his theology and practices. Indeed his opponents spent extraordinary energy in combating his influence, attacking his theology, and constructing alternatives to his practices. It was a massive effort, not only because many people found Marcionite Christianity attractive, but also because his was a complex challenge that, if met at all, had to be engaged on several fronts at once. Marcion's opponents rightly saw that the very definition of the Christian movement was at stake in the outcome.

If they were to meet Marcion's challenge, leaders such as Irenaeus and Tertullian would need to have a clear conception of the relation of the gospel to past history. Is it absolutely new, as Marcion would claim, or are there anticipations and predictions of it in the Hebrew Scriptures? Denying the newness of the Christian gospel might imply a doubt about its significance, and so Irenaeus and Tertullian would need to uphold the crucial significance of the gospel while at the same time affirming the sacred character and authority of the Hebrew Scriptures. Moreover, they would need to show that these writings could not be taken in strictly literal fashion, as the Marcionites did. They would need to show that the Hebrew prophets predicted the coming of Jesus Christ, and they would find that symbolic, allegorical, and typological interpretations provided the most reliable ways to understand their writings. Retention of the Hebrew Scriptures also would support the proclamation of monotheism and, hence, a theology of a single God, who not only created the world and gave Torah to the people of Israel, but also revealed divine grace through Jesus Christ.

A most difficult aspect of Marcion's challenge had to do with Paul. As we have already seen, Paul's letters were not collected until late in the first century and must not have been widely known for some time afterward. Admittedly, the author of *1 Clement* knew at least one of the letters, but Justin, writing several decades after the collection, makes no reference either to Paul or to any of the letters. Some of the letters reveal that there was serious contention about Paul's theology and activity even during his lifetime, but afterward there seems to have been a long silence about him. Little attention seems to have been paid to him, except by Marcion and his followers. But Marcion would make Paul the only apostle, and Paul's theology, as Marcion interpreted it, the only acceptable form of Christian thought. What would happen to the legacy of Peter and the other apostles, said by Marcion to be false apostles?

Knox adeptly elucidated the problem the non-Marcionite churches faced. He wrote: "The fact is that the more conservative churches (and this means Rome principally) in the middle of the second century were confronted with the necessity of a crucial choice as far as Paul is concerned: either they must canonize him or repudiate him (or at least seriously discredit him)."[118] Knox went on to say that this was not a real choice and that it was necessary for the more conservative churches to claim Paul, but not at the risk of casting off Peter and the other apostles.

Closely related to issues about the role of Paul are those related to his theology. It would have been known that Marcion drew his core convictions from Paul's writings about the opposition of law and grace. Marcion's exclusive adherence to grace meant that the law (and the Hebrew Bible that contained it) was not authoritative for Christians. For Marcion the church had to be seen as something over against Judaism. Even Jesus was shown to be distant, with no Jewish connections. Marcion's insistence on the newness of the revelation of Jesus Christ carried with it an inevitable denial of any vital relationship between Christians and Jews, between Christianity and Judaism. Certainly Marcion's opponents would not have wanted to deny the grace of God in sending the Christ and saving his people. But they were not ready to stress grace to the point that Torah, Hebrew Scriptures, and Jesus' Judaism would be relegated to oblivion.

Christian leaders, including Irenaeus and Tertullian, were quite explicit in their attempts to meet the challenge of Marcionite Christianity, and in their efforts they found the Acts of the Apostles to be of significant help. In the following chapters I intend to show that one of the purposes of the author of Acts and the editor of canonical Luke was precisely to provide ammunition for meeting the Marcionite challenge. These writings constitute early chapters in the response to Marcion, and they played a major role in what turned out to be a defining struggle for second-century Christianity.

CHAPTER 3

A Context for the Composition of Acts

In chapter 1 we concluded that the book of Acts was most likely written some time during the first half of the second century, that is, 100–150 C.E. We also observed that, in order to narrow the range of this period, we need to explore the possible context within which it was written. The chapter ended with the question whether it might be possible to find, in the first half of the second century, a plausible context for the composition of this book. We must, of course, keep in mind the fact that texts are composed within complex contexts and may be intended to serve multiple purposes. Thus our question is: given the probability that Acts was written in the first half of the second century and given the likelihood that its author wrote with more than one purpose in mind, is it possible to speak of at least one phenomenon that might provide an appropriate context for this composition? In chapter 2, we examined the challenges presented by the emergence in the early second century of Marcion and Marcionite Christianity. The present chapter will explore the proposition that the challenge of Marcion was one ingredient in the context of the composition of Acts, indeed the primary one.[1]

Although it is not often acknowledged, the context of Acts has been a problem for New Testament scholars. Ernst Haenchen alludes to the problem and indirectly hints at a solution, without embracing it. After a careful survey of possible quotations and allusions to Acts in second-century writings, he concludes that Justin is the first writer whose knowledge of Acts is certain. He adds that "until the middle of the second century Acts was not considered an authoritative book to which one might appeal."[2] Then he asks why it was not acknowledged earlier and concludes: "The only answer is that, unlike the gospel, it had no 'life-situation' in the Church at all. In Acts the Christian reader encountered a book unlike any he had previously known, and one which was neither necessary nor customarily used in preaching or instruction. Only because of its connection with the third gospel, then, was Acts allowed to cross the threshold of the Canon."[3] Haenchen notes further that Acts first proved useful to the church in the struggle against Gnosticism and that it was used extensively by Irenaeus.[4]

Haenchen's inquiry is directed to the reception of Acts in the church, but his comments raise questions about its composition as well. Indeed Haenchen creates a problem by holding to a first-century date for the composition of Acts but failing to find a proper context for its reception before the late second century. The neglect of

Acts by writers before Justin is better explained by its not being available than by an assumption that no earlier writer knew what to make of it. In any event a question about the context of reception has implications about the context of composition. If, as Haenchen asserts, Acts found no audience at the time it was composed and for several decades thereafter, the question of the context for its composition becomes serious indeed. Perhaps it is impossible for us, at this late date, to discern all the factors that may have prompted Luke to write this book, but it should be possible to find a context that would give meaning to both its composition and reception. Of course one cannot argue that because Acts was found useful in the struggle against heresy it must have been composed to serve this purpose. Other writings have served purposes not imagined by their authors. There is no compelling reason to assume that the context of reception is also the context of composition, but neither is there a compelling reason to avoid exploring the possibility that Acts was written primarily to serve one of the purposes for which it soon became so useful. This chapter explores the probability that the Marcionite challenge formed a major aspect of the context within which Acts was written and that it was written, at least in part, as a reaction to this challenge.[5]

The search for an appropriate context for Acts should begin with an examination of the literary aspects of the text. An examination of this sort will help us gain a clear perception of such things as the themes that control the narrative, the literary patterns, and the methods of characterization that the author used. Studies of the literary aspects of a text usually do not make assumptions about its date of composition or its context, but these are helpful in our quest since it is essential to understand what is going on in this text if we are going to ask about its context. The questions to be faced are: What are the themes in Acts? What literary patterns are employed? How are the characters portrayed? Why does the author adopt these themes and shape these characterizations? And, finally, in what historical context does this kind of presentation best fit? We begin this exploration with a discussion of themes and literary patterns in Acts.

Themes and Literary Patterns in Acts

Scholarship on Luke and Acts, especially in the commentaries, usually includes a listing and discussion of significant themes, but rarely is there a consideration of methods for determining them. Without some consideration of method, readers of commentaries and monographs probably gain the impression that the themes listed are obvious and incontestable; yet there is little agreement among scholars on just what these themes are. Robert J. Karris is one of only a few scholars who raise methodological issues in connection with the task of identifying themes in Luke. In his study of the literary characteristics of Luke 23 he includes a definition of "motif," drawn from William Freedman: "A motif, then, is a recurrent theme, character, or verbal pattern, but it may also be a family or associational cluster of literal or figurative references to a given class of concepts or objects"[6] But without further explanation Karris moves to the listing of major themes ("the faithful God, justice, and food"), and then he lists in alphabetical order some twenty apparently minor themes in Luke's gospel as a whole: "banquet, conversion, faith, fatherhood, grace, Jerusalem, joy, kingship, mercy, must, poverty, prayer, prophet, salvation, Spirit, temptation, today, universalism, way, and witness"[7] It is not clear how Karris determined that these are the controlling themes in Luke.

The danger of subjectivity in determining themes in an ancient narrative is quite real and should caution us to be self-conscious in our efforts. In my view the determination of dominant themes involves the utilization of literary-critical approaches that make few assumptions about the text. What is needed is a consideration of the text itself, not of course as a disembodied entity but as a document whose meaning is not dependent on hypotheses concerning its social, historical, cultural context, the identification of its author, the historical accuracy of the text, or the nature of the traditions on which the author may have drawn. It is not that these matters are unimportant—far from it—but that they may be bracketed for the purpose of reading the text.

It is often claimed that at least two preliminary matters must be settled before the reading can begin. The issue of genre is fundamental to any reading of a text, since different works are to be read in different ways. If Acts is general history, we read it with interest in the events being reported and with questions about the meaning of the events.[8] But if Acts is a narrative intended to instruct and entertain, we may be less interested in probing the reported events than in reading the text for the value of its story.[9] As important as it is to determine the genre of the Acts of the Apostles, the fact of the matter is that even this determination requires a prior reading of the text and is partially affected by the identification of major themes.[10] Other factors also must be considered, of course, such as the form and content of the narrative, but we recognize these also by a close reading of the text.

Determination of the intended readers may also be seen as a preliminary task.[11] If the Acts of the Apostles is directed to Roman officials, we would expect one of its dominant themes to have something to do with the political inoffensiveness of the early Christian movement. If the intended readers are members of the Greco-Roman intelligentsia, we might expect some stress on the correspondence of Christian beliefs with those among the cultural elite. If the intended readers are Christians, we might expect to find a compelling stress on divine confirmation of basic beliefs and practices. If the intended readers are potential converts, we might expect to find examples of conversions on the part of characters in the text. In fact we find all of the above, and so identification of the intended readers is very difficult. Like assumptions about genre, assumptions about intended readers should be bracketed in the effort to determine the dominant themes in Acts. As in the case of the genre question, our conclusions about intended readers are, in the first instance, dependent on our reading of the text. Therefore I want to test the hypothesis that it is possible to read Acts and to determine some of the dominant themes in it without first resolving questions about its genre or its intended readers.

We may initially seek thematic aspects of a narrative by examining the sections that appear to be redactional. Those places where the author speaks in his or her own voice, by summarizing or interpreting events and characters, should be particularly useful in determining dominant themes. But themes also appear in connection with repeated literary patterns, as well as in exemplary episodes that convey points of stress to which the author returns on several occasions. For the most part dominant themes will not be confined to the report of a single episode but will appear and reappear either throughout the narrative or in connection with several different stories. Some themes may form parts of the structure of the narrative, while others simply impress themselves on the reader by virtue of their recurrence.

A number of major themes appear in the opening chapters of Acts, especially Acts 1–5, chapters that establish a foundation for understanding themes throughout the book. This section of Acts is notable for its description of the idyllic beginnings of the Christian movement. Gerhard Lohfink coined the apt descriptive term "Jerusalem Springtime" to designate these opening chapters of Acts.[12] No reader would be likely to miss the stress here on the pristine beginnings of the Jesus movement. The narratives included in this section show the believers in prayer and the apostles healing the lame, performing wonders, and escaping from prison. About these chapters C. K. Barrett wrote persuasively: "Luke wished to hold up before his readers a set of Christian ideals which would show them what their own Christian life should be and at the same time supply them with a strong motivation for following the example"[13]

This opening section of Acts also contains a number of summaries that reveal matters the author wishes to stress (see Acts 2:42–47; 4:32–35; 5:12–14). In them we hear the narrator speaking in his own voice, and it is highly probable that Luke intends to use the summaries for the precise purpose of stressing the themes that are most significant for his project. Henry J. Cadbury was reluctant to attribute the summaries to the final redactor of Acts and held out the possibility that they may have been in sources at the author's disposal. He wrote: "How far the summaries came to our author along with his materials cannot now be determined. Whether thus derived or whether added by the final author, they give us tantalizing suggestions for determination of sources."[14] But Cadbury also was convinced that the summaries "are peculiarly liable to free treatment by the final editor and especially to combination."[15] A strictly narratological approach, which makes no assumptions about the use of sources or traditions, would regard the summaries as clues to the readers of the major themes to be observed.[16] So, drawing on the summaries, literary patterns, and narratives in the opening chapters of Acts, we learn of a number of important themes.

The summaries lay great stress on the *growth of the community* (see Acts 2:47; 5:14). Luke seems especially intent on emphasizing the phenomenal increase in the number of adherents in Jerusalem (see also Acts 2:41; 4:4; 6:1, 7; 21:20) and beyond (see Acts 9:31; 11:21, 24; 12:24; 14:1; 19:20).

Together with the phenomenal growth of the community there is stress on the *order of the community* (see Acts 2:42, 43; 4:33, 35; 5:12). Luke intends to present to the reader a portrait of a well-ordered believing community. Community order is provided by the leadership of the apostles, who were appointed by Jesus (Acts 1:2) and who continue to proclaim the word of his resurrection and perform signs and wonders. In this connection we should observe the care with which Luke tells the story of the selection of Matthias to replace Judas among the apostles (Acts 1:15–26). Luke is careful to state that the number of apostles is not only limited to twelve but must also be maintained at this level. The requirements are set out with exactitude, and the selection is made within the context of prayer and is shown to be dependent on divine direction. For Luke the requirements for leadership in the community must be clear, and the names of the leaders public. In the important practice of community ownership of property and distribution of provisions, the apostles exercise control (see Acts 4:35; 5:1–11). They speak for the community both to potential converts and to political and religious authorities.

Divine leadership of the community is also emphasized in the summaries (see Acts 2:47; 4:33) and episodes in the first several chapters of Acts. The guidance of the spirit in the choice of a replacement apostle (Acts 1:15–26) and the descent of the spirit at Pentecost (Acts 2:1–13) are remarkable demonstrations of divine activity.

Another of the major themes in this section of Acts is that of the *internal harmony of the community*. Internal harmony is especially stressed in Acts, in which a characteristic description of the community is the Greek word ὁμοθυμαδὸν, which expresses the idea of unanimity, concord, agreement, and of a group having one mind and intent (see Acts 1:14; 2:46; 4:24; 5:12). It is not a rare word in contemporary literature and the LXX, but it is found only once in the New Testament (see Rom 15:6) outside of Acts, where it appears ten times and seems to be a favorite Lukan term. For the author of Acts authentic Christianity is marked by peace and concord among the leaders and members. In the "Jerusalem Springtime" section the major illustration of internal harmony is the community's practice of common ownership of property and distribution of proceeds. The story of Ananias and Sapphira (Acts 5:1–11) reveals the author's awareness of violations of the practice and hence of threats to the internal harmony, but it also shows that such problems are quickly resolved.

Supporting the theme of internal harmony, the author of Acts employs a notable literary pattern to report the resolution of certain problems.[17] A number of specific episodes in this and later sections of Acts illustrate the theme of harmony as the essence of the early Christian movement, while showing various threats to it and the ways in which they are resolved. Each of these narratives has four components: (1) harmony; (2) threat; (3) resolution; and (4) restoration. The story of Ananias and Sapphira exhibits the pattern clearly.

(1) *Harmony.* All the believers are of one heart and soul; no one regards anything as his or her own, and all things are held in common. The apostles witness to the resurrection; no one is in need, and distribution is made according to need. The action of Barnabas is cited as an illustration—Acts 4:32–37. This is a rather full

description that serves both as a general summary and as an introduction to the story of Ananias and Sapphira.

(2) *Threat.* Ananias and Sapphira lie about retaining some of the proceeds from a sale of property—Acts 5:1–2.

(3) *Resolution.* Peter condemns the two and they both die; thus the threat is eliminated from the community—Acts 5:3–10.

(4) *Restoration.* Awe comes upon the whole community—Acts 5:11.

The same pattern may also be found in Acts 1:12–2:1; 5:12–42; 6:1–7; 8:6–13; 8:14–25, and elsewhere. The use of this literary pattern reveals our author's predisposition for harmony, which he conceives to be the original and continuing state of the church. There are threats, but they are quickly met and resolved, and the church then returns to its accustomed state of harmony.

Another important theme in the early part of Acts is *the community's fidelity to Jewish traditions and practices.* The believers gather in the temple (Acts 2:46; 5:12), which is the setting for many of the episodes in Acts (see Acts 2:46; 3:1, 2, 3, 8, 10; 4:1; 5:20, 21, 22, 24, 25, 26, 42). The believing community enjoys popular goodwill and esteem (see Acts 2:47; 5:13), and apostolic healings are in great demand throughout the city (see Acts 5:14–15). The participation of the apostles in the temple ritual is assumed. Peter and John go there "at the hour of prayer, at three o'clock in the afternoon" (Acts 3:1), where they heal a man who had been lame from birth. Peter speaks in Solomon's portico (Acts 4:1), which subsequently becomes a regular meeting place (Acts 5:12). But the temple also becomes a place of contention. After the apostles are arrested, an angel appears, releases them, and commands them to speak to the people in the temple (Acts 5:20). They do so but are again captured and arrested in the temple (Acts 5:21–26).

Good narratives include stories of conflict, and Acts is no exception. Despite the goodwill and esteem that the community enjoys, it encounters *Jewish opposition,* another theme in Acts. Opposition in Acts 1–5 comes not from the people but from the leaders. Priests, chief priests, the στρατηγὸς of the temple, Sadducees, elders, and scribes are listed among the groups of leaders who attempt to restrict the apostles (see Acts 4:1, 5, 8, 23; 5:17, 21, 24, 26). Individual opponents—Annas, Caiaphas, John, Alexander (Acts 4:6)—are also named. The apostles are brought to appear formally before the Sanhedrin (Acts 5:27), and the members are prepared to execute them (Acts 5:33). But even in the hearing before the Sanhedrin the apostles gain support from Gamaliel, who is described as a Pharisee, a member of the Sanhedrin, and a teacher of the law (Acts 5:34). Gamaliel argues successfully that the apostles should be left alone in the event that they have divine support (Acts 5:35–39).

The story in Acts 1–5 is generally idyllic. Major themes are (1) the growth of the believing community; (2) the order of the community; (3) the divine leadership of the community; (4) the internal harmony of the community; (5) the community's fidelity to Jewish traditions and practices; and (6) Jewish opposition to the believing community. These themes reappear and undergo development in the rest of Acts. Space does not allow a full discussion of every incident in Acts and its contribution to the development of a theme, and so I intend to select a few episodes as illustrations of important thematic developments.

Once we leave behind the idyllic descriptions of the "Jerusalem Springtime" in Acts, we become increasingly aware of internal threats and external opposition affecting the early Christian movement. But the internal threats are quickly met, problems are easily resolved, and the accustomed harmony is restored. In Acts 6:1–7, for example, a serious internal threat is posed by two contending groups—Hebrews and Hellenists. Here the reader comes upon the literary pattern that was first used in the story of Ananias and Sapphira.

(1) *Harmony.* There is growth as the number of disciples increases—Acts 6:1a.

(2) *Threat.* The Hellenists grumble against the Hebrews because their widows are being overlooked in the daily service—Acts 6:1b.

(3) *Resolution.* The Twelve call the community together and propose a plan. The community accepts the plan, and seven men are ordained by the apostles—Acts 6:2–6.

(4) *Restoration.* The number of disciples continues to multiply, and priests become obedient to the faith—Acts 6:7.

The identification of the two contending groups is by no means clear, but, at a minimum, the narrative tells the reader about diversity within the believing community, diversity that threatens the internal harmony. Further, the narrative continues an emphasis on themes that were introduced in the earlier chapters of Acts. The growth of the community forms the frame for the narrative (Acts 6:1a, 7). The order of the community is shown by the apostles' convening the believers, proposing a plan to resolve the threat, and executing the plan. The ordination of the seven in Acts 6:6, which allows the apostles to continue their activities, is especially important in supporting the theme of order. It means that although attention may be focused on a new group and new characters, their activity does not constitute any disruption of order. What they do has the blessing and approval of the leaders of the believing community.

The story of Stephen (Acts 6:8–7:60) abruptly focuses attention on Jewish opposition to the early Christian movement, while maintaining stress on the movement's fidelity to Jewish practices. The opposition to Stephen comes originally from diaspora Jews who belong to a synagogue in Jerusalem. Their charges against Stephen are that he has committed blasphemy against Moses and God (Acts 6:11), that he has spoken against the temple and the Torah (Acts 6:13), and that he has claimed that Jesus will destroy the temple and change the practices decreed by Moses (Acts 6:14). But Jerusalemite people and leaders are soon implicated in the narrative as well, as the accusers gain the involvement of people, elders, scribes, and finally the Sanhedrin (Acts 6:12).

Stephen's speech (Acts 7:2–53) begins with emphasis on the common heritage that he shares with the Jewish auditors but ends with severe accusations against them. The speech is packed with quotations from and allusions to Scripture—most of them from the Pentateuch—and references to ancient Hebrew figures—Abraham, Isaac, Jacob, Joseph, Moses, Aaron, Joshua, David, and Solomon. Most of the speech constitutes a retelling of the history of Israel, and the speaker maintains his own identity with the people of Israel, many times speaking of "our ancestors" (Acts 7:2, 11, 12, 15, 38, 39, 44, 45) and "our nation" (7:19). Nothing here disturbs the theme of the fidelity of the Christian community to Jewish traditions and practices. To underline this theme our author states that the charges against Stephen were generated by *false* witnesses (Acts 6:13), implying that Stephen did not teach against the temple or Torah and did not claim that Jesus would destroy the temple or change Mosaic practices. The author will make the same point later in regard to Paul (see especially Acts 21:18–28).

The speech of Stephen connects Jewish opposition to the believing community with historic attitudes of Hebrew people, going back to the time of Moses. It tries to persuade the readers that opposition to the will of God has always been characteristic of Jewish people. Stephen maintains that Moses' fellow Hebrews rejected him as judge even when he defended a man who was being oppressed by an Egyptian (Acts 7:23–29). Later he says that after the exodus the people rejected Moses, intended to return to Egypt, and worshipped images (Acts 7:39–41). Then, without citing specific incidents, Stephen charges that the ancient Hebrews murdered all the prophets (Acts 7:52), and he concludes by identifying his present audience with the rebellious Hebrews of the past. He describes them as "stiff-necked people, uncircumcised in heart and ears" (Acts 7:51), and he says, "You are forever opposing the Holy Spirit" (Acts 7:51). He charges them with the betrayal and murder of Jesus (Acts 7:52) and with not observing Torah (Acts 7:53).

It is significant that the expressions of a common heritage ("our ancestors") that we find through most of the speech give way to a distancing at the end ("your ancestors," Acts 7:51, 52). Stephen's stress on the historic Jewish opposition to God, culminating in the charge that Jews did not keep Torah (Acts 7:53), is an ironic answer to the charge against him: "This man never stops saying things against . . . the law" (Acts 6:13). The reader of Acts is being persuaded that it is Stephen and his fellow believers who are faithful to the traditions and practices of Moses, not the Jews, who have always opposed God and now stand in opposition to the believing community.

After the death of Stephen there is a scattering of the believers, although the apostles remain in Jerusalem. This scattering results in an enlargement not only of the geographical setting in Acts 8–12 but also of the ethnic diversity among believers. In these chapters Christian missionaries go out to Judea and Samaria; a convert comes from Ethiopia; we learn that there are believers in Damascus; a centurion from the Italian regiment at Caesarea is converted; and Hellenists at Antioch accept the gospel. We may be tempted to designate this section as an illustration of the by-now-familiar theme of the growth of the community. That would not be inaccurate, but such a designation would overlook important aspects of this section of Acts, in which the spread of the Christian movement beyond Jerusalem and Jews to diverse people in distant lands is the real subject. The prime exemplary story is the conversion of Cornelius, regarded by Luke as the first Gentile.[18] The question of how a movement made this kind of major ethnic change is answered here in an anecdotal fashion that shows how the change was prepared for by missionary enterprises among Samaritans and diaspora Jews, people who, from the perspective of Jerusalemite Jews, were regarded as peripheral. Since the goal of the entire section is to move toward the conversion of non-Jews, we may refer to this theme as *the community's inclusion of Gentiles.*

This theme governs the story of the Pauline mission in Acts 13–28. For many of the narratives that describe Paul's missionary efforts Luke employs a literary pattern that not only focuses on the mission to the Gentiles but also calls special attention to the Jewish component of early Christianity. When Paul arrives in a city he goes immediately to the synagogue, where he speaks to Jewish people and God-fearers, interpreting the Scriptures to show that the Christ is Jesus. He meets with some success in the synagogue, but the overwhelming response is Jewish rejection. Paul then presents his message to the general public, apparently consisting entirely of Gentile people, and meets with a great deal of success. The success breeds increased Jewish opposition, which, sometimes coupled with official repression, forces Paul's departure. Although there are variations the general pattern establishes itself clearly and forcefully (see especially Acts 13:13–52; 14:1–7; 17:1–9, 10–15; 18:1–17). The visit of Paul and Barnabas to Pisidian Antioch in Acts 13:13–52 develops the pattern fully and may be seen as paradigmatic for many episodes of the Pauline ministry. Notably, it concludes with a solemn statement that serves as a summary of the events at Pisidian Antioch and as a programmatic statement of first importance. The missionaries say: "It was necessary that the word of God should be spoken first to you. Since you reject it and judge yourselves to be unworthy of eternal life, we are now turning to the Gentiles" (Acts 13:46; see also 18:5; 28:28).

It is important to observe the force of the first sentence in Paul's announcement in Acts 13:46. It is a statement that controls the way the author of Acts tells the story, as he has Paul, almost invariably, begin his mission in a new city with a visit to the synagogue. The statement reinforces the theme that appears throughout Acts, namely, the fidelity of the believing community to Jewish traditions and practices. This theme plays a prominent role throughout the story of Paul, and we shall encounter it again in exploring the characterization of Paul in Acts, below.

Yet another theme that affects the narrative in the later chapters of Acts and particularly in the story of Paul is the *Jewish rejection of the Christian message.* The earlier chapters of Acts are marked more by Jewish acceptance than rejection, but increasingly in the story of Paul the reader learns that community growth is due to acceptance by Gentiles, not Jews. Offstage, growth continues in the Jerusalem community, which remains faithful to Jewish practices and traditions (see Acts 21:20). But in Paul's theater of operations, although there is no diminution in his efforts to convert Jews, and although there is always some positive response, the narratives repeatedly call attention to Jewish rejection in the Diaspora.

Thus the literary pattern that the author of Acts uses for so many of the episodes telling of the mission of Paul ties together four major themes: *the fidelity of the believing community to Jewish traditions and practices*—Paul almost always opens his mission by preaching to Jews in synagogues; *the community's inclusion of Gentiles*— increasingly these narratives point to the success of Paul and his colleagues in contributing to the growth of the community by converting Gentiles; *Jewish rejection of the Christian message*—although Paul makes strong efforts to convert Jews, and although there is always some positive response, the narratives repeatedly call attention to the negative response of the Jews; and *Jewish opposition to the community*— Paul and his fellow missionaries are often compelled to leave town as a result of disturbances instigated by Jewish opponents.

These then are, in my judgment, the major themes in Acts. For convenience they are listed below without additional comment.

(1) Growth of the community
(2) Order of the community
(3) Divine leadership of the community
(4) Internal harmony of the community
(5) The community's fidelity to Jewish traditions and practices
(6) Jewish opposition to the community
(7) The community's inclusion of Gentiles
(8) Jewish rejection of the Christian message

We must not lose sight of these themes when we come to examine the characterizations in Acts. But some comments are in order at this point. If we should ask why the author of Acts chose to use these particular themes to construct the narrative of Christian beginnings, several possible answers are available. We could assume that the author made use of available traditions which allowed him to read the story the way he did, but this assumption does not help to answer our question, since themes and literary patterns are under the control of the authors who employ them. Some of the themes may be accounted for as usual and useful rhetorical devices.[19] To present a movement positively, it would have been most appealing to show its growth, order, internal harmony, inclusiveness, and divine leadership. The community's fidelity to Jewish practices would affirm its ancient roots, while Jewish rejection and opposition would tend to distance the movement from contemporary Jews and underscore the anti-Semitism of the ancient world.

In my judgment, however, many of these themes may be best explained as motivated by the need to counter the Marcionite challenge. Assuming that Acts was written in the first half of the second century, we find that there is a ready explanation for the use of a number of these themes. The emphasis in Acts on the internal harmony of the community addresses the issue raised by Marcion that would posit a split between Paul and the older apostles. The theme of order likewise points to the leadership of the community by the apostles. The theme of the community's fidelity to Jewish traditions and practices, together with the literary pattern that supports it, would also have served as a powerful counter to Marcionite claims. Marcion, who would totally distance Christian faith from Jewish traditions, is here met by an author who makes every attempt to show that the faith of Peter, Stephen, Paul, and all the Christians was the supreme expression of fidelity to the Hebrew Bible and Mosaic teachings and that Jesus was the fulfillment of Hebrew prophecy and Jewish messianic expectation. The author's characterization of Peter and Paul, which we will examine below, lends support to this explanation.

Characterization in Acts

Acts is thickly peopled with characters who appear and disappear as the narrative progresses, but clearly there are two major characters: Peter and Paul. It is not implausible to refer to the Acts of the Apostles as the Acts of Peter and Paul.[20]

The Characterization of Peter

Peter is the dominant character in the opening chapters of Acts. He is portrayed as the leader of the Jerusalem community, worker of miracles, persuasive speaker, and representative to powerful Jewish leaders. He has pride of place in the list of apostles in Acts 1:13. He devises a way to reconstitute the apostolic group after the defection and death of Judas (Acts 1:15–26). He interprets the events of Pentecost to the Jerusalem citizenry, and after his speech three thousand of them convert (Acts 2:14–42). He speaks again to the people of the city after the healing of the lame man at the temple (Acts 3:12–26) and then to the rulers and priests (Acts 4:8–12). He questions Ananias and Sapphira about the proceeds from their sale of property (Acts 5:1–11). These chapters give us an image of a man of exceedingly strong conviction and rhetorical skill. He is confident in his ability to quote and interpret the Scriptures and unafraid in appearing before authorities.

If the author of Acts knew the letter to the Galatians, he was aware that Paul had not always portrayed Peter in a favorable light.[21] Paul acknowledged that Cephas (that is, Peter) was an apostle, along with James the Lord's brother (Gal 1:19; cf. 1 Cor 15:7). He emphasized Peter's role as the first witness to Jesus' resurrection (1 Cor 15:5). But in Gal 2:11–21 Paul makes no effort to hide his theological differences with Peter. He claims that Peter acted with hypocrisy, and he gives him a royal dressing-down. In this episode Peter appears to be neither a leader of the believing community nor a person of deep conviction. He first participates in meals with Gentiles but then departs in the face of criticism from the associates of James.

We do not know what materials about Peter were available to the author of Acts, apart from Galatians and other Pauline letters. In any event his treatment of these sources is perplexing. Unless he had some additional information about Peter or unless he had some other agenda to pursue, why would the author of Acts have so altered the characterization of Peter to contrast with that in Galatians? It is possible that this author had seen *1 Clement*. There both Peter and Paul are elevated to a heroic status. This letter, usually dated about 95 C.E., written from the church at Rome to the church at Corinth, cites a number of examples of the dangers of jealousy. One such example is that of "Peter, who because of unrighteous jealousy suffered not one or two but many trials, and having thus given his testimony went to the glorious place which was his due"[22] The author of Acts may have derived from Clement that Peter endured trials, but *1 Clement* does not provide any information about the preaching of Peter or his leadership of the Jerusalem church.

It seems more likely that the author of Acts has an agenda that was formed by the Marcionite challenge. We know that one of Marcion's major contentions was that Peter and the other Jerusalem leaders were false apostles. It is reasonable to suppose that Marcion obtained this view of Peter from Galatians and others of Paul's letters. He probably also concluded from 2 Cor 11:1–15 that the so-called super apostles (2 Cor 11:5) and the false apostles (2 Cor 11:13) that Paul mentioned there included Peter and the others from Jerusalem. Paul suggested here that they were preaching a different gospel (2 Cor 11:4), a charge similar to the one he made in Gal 1:6–7.

We also know that Marcion had a gospel in which the characterization of Peter was not flattering. Although it is unclear that this gospel had the story of Peter's denial (Luke 22:54–62), it almost certainly had Jesus' prediction about it (Luke 22:34). We have already seen that the narratives in Gos. Mar. 24 do not give us a clear picture of this chief apostle as a witness to Jesus' resurrection. The note in Luke 24:12 that says that Peter went to the tomb of Jesus but did not know what to make of it was almost certainly missing in the Gospel of Marcion and is even textually unclear in canonical Luke.[23] The situation of Luke 24:34, in which we have a report that there had been an appearance to Simon (apparently meaning Peter), is similar. This verse was probably not in the Gospel of Marcion, and even in canonical Luke there is no description of an appearance to Peter.

These materials would have served as powerful reinforcements of Marcion's view that Peter and the Jerusalem leaders were false apostles. Marcion's gospel would have shown that Peter himself was an undependable disciple of Jesus and not a witness of the resurrection. An author who intended to dispute Marcionite claims would need to characterize Peter and the other leaders as bold proponents of the faith that Jesus imparted to them. He would have to make it clear that they were witnesses to the resurrection and reliable interpreters of the tradition. The Marcionite challenge provides the perfect foil for our author. If the author of Acts was aware of the Marcionite contention that Peter was a false apostle, and if he was intent on correcting this charge, the characterization of Peter in Acts is perfectly plausible. Our author wrote to show the falsity of what Marcion said about Peter. He portrayed the apostle in bold colors to provide a stark contrast to Marcion's claims and to correct impressions that an audience may have gained from reading or hearing about Marcion's gospel. A reader of Acts who also knows what Marcionite Christians have been saying would come away with a picture of Peter as the very opposite of a false apostle. Far from being false Peter is a forceful witness to Jesus' resurrection and a compelling preacher of repentance.

The Characterization of Paul

An intriguing aspect of the characterization of both Peter and Paul in Acts is the parallelism between them. Both characters deliver speeches, perform healings and resurrections, defeat workers of magic, correct inadequate teaching, are miraculously released from prison, and witness the giving of the spirit and the phenomenon of glossolalia among converts. In reference to the miracles Andrew C. Clark correctly observed that "every miracle performed by Peter has its parallel in one wrought by Paul" and "nearly all the miracles narrated in Acts were performed by these two (and their companions)."[24]

The parallelization of Peter and Paul in Acts has been long noted.[25] We should recall that it was the work of Matthias Schneckenburger on these parallels that inspired Ferdinand Christian Baur to characterize Acts as an attempt to harmonize Jewish and Gentile Christianity.[26] In his recent dissertation, published in 2001, Clark subjects the parallels to an exhaustive treatment.[27] He attempts to be self-conscious about the methodology to be employed in identifying the parallels, and he employs useful criteria. In addition he maintains that the writing of Plutarch, a near contemporary of the author of Acts, shows that parallelization was a recognized literary device. Drawing on the work of D. H. J. Larmour, Clark notes the various ways in which Plutarch manipulated his sources to produce the parallel lives: selection and exclusion, simplification and amplification, and alteration and fabrication.

> As regards the former, there is ample evidence that Plutarch can "select certain elements of the tradition for inclusion, and happily ignore those he finds uncongenial, inconvenient or unnecessary." As regards simplification, while things may be left out for aesthetic reasons, or because it was unnecessary to re-tell a well-known story at length, more often both simplification and amplification were tied to the didactic requirements of the narrative. Alteration on a bolder scale, such as the transferal of an action from one character to another as occurs in some narratives, often appears to be motivated by the desire to give more prominence to a hero. Chronological sequence is sometimes radically altered for similar ends. Although outright fabrication is difficult to prove, it seems very likely that sometimes details are made up with no basis other than Plutarch's imagination.[28]

Since Plutarch had an ethical purpose in writing the *Parallel Lives* and manipulated his material in order to support that purpose, it seems probable that Luke would have used the device of parallelization for a similar end. Clark writes: "If this analysis is accepted as convincing, and it would seem difficult to refute it, the intriguing possibility is raised that his portraits of Peter and Paul may have been intended by Luke at least in part as symbols of his overall message."[29] Clark then analyzes the parallelization of Peter and Paul in Acts and concludes that the device is intended to impress upon the reader the point that these two leaders acted harmoniously, that the history of the early church was marked by continuity and unity.[30] He understands that emphasis on these themes brings the narrative into line with the purpose stated in the prologue to Luke's gospel. Luke intended to give Theophilus assurance about the gospel, and "the greatest obstacle to Theophilus' continuing acceptance of the gospel" was his doubt "as to the continuity of God's purposes in Israel and the church, and the question of whether there was true unity between the Jewish and Gentile sections of the church."[31]

Clark has performed an important service for Acts scholarship in highlighting the criteria for identifying parallels and by his analysis of the relevant material in Acts. He has also succeeded in showing that the device of parallelization was used by the author of Acts in service of important themes—continuity and unity—themes which are readily associated with the writing of Acts. It should be noted, however, that the influence of Plutarch on the writing of Acts is more credible if we date Acts after ca. 115 C.E., since it is probable that the *Parallel Lives* was not published before that date. Further, the reason given by Clark to account for Luke's use of the device of parallelization and for his emphasis on the themes of continuity and unity lacks objective reference. It relies only on internal evidence and a plausible interpretation of the link between Luke's prologue and the use of the device of parallelization in Acts. An explanation that sees the reason for the employment of certain themes and devices of characterization as rooted in a known historical challenge, such as that of Marcion, would be more credible.

The characterization of Paul in Acts, affected by the device of parallelization, has constituted an issue in the interpretation of Acts for some time. We have already taken note of the importance this issue had for F. C. Baur and the Tübingen School. Baur was certain that the characterization of Paul was completely under the control of the author of Acts, who was intent on harmonizing Pauline and Petrine Christianity. Noting the significant parallels between Peter and Paul, Baur claimed that the author of Acts intentionally distorted the portraits of both in order to support his own theological tendencies. Thus the author of Acts stressed Paul's adherence to Torah observance and de-emphasized those convictions that may have called Torah into question. In the Tübingen view the Paul of Acts was far closer to Jewish Christianity than was the actual Paul.[32]

Adolf von Harnack faced the objections of Baur and his colleagues in an effort to minimize the distance between the Paul of Acts and the Paul of the letters. As we have seen Harnack defended the traditional view of the authorship of Acts and maintained that it was written by a companion of Paul. But he was aware of the objection that a companion of Paul would not have erred significantly in dealing with historical information and would not have portrayed Paul in ways that appeared to contradict the impressions we gain from the letters. But here Harnack questions these modern impressions of Paul. He argues vigorously that, although the author of Acts is no more immune than any other writer from making historical errors, we have no right to substitute our impressions, drawn from the Pauline letters, for his.[33] "If he [the author of Acts] has here assigned less honour to St. Paul than from his epistles seems to be due to him, and if in chaps. xxi ss. he makes him appear more Jewish in his behaviour than we, judging from the same epistles should imagine possible, it is at least permissible to ask which is right—our imagination or the representation given in the Acts."[34]

Harnack also contrasts Luke and Paul in respect to their religious backgrounds. Luke had not come to grips with the problem of Torah in the way that Paul had. In addition Harnack maintains that we should not simply interpret Paul's letters as anti-Torah. He calls attention to some things in the letters that suggest that Paul's attitude was more complex than it has been represented to be. Even in Gal 5:11 Paul is accused of still preaching circumcision, and, says Harnack, there must be some ground for the accusation. In 1 Cor 7:18–20 Paul implies "that the converted Jew should remain faithful to the customs and ordinances of the fathers."[35] Romans 9–11 constitutes a serious qualification to Paul's judgments in Galatians, since here he holds out a future hope for historical Israel. Strict logic would have required Paul to abandon this hope, but, in Harnack's words, "the Jew in him was still too strong and his reverence for the content of the Old Testament still too devoted!"[36] Also in 1 Cor 9:20 Paul says, "To the Jews I became a Jew, in order to win Jews." Harnack maintains that this was not simply a pragmatic consideration. "*His limitation lay in this, that he had not thought this conception out to the end, and accordingly held fast to an indefinite compromise with Jewish convictions; and that, instead of carrying on the fight along the whole line, he on important points yielded to the Jew in the Jewish Christian—not from cowardice or insincerity, but because the Jew in himself was too strong.*"[37] Harnack concludes that there were more pro-Jewish tendencies in Paul than most critical commentators had heretofore recognized and that Acts brings out these tendencies in ways that the letters, because of their occasional contexts, leave only implicit.

The issue was most sharply treated by Philip Vielhauer in the article "Zum 'Paulinismus' der Apostelgeschichte."[38] His work has been influential on a generation of Acts scholarship. Vielhauer intentionally ignored the historical and chronological comparisons between Acts and the Pauline letters and concentrated exclusively on the theology. He maintained that the theology attributed to Paul in Acts was unrelated to that found in the letters on four major issues: natural theology, the law, Christology, and eschatology. On natural theology Vielhauer maintained that Luke drew especially from Stoic thought in writing the speeches of Paul, especially the speech on the Areopagus (Acts 17:22–31). Here knowledge of God apart from revelation is positively valued and treated as something of a forerunner of

Christian faith. Paul even adopts the idea of human kinship with God (Acts 17:28–29). In the letters of Paul, however, only a small hint about natural theology is present in Rom 1:19–21, in which knowledge of the divine serves to demonstrate human responsibility. Vielhauer states that the Christology in Acts, which comes from earlier traditions, is "adoptionistic, not a Christology of preexistence."[39] For Paul the death of Jesus means judgment and reconciliation, but in Acts, Jesus' crucifixion is "an error of justice and a sin of the Jews."[40] The "suffering and death of the Messiah were prophesied, and the Jews unconsciously did their part toward the fulfillment of this prophecy. Nothing is said of the saving significance of the cross of Christ; and consequently also nothing of the reality of 'in Christ' and of the presence of the whole of salvation."[41] Thus Vielhauer maintains that "Luke himself is closer to the Christology of the earliest congregation, which is set forth in the speeches of Peter, than he is to the Christology of Paul, which is indicated only in hints."[42] But on the issue of eschatology Luke is post-Pauline rather than primitive, since he moves it from the center of Paul's thought to the periphery.

It is on the issue of Torah observance and connection with Judaism that Vielhauer finds the most dramatic contrasts between the Paul of Acts and the Paul of the letters. In Acts Paul is a faithful Pharisaic Jew, believing everything in the Scriptures and devoutly adhering to the customs and requirements of his faith. Vielhauer catalogues the practices in Acts that demonstrate Paul's adherence to Jewish customs:

1. By his missionary method: beginning at the synagogue; only after a formal rejection by the Jews does he turn directly to the Gentiles;
2. By his submission to the Jerusalem authorities;
3. By the circumcision of Timothy (16:3);
4. By spreading the apostolic decree (16:4) (nonhistorical);
5. By assuming a vow (18:18);
6. By trips to Jerusalem to participate in Jewish religious festivals (18:21; 20:16);
7. By participating, on the advice of James, in a Nazirite vow with four members of the Jerusalem congregation (21:18–28);
8. By stressing when on trial that he is a Pharisee (23:6; 26:5) and that he stands for nothing other than the "hope" of the Jews in the resurrection of the dead.[43]

All of these practices underscore Paul's observance of Torah and his connection with Judaism and the Jewish people. And, to cap it off, Paul never in Acts hints at any critical attitude toward Torah. Only two verses in Acts may be cited as alluding to Paul's views. In Acts 13:38–39 Paul announces: "Let it be known to you therefore, my brothers, that through this man forgiveness of sins is proclaimed to you; by this Jesus everyone who believes is set free from all those sins from which you could not be freed by the law of Moses."[44] The other verse is actually attributed to Peter rather than to Paul: "We believe that we will be saved through the grace of the Lord Jesus, just as they will" (Acts 15:11). But Vielhauer insists that even in Acts 13:38–39 we do not have a reflection of the genuine Pauline message, since in 13:38 the author substitutes the term "forgiveness" for the Pauline "justification." Paul's theology of the Torah, Vielhauer notes, is far more complex than the author of Acts represented it to be.

Writing only a few years after Vielhauer, Haenchen comes to essentially the same conclusions. He stresses that Paul and the author of Acts are in basic agreement on the legitimacy of the Gentile mission without the law. Luke, says Haenchen, takes it for granted but is *"unaware of Paul's solution"*[45] and unable to justify it "from within," as Paul was.[46] "He must therefore seize on a justification 'from without'— God willed the mission, and that was sufficient."[47] Furthermore, in Haenchen's view, Luke's portrait of Paul differs from the Paul of the letters in significant ways: in Acts Paul is a miracle worker and a great orator, but not an apostle. Further Acts misses the real point of Paul's theology: "From beginning to end, according to Acts, the Jewish hostility to the Christians was kindled by the latter's preaching of the Resurrection (Acts 4.2, 28.23)."[48] But, in fact, says Haenchen, the real bone of contention was Torah. This point surfaces from time to time in Acts, but only as a charge against Paul, a charge of which Paul is said to be not guilty.

The challenges of Vielhauer and Haenchen have not gone unanswered. Jacob Jervell reminds us that the letters of Paul were occasional letters, which do not require full biographical information. He writes: "As such they [the Pauline letters] obviously conceal parts of Paul's preaching and activity, since it was not necessary to treat such in a letter."[49] Jervell maintains that "the Lukan Paul, the picture of Paul in Acts, is a completion, a filling up of the Pauline one, so that in order to get at the historical Paul, we cannot do without Acts and Luke."[50] He emphasizes the Lukan treatment of Paul as a practicing Pharisee and calls attention to those places in the Pauline letters where Paul claims to have lived as a Jew (Rom 9:7; 11:2; Gal 2:15; 2 Cor 11:22; and especially 1 Cor 9:20). In general these references certify the context in which Paul saw himself. And it is as a Pharisee faithful to Torah that Paul is represented in Acts. Jervell concedes that Luke has built his portrait of Paul "on material to be found in the marginal notes in Paul's letters."[51] But the Acts picture can be harmonized theologically with an important section of one of Paul's letters, namely Romans 9–11. Here Paul emphasizes the irrevocable covenant of God with Israel and projects the expectation of the eventual inclusion of all Israel in the believing community. Jervell concludes: "I am therefore inclined to assert that what Luke writes on the subject of Paul is historically correct, even if not in detail—and we have in Luke of course not the whole of Paul. But the practicing Jew Paul, the missionary of Israel and to Israel, the theologian for whom Israel's salvation is the goal of his work—all these important Lukan views can be found in Paul's letters."[52]

Stanley E. Porter faced the challenges from Vielhauer and Haenchen directly in a book published in 1999.[53] He notes Haenchen's claim that the Acts portrait of Paul stresses him as miracle worker and orator but not an apostle and contends that there is no necessary contradiction with Paul's letters on the first two points. On the matter of apostleship Porter calls attention to Acts 14:4, 14, in which Barnabas and Paul are called apostles. Haenchen said that these verses were unimportant, but Porter notes that of the twenty-eight uses of the word "apostle" in Acts, two apply to Paul, and he maintains that this cannot be overlooked as unimportant.[54] Porter also questions Haenchen's claim that the author of Acts was unaware of Paul's solution to the issue of the Gentile mission without the law: "In Acts 18:13, 21:28, 22:3, 23:29 and 25:8, in each of these instances, Paul is either being accused of disobeying the law or of instructing others to disobey the law, or defending himself against such accusations. This evidence indicates that it is an unfair generalization to claim that Acts is concerned with resurrection and the letters of Paul with the law, when both are issues of concern in each corpus."[55]

Porter concludes that whatever differences may be found between the letters and the Acts are not as significant as Vielhauer and Haenchen maintained and that they simply occur when different writers use different literary genres. He writes: "The conclusions of this chapter are traditional ones. The first is that the standard arguments marshaled in defense of the differences between the Paul of Acts and of the letters regarding his person and work, once analyzed in detail, simply do not point to significant and sustainable contradictions. The second is that the standard arguments marshaled regarding differences in theology between the Paul of Acts and of the letters, again when scrutinized in detail, are also inconclusive for this hypothesis."[56]

In some respects the emerging new perspective on Paul, based in part on the work of E. P. Sanders, allows scholars to address questions about the Paul of Acts in different ways.[57] A major study related to this new perspective is that of Mark D. Nanos on Galatians.[58] Although it is not directly concerned with the apparent conflicts between the Pauline letters and Acts, his work has a significant bearing on the issue. Nanos's interpretation of Paul's letter to the Galatians opens the possibility that the author of Acts may not be so far distant in his presentation of Paul. Nanos understands Galatians as an "ironic rebuke" of Paul's converts. These converts from paganism had been drawn to Paul's promise that they could become members of the community of God's people simply by believing in Jesus. Opponents of Paul, designated by Nanos as "influencers," disagreed and attempted to persuade Paul's converts that they must become something more than guests in the house of Israel. They maintained that to be part of the people of God entails becoming full proselytes, which requires circumcision. Paul, of course, objected and reaffirmed his conviction that faith in Jesus is sufficient and that circumcision and Torah-observance are not required. This way of shaping the context and problematic of Galatians has significant implications. The resulting issue is not faith in Christ versus Torah-observance, and Paul neither attacks Torah-observance per se, nor questions its appropriateness for non-Christian Jews. Those influencing the Galatian converts are not attacking belief in Christ; they are rather saying that it is not sufficient for membership in Israel. Further, it is notable that the goal of the pagan converts is to be members of the people of Israel and that Paul affirms this goal. Nanos's conclusion, which he states at the beginning of the book, brings the epistolary Paul very close to the Paul of Acts: "In fact, nothing I have encountered in Galatians has led me to question the working assumption that the Paul who writes this letter is a Torah-observant Jew, known as such by his addressees when he had lived among them."[59] Nanos's study suggests that a solution to the problem we face here may well come from the side of scholarship on Paul rather than from that on Acts, but we must await further developments from that area.

The studies that compare the Paul of Acts with the Paul of the letters may not solve the problems about apparent differences, but they help to illuminate features of the characterization of Paul that we find in Acts. However he might appear in the letters, in Acts Paul is a missionary, a miracle worker, an impressive speaker, and a hero who is willing to suffer for his faith. Both before and after his conversion the Paul of Acts is a faithful Jew who observes Torah and the customs of his people, believes the Hebrew Scriptures, and intends to convince one and all that Jesus is the fulfillment of Jewish expectations. The Paul of Acts is a Pharisee, who, like other Pharisees, believes in resurrection.

This characterization of Paul conforms to the dominant themes in Acts that we examined previously. The missions of Paul obviously demonstrate the themes of Gentile inclusion and the growth of the community. But it is the theme of the community's fidelity to Jewish traditions and practices that is most problematic for us. This is, after all, the bone of contention in the debate about the Paul of the epistles and the Paul of Acts. In my judgment the employment of this theme in Acts creates a characterization of Paul that distances him from his letters. Even if Nanos is right about Galatians, it is difficult to reconcile the views expressed there with a Paul who in Acts 16 would circumcise Timothy. Further, how might one reconcile Paul's rejection of his past in Phil 3:1–11 with his maintenance of it in Acts 23:6? In the former passage Paul refers to his life as a Pharisee in highly derogatory terms, but the latter reference conveys only a sense of pride. In the former it is clear that Paul looks upon his Pharisaic identification as past, a stage of his life not to be continued, but in Acts 23:6 he announces his Pharisaic identification as a matter of the present: "I am a Pharisee, a son of Pharisees." How can one reconcile Paul's vehement definition of himself as an apostle in Gal 1:1 and his repeated claims to the designation in Rom 1:1; 11:13; 1 Cor 1:1; 9:1, 2; 15:9; 2 Cor 1:1; 12:12 with the almost total denial of the title to him in Acts?

Although the issue of Paul in Acts versus Paul in the epistles remains important, a final settlement appears out of reach at the present time. It is, however, possible to frame the question in a different way. If Acts was written in the first half of the second century, as claimed in chapter 1, its characterization of Paul and Pauline theology may be understood as an extraordinarily appropriate attempt to correct the teachings of Marcionite Christianity. The author of Acts is not dealing directly with the real Paul but with the Paul of the Marcionites. In this respect the issue is not the accuracy of his characterization of Paul, but the adequacy of his response to Marcion. We can grant that the historical Paul was a complex figure, not easily understood by his contemporaries. Nor is it at all clear in what ways his contemporaries understood him. But we know that in the second century Marcion made abundant use of Paul's letters, especially Galatians, and that he understood Pauline theology as a denial of the religious validity of the Hebrew Bible, Torah, and Judaism. Whatever role Paul played during his own lifetime, there appears to be a struggle for his legacy in the second century.[60] By the early second century it became clear that Paul was being co-opted by Marcionite Christians and interpreted as an opponent of the Hebrew Scriptures, the Torah, and Jewish customs. The author of Acts, in the effort to rescue Paul from the Marcionites, portrayed a Paul who was a faithful Jew and a devout Pharisee.

If Acts was written, at least in part, as a reaction against the Marcionite use of the Pauline letters, it is not difficult to understand the characterization of Paul in this book. To explore this point it will be useful to focus on a few major features of Luke's characterization and to show how they may have been intended to counter Marcionite claims. In what follows I will comment on three of the major items in the characterization of Paul in Acts, drawing partly from the list of features that Vielhauer emphasized as divergences from the epistolary Paul.[61] I intend to examine them in the light of the themes that govern Acts and the literary patterns used by the author, in an effort to show that they are aspects of Luke's response to the Marcionite challenge.

Paul's Missionary Method. In episode after episode Paul begins his visit to a locality with a visit to the synagogue, where he presents his message to Jews. We have already noted the literary pattern used for many of these narratives and the ways in which it supports major themes in Acts. The narratives that describe Paul's missionary method are governed by the themes of the Jewish rejection of the Christian message, Jewish opposition to the community, the community's inclusion of Gentiles, and the community's fidelity to Jewish traditions and practices. The heart of Paul's message in the synagogues is that Jesus is the fulfillment of Jewish expectation and prophetic promises. A reader may conclude from these narratives that they firmly establish a parting of the ways between Judaism and Christianity, but it should also be clear that the reason for the parting is Jewish rejection of Paul rather than Pauline intention.[62] The Paul of Acts returns to the synagogue again and again, proclaiming that Jesus is the fulfillment of Jewish expectations.

Why does the author of Acts portray Paul in this way? If he wrote in the early second century, it is plausible to suggest that he would have been familiar with Marcion's elevation of Paul and his denial that Jesus was the Christ of Jewish expectation. The missionary method used by the Paul of Acts and his message to Jews stand in stark contrast to Marcionite theology. What better way to counter the Marcionite claims than to have the apostle they revered make repeated attempts to convince Jews that Jesus is the fulfillment of the biblical prophets and that belief in Jesus is harmonious with Jewish theology? Paul's failure to convert masses of Jews is not due to the character of the message he preached but to the recalcitrance of the people (see Acts 28:25–27).

Paul and the Jerusalem Apostles. Two interrelated issues are involved here: the question of Paul as apostle and his relationship to the Jerusalem leaders. It is known that Marcion maintained that Paul was the only true apostle of Jesus and that Peter and the Jerusalem leaders were "false apostles." Luke employed a number of literary techniques to dispute this claim. We need only remind ourselves of the characterization of Peter as the leader of the early community and chief of the apostles. Further, the parallelization of Peter and Paul reinforces the themes of order and harmony in the early Christian community and negates any concept of Pauline independence. But the parallelism between Peter and Paul is not complete, since the title "apostle" is almost totally confined to Peter and the Jerusalem leaders and used apparently to designate Paul (and Barnabas) only in two verses (Acts 14:4, 14). Is this not a direct reversal of the Marcionite claims? For Marcion Paul is *the* apostle, and he stands opposed to the Jerusalem authorities, who are false witnesses to the gospel. For the author of Acts there is complete harmony between Peter and Paul; the Jerusalem leaders are undoubtedly apostles, but Paul's position is technically more ambiguous.

The question of the apostleship of Paul in Acts is a particularly thorny one that has elicited a great deal of debate. A discussion of it should begin with the observation that the requirements set forth by Peter in his first speech in Acts 1:21–22 define apostleship in such a way that Paul could not have been accorded the title: "So one of the men who have accompanied us during all the time that the Lord Jesus went in and out among us, beginning from the baptism of John until the day when he was taken up from us—one of these must become a witness with us to his resurrection."[63] Further, the narrative in Acts 1 makes it clear that the apostles must be twelve in number, since the twelfth apostle, Judas Iscariot, must be replaced. Given these stipulations there is no way for Paul to be called an apostle in Acts. He was not appointed by Jesus; he was not with the other disciples/apostles from the time of Jesus' baptism by John to the time of the ascension; and his inclusion as apostle would expand a group whose number must remain constant.

As is well known, however, the title is apparently applied to Paul and Barnabas in Acts 14:4, 14. How can one account for this? A number of possibilities lie at hand, but before we examine them it is necessary to take note of a text-critical matter affecting Acts 14:14. The so-called Western text of this verse omits the term "apostles" (ἀκούσας δὲ Βαρναβᾶς καὶ Παῦλος). This is a difficult reading, and some texts correct the singular participle to the plural ἀκούσαντες.[64] If the more difficult Western text is acceptable, as it is to a number of scholars, the problem has been reduced to one verse, Acts 14:4, for which readers must rely on the context to determine the identity of those called apostles. The verse itself, indeed the entire pericope that deals with the mission to Iconium, has a number of indefinite references. In Acts 14:1 "they" speak in the synagogue at Iconium;[65] in 14:2 the unbelieving Jews stirred up trouble "against the brothers;" 14:3 has only the third-person pronoun. When the reader gets to Acts 14:4 and learns that the people of Iconium were divided, some siding with the Jews and some "with the apostles," it is necessary to go back six verses to the previous episode in Acts 13:50 to determine who is meant by the title. A hearer of the text would have even greater difficulty. Acts 13:50 is the last time before 14:4 that actual names, Paul and Barnabas, are used. Is this perhaps a subtle distancing of the title from the persons?

Despite the language the most likely reading of Acts 14:4 is that Paul and Barnabas are the apostles there designated: some Iconium residents sided with the Jews and some with Paul and Barnabas. How then may we account for Luke's use of the title *apostle* for two persons who, according to his own definition, did not qualify? Most interpreters attribute the problem to Luke's uncritical use of a tradition.[66] This is a solution similar to that frequently used for the "we" sections: Luke found this material in a source and used it without editing it. Another possibility is that Luke intended readers to understand that the title designated a group wider than the one he had described in Acts 1 or that he used it as a subtle hint that Paul and Barnabas were equivalent to Peter and the Jerusalem apostles, except in terms of jurisdiction. Günter Klein, who stressed the Lukan exclusion of Paul from the twelve apostles, downplays the significance of Acts 14:4 (14). He says that Luke would have had no fear that his readers would have been confused. The definition of *apostle* should by now have become so clear that no reader would have thought that Paul and Barnabas were to be included with Peter and the others.[67] Clark has recently suggested that the two verses in Acts 14 reflect a Lukan view that Paul and Barnabas functioned in the Gentile mission in the same way as Peter and the Jerusalem group did in the Jewish mission. Clark points out that Acts 14:4 (14) reinforces the impressions made by the parallelization of Peter and Paul: the reader is to think of them as equivalents, except in terms of jurisdiction.[68]

The problem with Acts 14:4 (14) is one of consistency. If Luke had been strictly consistent, he could not have used the term *apostle* to designate Paul and Barnabas, unless he intended for the reader to understand the term as meaning something different from the definition given in Acts 1:21–22. Since, however, the author provides no help for the reader to formulate a new definition, it seems unlikely that this was his intention. For good reasons modern interpreters are hesitant to impute inconsistency to Luke without first examining every conceivable alternative explanation. But in this case the inconsistency at the logical level is so clear that hesitancy to recognize it seems due to other assumptions about the author. If, however, critical scholars generally make no assumptions about the historical accuracy of the author of Acts, why should we expect logical consistency? If Luke is capable of historical errors, is he not also capable of logical ones?

There is, however, a different way of approaching the problem of Acts 14:4 (14). We know that Marcion regarded Paul as the only apostle and called Peter and the Jerusalem leaders false apostles. In my judgment Acts was written as, in part, a response to the challenge of Marcion and Marcionite Christianity. If this is the case, the author's major problem was not with Paul but with Peter and the Jerusalem leaders. He needed to show that Marcion was wrong in his estimation of these men and that they were the real apostles, appointed by Jesus himself, fully prepared and fully credentialed. The author's task was not to argue for Paul as apostle, but to show that he was not the only apostle. To fulfill this task he "rehabilitated" the Twelve as the authorized bearers of tradition, and he showed that Paul was in every respect in line with them and at some points subservient to them. If he occasionally used the title *apostle* for Paul, this is only because of the fact that, despite his own definition that would exclude Paul from the group, he never doubted its appropriateness. We may regard the author of Acts as inconsistent at this point, but his inconsistency is understandable.

The Peter-Paul parallelism and the author's emphasis on the apostolicity of the Jerusalem leaders has yet another consequence. The community's inclusion of Gentiles, a major theme in Acts, is first exhibited in the work of Peter, not Paul (Acts 10:1–11:18). This section of Acts is particularly important for our author, as its size and complexity make clear. The story of Cornelius and Peter is the story of the conversion of the first God-fearing Gentile. We learn from the story that Cornelius is a devout worshiper of God, who gives generously to the people and prays to God (Acts 10:2); he is highly regarded by Jews (Acts 10:22), and he observes the Jewish times of prayer (Acts 10:30). But the conversion of this God-fearer is unlike the conversion of Jews as described in the previous chapters of Acts.[69] Something more is necessary, something that will permit both Jews and Gentiles to be members of the community without disrupting its unity. The necessary permission comes through Peter's vision, in which the distinction between clean and unclean foods is abolished, and in Peter's interpretation of the vision, "God has shown me that I should not call anyone profane or unclean" (Acts 10:28; cf. 11:18; 15:9).[70]

In addition to the theme of the community's inclusion of Gentiles, a number of by-now- familiar Lukan themes govern the narrative of Peter and Cornelius. The need to preserve the harmony of the community is certainly stressed. The divine leadership of the community is prominent in visions, angelophanies, and commands. At every moment Cornelius and Peter are guided by heavenly instructions (Acts 10:3–6, 9–16, 19–20, 44–46). Of equal importance is the theme of the order of the community. In his speech at the home of Cornelius, Peter stresses his role as witness to all that Jesus had done, from the time of the baptism by John (Acts 10:37) to the resurrection (Acts 10:40), and he recalls the choice of the witnesses and the commission given to them (Acts 10:41–42). The reader would be reminded of the requirements for apostleship from Acts 1:21–22.[71] But for the author of Acts there must be an authoritative confirmation of the validity of the new move of Peter, and that is given in Acts 11:1–18. Here Peter is called to give account of his actions in regard to this God-fearing Gentile, and after he does so the Jerusalem apostles agree that repentance has also been granted to Gentiles (Acts 11:18). It is important to observe that, for the author of Acts, the story is not over until the Jerusalem apostles have agreed that Gentiles may be members of the community and that their admission will not create disharmony.

Interpreters of Acts have long regarded it as curious that the one who in his letters claimed to be the apostle to Gentiles played no role in that momentous first conversion.

But in fact the narrative in Acts 10:1–11:18 is fully controlled by a theme that plays out in the book as a whole. For the author of Acts the importance of order in the community requires that the conversion of the first Gentile be the work of an apostle and that it be authorized by the entire group of Jerusalem apostles. After that authorization the story can proceed, and the marvelous ministry of the nonapostolic Paul may be praised. Such an important event as the inclusion of the first Gentile cannot be seen as an unauthorized departure or a disruption of order and harmony in the early community.

The relation of Paul to the leaders in Jerusalem is most vividly treated in Luke's narrative of the apostolic conference in Acts 15. In chapter 1 we concluded that the author of Acts used Paul's letter to the Galatians as a source for his narrative in Acts 15 and that he intentionally subverted the Pauline letter.[72] Why would he do so? It would be difficult to explain the reasons for this treatment of Galatians if Acts had been written by a companion or follower of the historical Paul. The treatment in Acts is born of an effort to read Galatians in such a way that it would not call attention to rifts between Paul and the other apostles and would not lead readers to think that Paul and his followers were unfaithful to Jewish traditions and practices. It is not unreasonable to think that such a treatment resulted from an effort to reconcile followers of Paul with followers of Peter, as the Tübingen School maintained. One of the most notable aspects of the chapter is the short speech in Acts 15:7–11, which puts Paul's words into Peter's mouth.[73]

It seems more reasonable, however, to think that there was a serious and specific challenge that the author of Acts intended to meet, a challenge that stressed the distance between Jewish and Christian practices and the opposition of Paul to the imposition on Gentile Christians not only of circumcision but of any requirements coming from Torah as well. Such a challenge came from Marcionite Christians, who emphasized Paul's claim not to yield to the opponents of Gentile freedom for a moment (Gal 2:5). How better to counter these Marcionite assertions than by publishing a narrative of this very meeting that Paul described in Galatians and by showing that there was no genuine disagreement between Paul and the other apostles but that the meeting ended in full accord with an agreement that some requirements from Torah were to be imposed on Gentile believers. The fact that the requirements as listed in Acts are said to be minimal is not the issue. Rather, the imposition of any such requirements on Gentile believers would signal to Luke's readers that Marcionite Christians are in error. Their total separation of Jewish and Christian practices is not to be countenanced; Peter cannot be regarded as a false apostle; and the distance between Jewish and Christian practices is not as great as Marcion had said. Paul's spreading of the apostolic decree (Acts 16:4) underscores his own agreement with it and leads the reader to understand Paul as quite different from the way the Marcionites portrayed him. Again, it is difficult to see why Luke would have so altered the material from Galatians except under the threat of a serious challenge such as that of Marcion.

Paul as a Faithful Jew and a Pharisee. For Vielhauer and many other scholars the assertion that Paul continued to think of himself as a Pharisee even toward the evident end of his life rings false to the assertions Paul makes about himself in the letters. I agree, but I also think that the claims of Paul in Acts sound very much like anti-Marcionite assertions. In addition the content of Paul's preaching in Acts is anti-Marcionite. While Marcion would totally divorce the Hebrew Scriptures, the prophets, and Jewish messianic expectations from Jesus, Paul in Acts asserts that Jesus is the fulfillment of these expectations.

A major objective of the scenes in Acts in which Paul is on trial appears to be to portray him as a Torah-abiding Jew. In his appearance before the Sanhedrin in Acts 23 Paul submits to the Jewish high priest, quoting from Exod 22:28: "You shall not speak evil of a leader of your people" (Acts 23:5). In the next Pauline speech, before the Roman governor Felix, Paul describes himself as a loyal Jew: "I worship the God of our ancestors, believing everything laid down according to the law or written in the prophets" (Acts 24:14). Paul reiterates his hope in the resurrection and calls attention to this hope as Jewish (Acts 24:15). He emphasizes his return to Jerusalem to bring alms to his people and make sacrifices in the temple. He reminds us that he was seized while engaged in a ritual of purification (Acts 24:17–18). In the hearing before Festus Paul defends himself by saying that he has done nothing against the Jewish law or the Jewish people (Acts 25:8, 10). In the climactic hearing before Agrippa and Bernice Paul firmly proclaims his Jewish allegiance: "All the Jews know my way of life from my youth, a life spent from the beginning among my own people and in Jerusalem. They have known for a long time, if they are willing to testify, that I have belonged to the strictest sect of our religion and lived as a Pharisee. And now I stand here on trial on account of my hope in the promise made by God to our ancestors, a promise that our twelve tribes hope to attain, as they earnestly worship day and night. It is for this hope, your Excellency, that I am accused by Jews! Why is it thought incredible by any of you that God raises the dead?" (Acts 26:4–8).[74] When in Acts 26:22 Paul asserts that he says "nothing but what the prophets and Moses said would take place," we know that the Paul who speaks here has nothing whatsoever to do with the Marcionite Paul. The reader of Acts, however, should not be surprised at this claim, because the author has prepared for it by portraying a number of incidents in which Paul is shown to be just what he claims to be in his trials, the most important of which are Acts 16:1–3 and 21:18–28.

In Acts 16:1–3 Paul has Timothy circumcised.[75] Luke explains that Timothy's mother was Jewish and his father was Greek and that Paul wanted him to travel with him and had him circumcised because of pressure from the Jews of Lystra. Again we see the significance of the Lukan theme of fidelity to Jewish traditions and practices. Whether this act would have been anathema to the historical Paul may not be certain, but it would surely have been contrary to the Marcionite Paul. A Paul who would preach a message of release from the God of Torah would hardly participate in or even approve an act that so clearly fulfills the requirements of this God. A Paul who rejects the God of creation would not bring himself so close to this physical Jewish act. A second-century reader of Acts who was aware of Marcionite teaching would surely have seen here a deliberate rejection of that teaching.

Viewed as a response to the Marcionite challenge the narrative of Acts 21:18–28 is very interesting. It tells of Paul's arrival at Jerusalem and of the news that greeted him there. First we learn categorically that there are myriads of believers among the citizens of Jerusalem and that "they are all zealous for the law" (Acts 21:20). This would be an impossibility for Marcion, who saw the role of Jesus as freeing believers from the domination of Torah. Then we learn that Paul has been accused of teaching diaspora Jews to forsake Moses, to forego circumcision for their sons, and not to observe the customs (Acts 21:21). This is clearly regarded as a false charge against Paul, and he is to demonstrate its falsity by participating in a ritual of purification and paying the expenses of four men under a Nazirite vow. There should be no doubt that the purpose of this series of actions is to show that Paul did *not* teach the abolition of Torah. James's statement in Acts 21:25 makes the point explicitly: "Thus all will know that there is nothing in what they have been told about you, but that you yourself observe and guard the law."[76] It is as if the author of Acts is saying to the reader: "You may have heard Marcionite Christians say falsely that Paul did not observe Torah, but here is what he really did." Paul willingly engaged in the practices recommended by James but the charges against him persisted. He was seized by Asian Jews, who shouted: "This is the man who is teaching everyone everywhere against our people, our law, and this place" (Acts 21:28). The author of Acts knows this to be a vicious falsehood, and he here attributes it to Jews from Asia. But we know it also as a claim made by Marcionites. The message to the reader is that Paul was not as the Marcionites said he was, but he was arrested because people believed this falsehood.

A few additional items may also be observed in this connection. In Acts 18:18 Paul has his hair cut because of a vow. It is not clear that Luke intended the reader to understand this act as associated with Jewish tradition. But if ancient readers would have seen it as underscoring Paul's fidelity to Jewish practices, they would almost certainly have seen it as an indication of opposition to Marcionite Christianity. Acts 20:16 pictures Paul as eager to be in Jerusalem in time for the observance of Pentecost.[77] This note would serve to let the reader know that Paul is an observant Jew, and it would further distance him from the Marcionite portrait.

The characterization of Paul in Acts is internally consistent. He is a loyal Jew, obedient to Torah and faithful to Jewish practices. His message is that Jesus fulfills the words of the Hebrew prophets: he is the Messiah of Israel. Paul does not act unilaterally but only in harmony with Peter and the Jerusalem apostles. It is they who establish the authentic Christian tradition, and Paul neither adds to it nor subtracts from it. The characterization of Paul is also consistent with the major themes that the author used in writing Acts, among them: the order of the community; the internal harmony of the community; the community's inclusion of Gentiles; Jewish rejection

of the Christian message; and the community's fidelity to Jewish traditions and practices. The author of Acts has made use of these characterizations and themes to produce an engaging narrative that responds, almost point by point, to the Marcionite
challenge. Readers of Acts learn that the God of Jesus is the God of the Jews, that Jesus
was the fulfillment of Jewish expectations as announced by the Hebrew prophets, and
that the early Christian leaders continued to observe Torah and Jewish practices.

Acts as a Response to the Marcionite Challenge

In 1942 John Knox, building on insights from the Tübingen School, proposed that
Acts (and canonical Luke) was written as a response to the Marcionite challenge.[78]
He observed that the legacy of Paul posed serious difficulties for conservative
churches, such as that at Rome. Awareness of the contribution of Paul as apostle to
Gentiles was well known and could not be neglected. But the equally well known
association of the epistles of Paul with Marcion constituted a most difficult problem. Knox wrote: "Paul was at one time in grave danger of being lost to the heretics. Neither Justin nor Papias (as far as we can gather from Eusebius) so much as
refers to Paul. This silence, especially as it seems deliberate, can most naturally be
interpreted to mean that in some churches at least Paul was under suspicion; and
one of these churches must have been the church at Rome."[79] Thus churches such
as Rome "were confronted with the necessity of a crucial choice as far as Paul is
concerned: either they must canonize him or repudiate him (or at least seriously
discredit him)."[80] This was, however, no real choice: Paul had to be claimed even if
it meant shaping his legacy in a more proto-orthodox mold.

But, says Knox, if it was inevitable that epistles of Paul were to be canonized, "it
was likewise inevitable that they should not be canonized alone."[81] After all, the letters taken alone might tend to confirm Marcion's basic tenets. They might suggest,
as Marcion claimed, that Paul was the only apostle or that he was completely independent of the group in Jerusalem. Unless provided with a "proper" commentary,
the letters might lead readers to think that Paul's contrast of law and gospel implied
Marcion's theory of two Gods. Knox maintained that for the more conservative
churches to accept Paul and at the same time repudiate Marcion "meant to affirm
with all possible vigor that the Apostle to the Gentiles, far from being independent
of the Twelve, had acknowledged their authority, had been gladly accredited by
them, and had worked obediently and loyally under their direction. But the letters
of Paul gave only scant support to this view. Some book which, without reducing or
disparaging Paul, subordinated him to the Twelve was obviously required."[82]

This is precisely what the Acts of the Apostles does. Not only is Paul presented as
in agreement with the older apostles, but he reports to them on a regular basis,
accepts the apostolic decree, which imposes on Gentile converts certain restrictions
from Torah, and throughout maintains that he is a Pharisee. In Knox's judgment the
book of Acts appeared at precisely the point at which there was a need for separating
Paul from Marcion and provided the basis for doing so. The book of Acts, together

with other apostolic letters and the Pastorals, allowed for the acceptance of Paul as one among the apostles. Knox noted that in the Muratorian canon, Acts is called "The Acts of All the Apostles."[83]

The context that Knox evokes is one in which a second-century "Pauline" Christian comes out of Asia to Italy, armed with Paul's letters and a gospel associated with him and preaching a gospel in his name. Those who opposed him would have been significantly aided in their opposition if they also were armed with an authoritative text that interpreted Paul in a way that would counter the Marcionite position. Such a text would show Paul as in agreement with the apostles who had been with Jesus during his lifetime, as faithful to Torah and broaching no dichotomy between law and gospel. This is precisely what Acts does, and history shows that its conservative characterization of Paul fulfilled the church's needs admirably.

Confidence in Knox's case would be significantly increased if there were explicit references to the Marcionite controversy in Acts, but unfortunately this is not the case. There is no more explicit reference to Marcion than there is to the fall of Jerusalem or the death of Paul. Acts 20:29–30 refers to "fierce wolves" who will come in to the community and persons from among Paul's adherents who will lead away some of his disciples, but this reference is agonizingly vague. An enigmatic passage in Acts 16:6–8 may, however, contain an allusion to Marcion's homeland: "They went through the region of Phrygia and Galatia, having been forbidden by the Holy Spirit to speak the word in Asia. When they had come opposite Mysia, they attempted to go into Bithynia, but the Spirit of Jesus did not allow them; so, passing by Mysia, they went down to Troas" (Acts 16:6–8). Some of the local and regional names in these verses may be explained by Luke's use of a source, and the references to the "Holy Spirit" and the "Spirit of Jesus" support the theme of divine guidance for the early Christian mission. But the prohibition of preaching in certain areas is difficult to explain. It is worth observing that these verses come just before the first of the several "we" sections in Acts, but here the subjects are third person, implicitly Paul, Silas, and Timothy. No explanation of the spirit's action is given, but the implication is that there was no Pauline mission on this occasion in Asia or Bithynia. Since the author of Acts made no attempt elsewhere to mention places Paul avoided, the explicit reference here is striking. Further, the locations in Acts 16:6–8 are said to be neglected under the direction of the "Holy Spirit" and the "Spirit of Jesus." The avoidance of Asia is temporary, but that of Bithynia is, in the Acts narrative, permanent. Why so? A plausible suggestion is that in the second century Bithynia, which was generally connected with Pontus, was known as the place of Marcion's origin and that Luke wants to disassociate Paul from Marcion. He does so by affirming that in the very area where Marcion was born and began his preaching, there had been no Pauline mission, thus no association with earlier Christianity. The author of Acts would be signaling the reader that the claims of the Marcionites to be followers of Paul are mere fabrications, unsupported by the historical "facts" and, what is more important, contrary to the "Spirit of Jesus."

Conclusion

In chapter 1 I attempted to show that the most plausible date for the composition of Acts was 100–150 C.E. This chapter also noted that efforts to understand Acts as written either at an early or an intermediate date did not posit a context for its authorship that reflected a known historical situation. In the present chapter I claim that within the time frame of 100–150 C.E. the challenge of Marcion and Marcionite Christianity forms a remarkably meaningful and probable context for Acts and explains the use of many of the themes and literary features in the book and, in particular, the characterizations of Peter and Paul. If this claim is accepted, we can conclude that the Acts of the Apostles was probably written about 120–125 C.E., just when Marcion was beginning to attract adherents into what became the most significant heterodox movement of the second century.

In view of the generally accepted theory that the Gospel of Luke and the book of Acts belong together, any consideration of the composition of the latter involves that of the former. Chapter 4 will address some of the complex issues surrounding the composition of the Gospel of Luke.

CHAPTER *4*

The Composition of Canonical Luke

Any consideration of the date and context of Acts must include attention also to the composition of the Gospel of Luke. This is the case because of a fundamental agreement between early Christian tradition and modern critical scholarship. Irenaeus identified Luke as the author of both the third gospel and the Acts.[1] The Muratorian Canon did the same.[2] In both cases these documents stress the authorship of both Luke and Acts by an eyewitness and companion of Paul. As we have seen, critical scholars are divided on the identification of the author as a companion of Paul, but there is almost no disagreement on the authorship of Luke and Acts by the same person. Henry J. Cadbury coined the term *Luke-Acts* to describe the two texts and to emphasize their common authorship.[3] Indeed, Cadbury's term has come to be used pervasively by modern scholars, some of whom treat Luke-Acts as a single text with an underlying structure and literary themes that govern both parts.

A second factor that requires us to consider the Gospel of Luke is its alleged connection with Marcion. We noted in chapter 2 that, although our early Christian witnesses agree that the gospel that Marcion used was a version of what they knew as the Gospel of Luke, there are good reasons to doubt their charges that he "mutilated" the canonical Gospel of Luke. It is nevertheless clear that authorities such as Irenaeus and Tertullian recognized a relationship between canonical Luke and the Gospel of Marcion.

These two factors—the common authorship of Luke and Acts and the association of some form of Luke's gospel with Marcion—compel us to turn now to an examination of the Third Gospel. We do so, however, in the light of the studies of the previous chapters. If it is the case that the Acts of the Apostles was written in the first quarter of the second century as, in part, a response to the challenge of Marcion, what can we say about canonical Luke? Was it also written at about the same time and with the same intent?

It is important to keep in mind the fact that more than one edition of the Third Gospel was in circulation during the second century. Marcion's gospel was recognized as a version of canonical Luke, albeit a defective one. Further, it is probable that Marcion's gospel was based on an edition of a gospel known in Pontus, that is, a primitive version of Luke, and we shall suggest that the author of canonical Luke also used this text as a source. Thus at least two and more likely three versions of the Third Gospel were known and available in the second century.[4] Unfortunately only canonical Luke is directly available for modern scholarship, but this fact does not affect the existence in the second century of multiple versions of this gospel.

The focus of attention in this chapter will be on canonical Luke, that is, the version of the Third Gospel known to Irenaeus and Tertullian and the only edition that has survived to modern times. If, however, the early Christian fathers had the relationship between the Gospel of Marcion and canonical Luke, so to speak, backward, and if the companion volume—Acts—was written in part as a response to the Marcionite challenge, is it probable that the canonical version of Luke was also produced with the same challenge in mind? This chapter will attempt to show that the answer to this question should be yes.

The Date of Canonical Luke

Consideration of the date of the Gospel of Luke is complicated by the fact that multiple texts and versions were known in the second century. External references to it are almost never clear in indicating which version is intended.[5] Nevertheless it is useful to examine such references for whatever light they might shed on the date of composition. In chapter 1 we saw that there were no clear references to Acts before the middle of the second century and that the external references permitted a second-century date for Acts.[6] The lack of early external references applies also to the gospels in general. But what may we say about the Gospel of Luke specifically?

Martin Hengel has recently claimed that the first citations of Luke come from the early decades of the second century.[7] Hengel is idiosyncratic in his dating of the composition of Luke even before that of Matthew. The evidence he cites for Matthew's use of Luke as a source need not detain us at this point, but he also helpfully calls attention to what he considers to be the first citations of Luke outside the New Testament. The clearest is the quotation of Luke 16:10 in *2 Clement* 8:5, which reads: "For the Lord saith in the Gospel, 'If ye have not kept that which was small, who will commit to you the great? For I say unto you, that he that is faithful in that which is least, is faithful also in much.'"[8] The quoted phrase is found only in Luke, and Hengel argues that the author of *2 Clement* probably had the Third Gospel in mind when he quoted it. Hengel dates *2 Clement* "one or two decades before Justin and Marcion" (presumably 130–140 C.E.), but it is usually dated somewhat later, between 140 and 160 C.E.[9] In any event a quotation in a document that may with some probability be dated at or after the middle of the second century does not preclude an early-second-century date for canonical Luke.

A more problematic claim made by Hengel has to do with the use of Luke by Basilides, who was probably active in the first half of the second century. Hengel notes references to twenty-four books on the gospels that Basilides supposedly wrote, and then he states: "There are some indications that Basilides especially used the Gospel of Luke, but also other Synoptic texts and even perhaps John in this commentary."[10] Hengel is here dependent on the work of his student Winrich A. Löhr.[11] Löhr has a careful examination of fifteen testimonies and nineteen alleged fragments quoted in second- and third-century sources. Of these the most significant are two of the alleged fragments (numbers 1 and 19). Fragment 1 is from Clement of Alexandria, *Stromateis* 1,145:6–146:4. The reference appears within a long section on chronology, a matter of importance to Clement and presumably also to Basilides and his followers. The entire passage reads as follows:

> And the followers of Basilides hold the day of his [Jesus'] baptism as a festival, spending the night before in readings.
>
> And they say that it was the fifteenth year of Tiberius Caesar, the fifteenth day of the month Tubi; and some that it was the eleventh of the same month. And treating of His passion, with very great accuracy, some say that it took place in the sixteenth year of Tiberius, on the twenty-fifth of Phamenoth; and others the twenty-fifth of Pharmuthi and others say that on the nineteenth of Pharmuthi the Saviour suffered. Further, others say that He was born on the twenty-fourth or twenty-fifth of Pharmuthi.[12]

Löhr observes that not only is there an allusion here to Luke 3:1 but also that the Basilidean assumption of a one-year ministry for Jesus is based on Luke 4:19, where Jesus, drawing on Isa 58:6; 61:2, claims that he has been sent to proclaim "the year of the Lord's favor."[13] Löhr concludes that "the fragment is evidence for the supposition that the original Basilideans made use of a gospel rescension based on the Gospel of Luke and possibly neither knew nor recognized the Gospel of John."[14]

If Clement of Alexandria was actually dependent on a fragment from a Basilidean text at this point, we would be forced to conclude that members of this sect were aware of the tradition reflected in Luke 3:1 about the appearance of John and the baptism of Jesus in the fifteenth year of Tiberius. It should be stressed that Clement's comments, which refer to the followers of Basilides, do not require the conclusion that Basilides himself knew Luke 3:1. Further, Löhr's conclusion could be rephrased to say that the followers of Basilides made use of an edition of Luke that contained Luke 3:1. We know that Marcion's edition began with Luke 3:1, although it made no reference to Jesus' baptism. As we shall show later in this chapter there are good reasons to think that the source behind both Marcion and canonical Luke also started with Luke 3:1. Thus in view of the existence in the second century of multiple editions of Luke, we cannot be certain which one is indicated by the Basilidean allusion to "the fifteenth year of Tiberius Caesar."

Löhr's fragment 19 is from an obscure text probably from the first half of the fourth century, Hegemonius, *Acta Archelai* 67:4–12. The text as we have it is in Latin, probably a translation from the Greek, which was in turn a translation from a Syriac original. It purports to be a dispute of a Bishop Archelaus with Mani, leader of the Manicheans. At one point the author refers to Basilides, whom he regards as a kind of progenitor of the dualism of the Manicheans. He notes that Basilides lived only a short time after the apostles and wrote a treatise, the thirteenth book of which was extant at the time the *Acta Archelai* were written. The author quotes from the beginning of this thirteenth book: "As we write the thirteenth book of the treatise, the saving word provides for us a necessary and substantial example: Through the parable of the rich and the poor we are shown from where nature could spring up without root and without origin, appearing in phenomena."[15] Löhr says that this may possibly be a reference to the parable in Luke 16:19–31. Hegemonius uses the parable as a springboard for his discussion of good and evil, and Löhr notes that this topic may have been suggested by Luke 16:25, which refers to good and bad.

For our purposes the key phrase is the reference to "the parable of the rich and the poor." Does this phrase constitute evidence that Basilides was acquainted with the parable in Luke 16:19–31? Clearly Hegemonius knows the parable, since he quotes from it extensively at an earlier point in *Acta Archelai* in support of the contention that Jesus said nothing contrary to Moses.[16] The reconstruction of the Hegemonius text is critical here. The two main Latin manuscripts have *parvulam,* but Löhr elects to follow an early translation by M. Routh, who suggested that the text should read *parabolam.* S. D. F. Salmond, however, translates the phrase as, "the figures of a rich principle and a poor principle,"[17] and he notes that "Routh confesses his inability to understand what can be meant by the term *parvulam,* and suggests *parabolam.*"[18] From Routh's inability to understand a Latin term, Löhr moves to the contention that Basilides was possibly acquainted with the parable of Dives and Lazarus in Luke 16. I suggest that this case has not been shown convincingly.

Actually Löhr's conclusion is cautiously stated. "In view of fragments 19 and 1, the hypothesis of a gospel rescension based on the Gospel of Luke has a certain plausibility . . . and even the Jordan scene [Jesus' baptism] described in fragment 4, going back to the circle of disciples, points to Mark or Matthew rather than Luke."[19] This statement is far more modest than the claim that Hengel built on his student's work. Hengel cited Löhr to support his contention that "Basilides especially used the Gospel of Luke."[20] In my judgment the evidence cited by Löhr does not support the conclusion that Basilides was acquainted with canonical Luke.

Andrew Gregory, whose work was cited earlier, has produced an exhaustive study of the reception of Luke (and Acts) in the second century.[21] He carefully examines available citations and allusions by writers from Ignatius to Tertullian. Among other allusions Gregory notes a passage in Ignatius, *Smyrnaeans* 3:2, that has striking affinities with Luke 24:39. After calling attention to similarities between the two texts in terms of setting and language, Gregory finally agrees with William R. Schoedel in rejecting the view that Ignatius knew and used the Gospel of Luke.[22] He concludes that Justin and Marcion were the first to show an acquaintance with Luke but that probably neither was aware of the edition of Luke in its canonical form. Justin knew some sections of Luke, but not the birth narratives, and Marcion knew a gospel similar to our canonical Luke but shorter. In fact, claims Gregory, "of potential significance . . . is the possibility that Marcion is actually the first witness to sustained use not just of *Luke* but of any discrete Gospel, and that he may in fact have been a conservative editor of a shorter form of *Luke* than that known today, a form with strong affinities to the western text."[23] Gregory further concludes that the "earliest patristic reference to a gospel associated with the name of Luke" is that of Irenaeus.[24]

I conclude, with Gregory and others, that citations and allusions to the Gospel of Luke do not require us to date the canonical version before ca. 120–125 C.E., the date we suggested for the composition of Acts.[25] In order, however, to show that the canonical edition of Luke, like Acts, was probably composed in the first quarter of the second century at the time of the Marcionite challenge, it is necessary to examine more closely the relationship between Marcion and Luke, and the balance of this chapter will be devoted to this topic.

Canonical Luke and the Gospel of Marcion

In chapter 2 we concluded that there were good reasons to doubt the claims of Irenaeus, Tertullian, and Epiphanius that the Gospel of Marcion was derived from canonical Luke. This doubt was enthusiastically endorsed by a number of nineteenth-century scholars.

Albrecht Ritschl originally argued that the Marcionite gospel was the major source for canonical Luke.[26] Ferdinand Christian Baur drew heavily on Ritschl's study but thought that there was an original edition of Luke composed by a non-Marcionite Paulinist.[27] Baur maintained that "original Luke" was not the Marcionite gospel, but there was much in it that would have been compatible with Marcionite teachings. The author of canonical Luke also drew upon original Luke, incorporating some material from Matthew and some from his Sondergut, in order to provide for the church a clearly anti-Marcionite gospel.[28]

Baur vigorously challenged the contention of the church fathers that Marcion "mutilated" canonical Luke. He said that this judgment came from noncritical and biased authors, who were intent on portraying Marcion as a heretic. The charge of mutilating a text carries no more weight than the charge of seducing a virgin; a heretic may be presumed to have done both, and Marcion's opponents so accused him. For Baur the most convincing evidence for the derivative nature of canonical Luke consists of a number of inconsistencies that he perceived in it. For most of them he drew on Ritschl. One such inconsistency has to do with the order of pericopes in our Luke 4. In the gospel as we now have it the narrative of Jesus' rejection at Nazareth (Luke 4:16–30) comes before that of an exorcism at Capernaum (Luke 4:31–37). But the former narrative refers to an earlier visit of Jesus to Capernaum. In Luke 4:23 we have, "Doubtless you will quote to me this proverb, 'Doctor, cure yourself!' And you will say, 'Do here also in your hometown the things that we have heard you did at Capernaum.'" As the order in canonical Luke stands there is a reference to an event in Capernaum that has not yet been described. Baur also comments that Luke 4:24 makes better sense in a context in which the reader can see a contrast with Jesus' reception outside his hometown. Another alleged inconsistency is found in Luke 11:29–32, which contains two interpretations of the sign of Jonah and a seemingly irrelevant note about Solomon and the Queen of the South. Yet another inconsistency noted by Baur is Luke 16:16–17. Here in one verse Luke's Jesus says that the law has come to an end, and in the following verse says that "it is easier for heaven and earth to pass away, than for one stroke of a letter in the law to be dropped."

For Baur these and other inconsistencies do not support the contention that Marcion mutilated our Luke. Rather they result from the merging of "original Luke" with other materials in an effort to combat the influence of Marcion and to ameliorate the differences between Pauline and Petrine Christianity. For example, the author of canonical Luke created the problem of order in chapter 4, so that Nazareth comes before Capernaum. This author believed that Jesus would naturally have begun his ministry in his hometown. "For the second author [the author of canonical Luke] the event in Nazareth had more importance [than for the author of original Luke] not only because it demonstrated the fulfillment of the Old Testament prophecies in the person of Jesus (v. 21), but also because it gave him opportunity to introduce a saying of Jesus which seemed especially suitable."[29] The suitable saying is Luke 4:24, "a prophet is not without honor except in his own hometown." The canonical author connects the Nazareth episode with the Elijah / Elisha sayings to show that the ministry of Jesus is both to Israel and the Gentiles. Baur also maintained that in Luke 16:17 the canonical author changed the phrase from that in "original Luke," "It is easier for heaven and earth to pass away than for one of my words to fail," by substituting "the law" for "my words," thereby affirming the perpetuity of Torah over against Marcionite interpretations.

Baur's chief intent in calling attention to these and other problems was to challenge the view that Marcion's gospel was a mutilation of canonical Luke. Ritschl was able to make this point by comparing canonical Luke with a reconstruction of Marcion's gospel, and he was able to show that the inconsistencies that he found in canonical Luke disappear in the Marcionite gospel. But Baur had to rely not only on a reconstruction of Marcion's gospel but also on a reconstruction of a gospel he called "original Luke," which, at least in the comparisons he made, appears to be quite similar to the Marcionite gospel as Ritschl had described it. In fact, at many points it is difficult to know whether Baur is talking about the Marcionite gospel or "original Luke." In any case the episode at Capernaum comes before the episode at Nazareth in Marcion's gospel, although according to Harnack both narratives are greatly abbreviated.[30] Marcion omits both interpretations of the sign of Jonah from Luke 11:29–32, and in place of Luke 16:17, Jesus proclaims the eternality of his own words. For Marcion it is clear that the law has come to an end but that Jesus' words will endure forever. Presumably Baur's "original Luke" is also free of the kinds of inconsistencies that he found in canonical Luke.

Under the influence of the work of Adolf Hilgenfeld and Gustav Volckmar, Ritschl retracted his views about the direct relationship between the Gospel of Marcion and canonical Luke, and he finally came to a view similar to Baur's.[31] Although the simpler view of the early Ritschl may seem more attractive, it would require us to believe something that is highly improbable, namely that a proto-orthodox author would base his work on a writing that he regarded as heretical. Further, Volckmar maintained that both canonical Luke and Marcion's gospel were derivative. For example, he showed, in opposition to Ritschl and Baur, that the order of pericopes in Luke 4 was no more original in Marcion than in canonical Luke. Ritschl and Baur had noted that the canonical order—the Nazareth pericope (Luke 4:16–30) before the Capernaum pericope (Luke 4:31–37)—created problems. Volckmar, however, pointed out that the Marcionite order—Capernaum, then Nazareth—is also inconsistent. It provides no motivation for the Nazareth people to turn against Jesus, since the only thing preceding it is Luke 4:22, in which they hear him gladly and approve of what he says. Volckmar also noted that the statement of the Nazareth people (Luke 4:23) does not work after only the one Capernaum incident. Its reference to the "things [plural] you did in Capernaum" suggests a rather long history of wonders, not just one. Volckmar also observed that Luke 4:24 ("no prophet is accepted in the prophet's hometown") is meaningless at the beginning of the gospel. Jesus must first have been shown to be a great prophet, and so the saying makes sense only at a later point in the narrative, as in both Mark 6:4 and Matt 13:57. In this case it appears that both the Marcionite and canonical authors adopted the two pericopes from a common original. Volckmar concluded that there is no ground for the thesis that canonical Luke is derived from Marcion, and his studies bear out this conclusion. He also maintained that there was an original gospel that served as a basis for both the Marcionite and the canonical gospels. In his view the expanded canonical text of Luke existed, in its entirety, prior to Marcion,[32] but he nevertheless acknowledged the likelihood that some verses and pericopes that were lacking in Marcion were added at a later time to canonical Luke.[33]

John Knox summarized the nineteenth-century German controversy as ending "not in the vindication of the traditional position which [August] Hahn had defended but in the establishment of a new view which denied both that Luke was derived from Marcion and that Marcion was derived from canonical Luke."[34] Knox himself adopted something close to Baur's approach and argued "that the relation between Marcion's Gospel and the canonical Gospel of Luke is not accurately described either by the simple statement that Marcion abridged Luke or by the simple statement that Luke enlarged Marcion. The position would rather be that a primitive Gospel, containing approximately the same Markan and Matthean elements which our Luke contains and some of its peculiar materials, was somewhat shortened by Marcion or some predecessor and rather considerably enlarged by the writer of our Gospel, who was also the maker of Luke-Acts."[35]

This formidable scholarly tradition, which includes Baur, Ritschl, and Knox, has established grounds for serious doubts about the claims of the church fathers and has encouraged an alternative theory, namely that canonical Luke, although not based directly on Marcion's gospel, was composed, among other factors, in reaction to the preaching of Marcion.

This alternative theory is strengthened by observing some of the major differences between the Marcionite gospel, to the extent to which it may be reconstructed, and our canonical Luke. In his discussion of these relationships Knox noted that, on the traditional view, "Marcion 'omitted' a much larger proportion of the peculiar Lukan material than of the common Synoptic material. Why should he have done this? If he did not like what was distinctively Lukan, why did he choose this Gospel, when, according to the usual view, he had all the Gospels at hand, including Mark and John?"[36] If, however, canonical Luke appeared after Marcion's gospel was in circulation, and if the prevailing view of synoptic relationships is correct, it would not be surprising to find that a substantial portion of the material not in Marcion but in canonical Luke is from the Lukan Sondergut.[37] In this case the added material was not known to Marcion and so could not have formed part of the gospel he used.

Drawing on Harnack's reconstruction of the Marcionite gospel, Knox conveniently classified the sections of Luke into three groups:

A. Passages that seem to have a Marcionite equivalent;
B. Passages known to have no Marcionite equivalent;
C. Passages that are uncertain.[38]

Knox further classified the passages in terms of their relation to the other Synoptic Gospels—that is., some passages have synoptic parallels and others are peculiar to Luke—and he showed that a much higher proportion of the peculiar material was absent from the Gospel of Marcion than of the material with parallels. As a basis for his study of synoptic parallels Knox used the work of John C. Hawkins, which he adapted slightly.[39] During the last several decades it has been possible to redo studies such as those of Hawkins, with electronic support.[40] I have made use of these studies to re-examine Knox's contentions and have found that the results tend to confirm his claims.

The tables below display the results of my own study, based on that of Knox. I have made use of an analysis of the Synoptic Gospels that Thomas R. W. Longstaff and I prepared in 1978, and I adhered closely to Harnack's reconstruction of Marcion's gospel, as Knox also did.[41] I adopted Knox's classification of material from Luke in respect to its use or nonuse in Marcion's gospel, and the minor differences in our results are generally due to differences in judgment about the parallelism or nonparallelism of certain Lukan pericopes.[42] Table 1, below, shows the results in terms of the number of verses involved. "Source" refers to the issue of parallelism or nonparallelism. "Class" refers to the use or nonuse in Marcion's gospel, following the classifications of Knox.

The table shows that canonical Luke has 684 verses that may be considered to have parallels in Matthew or Mark or both and 467 that have no parallels in either of the other two Synoptic Gospels. Of the verses with parallels 71.7 percent of them probably appeared in the Gospel of Marcion. Of the verses peculiar to Luke only about 40.9 percent appeared in Marcion.

Table 2, below, is also based on Knox's work but attempts to refine the results by viewing the material in terms of the number of words rather than verses.[43] This study

TABLE 1. Canonical Luke and Marcion: Verses

Source	Class	# of Verses	% of Verses
Synoptic Parallels	A	490.5	71.7
Synoptic Parallels	B	85.5	12.5
Synoptic Parallels	C	108.0	15.8
Total		**684.0**	**100.0**
Peculiar to Luke	A	191.0	40.9
Peculiar to Luke	B	201.0	43.0
Peculiar to Luke	C	75.0	16.1
Total		**467.0**	**100.0**

does not imply that all of the words counted below have synoptic parallels or appeared in Marcion's gospel. The word count is included here simply as an indication of the proportion of agreement. Since verses are of unequal lengths, a comparison of the number of words should give a more accurate measure of agreement than a comparison of verses or it should confirm the results of studies which compare verses.

TABLE 2. Canonical Luke and Marcion: Words

Source	Class	# Words	% Words
Synoptic Parallels	A	8,473	72.3
Synoptic Parallels	B	1,496	12.8
Synoptic Parallels	C	1,747	14.9
Total		**11,716**	**100.0**
Peculiar to Luke	A	3,321	43.4
Peculiar to Luke	B	3,127	40.8
Peculiar to Luke	C	1,212	15.8
Total		**7,660**	**100.0**

The results in table 2 are similar to those in table 1. Whether we attend to verses or words the notable phenomenon is the high percentage of Lukan Sondergut material that is not present in Marcion compared with material that has synoptic parallels. About 12 percent of Lukan material with synoptic parallels is probably absent from Marcion's gospel. But 41–43 percent of Lukan Sondergut material is omitted.[44]

By any measure this is a striking phenomenon. Knox writes: "It need hardly be urged that these facts present difficulties for the traditional position. Even when allowance is made for error, for varieties of judgment at a few points of detail, and for the possibility that the verses in 'B' are shorter than those in 'A' (although a sampling here indicates that they run to about the same length on the average), it still remains clear that Marcion 'omitted' a much larger proportion of the peculiar Lukan material than of the common Synoptic material. Why should he have done this?"[45]

How, indeed, can we understand the lack in Marcion of such a high proportion of the Lukan Sondergut material? At first glance three explanations seem to be available: (1) Marcion had a copy of canonical Luke that was similar to our modern texts, and he selectively omitted sections of his source but omitted much larger portions of the material from Luke's Sondergut simply because it was distinctive. (2) Marcion had a copy of canonical Luke that was similar to our modern texts, and he selectively omitted sections of his source but omitted much larger portions of the material from Luke's Sondergut because here he found material that he considered highly offensive. (3) Canonical Luke included a large number of pericopes that were unknown to the authors of the other Synoptic Gospels and to Marcion.

(1) The first alternative explanation, that Marcion had a copy of canonical Luke that was similar to our modern texts and selectively omitted sections but omitted much larger portions of the material from Luke's Sondergut simply because it was distinctive, is untenable. If all of the canonical gospels were available to Marcion and he chose Luke from among them, then Knox's question, quoted above, is sufficient to dismiss this explanation as highly unlikely: why would Marcion choose the Lukan gospel as a source and then cut out so much of the distinctive material in it?[46] If, however, Marcion knew only the canonical Gospel of Luke, this first alternative explanation is impossible, for in that event Marcion would have no way to determine what in Luke was distinctive. The first alternative may be dismissed without further consideration.

(2) The second alternative explanation, that Marcion had a copy of canonical Luke that was similar to our modern texts and selectively omitted sections but omitted much larger portions of the material from Luke's Sondergut because he found it highly offensive, answers some questions while raising others. An examination of the Lukan Sondergut material that is not in Marcion's gospel shows that this second explanation is viable. We must acknowledge that any judgments we make on this score are hampered by the limited nature of our knowledge about Marcion and Marcionite theology. What we do know, however, suggests that there is at hand a way of understanding the alleged omission of many of the pericopes under consideration. The major L pericopes that are not in Marcion's gospel are the following:

Luke 1:1–4. The preface.
Luke 1:5–2:52. The infancy narratives.
Luke 3:10–14. John the Baptist replies to questioners.
Luke 3:23–38. The genealogy.
Luke 13:1–9. The Galileans and the tower of Siloam; the parable of the fig tree.
Luke 13:31–33. A warning against Herod.
Luke 15:11–32. The parable of the prodigal son.
Luke 19:41–44. Jesus' weeping over Jerusalem.

Luke 22:35–38. The two swords.

Luke 23:39–43. The two thieves.

Luke 24:13–53. Jesus' postresurrection appearances (with traces in Marcion's gospel).

In addition there are a number of brief notes that are peculiar to Luke and omitted by Marcion, such as Luke 9:31, in which Moses and Elijah appear at Jesus' transfiguration and discuss his ἔξοδος with him, and 19:9b, in which Zacchaeus is identified as a son of Abraham. Verses such as these may be understood as details connecting Jesus with ancient Hebrew worthies and thus inimical to the Marcionite claim that the divine father of Jesus was not the God of the Hebrew Bible. The genealogy, Luke 3:23–38, links Jesus with the Hebrew patriarchs and suggests a line of prophetic anticipation. The saying about the Galileans and the tower of Siloam (Luke 13:1–5) suggests that Jesus believed in a God of judgment rather than of mercy and love, and the parable of the fig tree (Luke 13:6–9) suggests a patience with the Jewish people that Marcion may have wished to downplay. Jesus' weeping over Jerusalem (Luke 19:1–44) would have implied a link that Marcionites would deny. These pericopes *may* be explained as intentional Marcionite omissions from his source text.

But other allegedly omitted pericopes are more problematic. It is not clear that the parable of the prodigal son (Luke 15:11–32), peculiar to canonical Luke and absent from Marcion's gospel, would have been offensive to Marcion. If he understood the figure of the father to represent God and that of the elder brother to be Jews, the father's statement to him, "You are always with me" (Luke 15:31), may have constituted a problem for Marcion.[47] But the main thrust of the parable affirms a major Pauline viewpoint, as Baur long ago recognized.[48]

The second alternative explanation, that Marcion intentionally omitted certain materials peculiar to Luke on the grounds that they were offensive, accounts for the absence of some pericopes, but questions remain about others. It does not account for the greater abundance of offensive material in the Lukan Sondergut than in material from other sources. Further, we have already noted the difficulty in explaining "omissions" in Marcion on doctrinal grounds. Recall Tertullian's perplexity about finding things in Marcion's gospel which he thought Marcion would have rejected.[49]

(3) Under the third explanation, that canonical Luke included a large number of pericopes that were unknown to other gospel writers, including Marcion, some of the pericopes discussed above and explained as Marcionite omissions may be just as well understood as additions made by the final editor of canonical Luke. Pericopes for which we can find no good reason for Marcionite omission may be better understood as material unknown to him and added in canonical Luke.

Thus two explanations are viable. That Marcion omitted some offensive material may well explain the absence of a number of pericopes. That some pericopes were added by an anti-Marcionite canonical author may explain others. In order to adjudicate between these alternatives it will be necessary to examine a number of pericopes in detail. Of all the Lukan Sondergut material that is absent from Marcion's gospel, the material in what is now Luke 1–2 provides the clearest example of material that, in my judgment, is best explained by our third alternative—that it appears to have been added by an anti-Marcionite canonical author. In addition material in Luke 24 requires special treatment in this connection. An exploration of the preface and the infancy narratives in Luke 1–2 and the postresurrection narratives in Luke 24 will help give us a handle on the problem.[50] Our exploration will begin with the infancy narratives; then we turn to the postresurrection accounts and the preface. After examining these sections, we will look briefly at the body of Luke, that is, Luke 3–23.

The Infancy Narratives—Luke 1:5–2:52

In the material from the Lukan Sondergut that is not found in Marcion's gospel the infancy narratives, together with the preface, form by far the largest and probably most significant block of material. We shall consider the preface below. Here we shall focus attention on the infancy narratives.

The Lukan infancy narratives (Luke 1:5–2:52) consist of 128 verses and 1,991 words, all unique to canonical Luke. This material is well over half of the Lukan Sondergut material that is lacking in Marcion's gospel.[51] Since we are on solid ground in respect to the absence of these materials from Marcion's gospel and in view of their size in proportion to other omitted Lukan Sondergut material, an exploration of these narratives will serve as a test case for determining the relation between canonical Luke and Marcion's gospel.[52] Commenting on these narratives, Knox wrote: "Marcion would surely not have tolerated this highly 'Jewish' section; but how wonderfully adapted it is to show the nature of Christianity as the true Judaism and thus to answer one of the major contentions of the Marcionites! And one cannot overlook the difficulty involved in the common supposition that Marcion deliberately selected a Gospel which began in so false and obnoxious a way."[53]

Quite apart from Marcionite issues there are good reasons to think that the infancy narratives were late additions to an earlier version of Luke's gospel.[54] Raymond E. Brown came to this conclusion in his magisterial study of the birth narratives. He wrote: "Although there have been occasional attempts to join the infancy story to the next two chapters, so that a continuous narrative-unit of the Gospel would extend from 1:5 to 4:15, the solemn beginning of the ministry in 3:1–2 could well have served as the original opening of the Lucan Gospel."[55] Joseph A. Fitzmyer agreed. Although he maintained that the Lukan infancy narrative is an integral part of the gospel, he contended that Luke 3:1 was its original beginning and that Luke 1–2 was a late addition. "Recognizing this feature of the beginning of chap. 3 makes it imperative to acknowledge the independent character of the infancy narrative and its telltale quality of a later addition."[56]

Brown and Fitzmyer are not alone in observing that Luke 3:1–2 forms a strikingly suitable beginning to the Lukan narrative. "In the fifteenth year of the reign of

Emperor Tiberius, when Pontius Pilate was governor of Judea, and Herod was ruler of Galilee, and his brother Philip ruler of the region of Ituraea and Trachonitis, and Lysanias ruler of Abilene, during the high priesthood of Annas and Caiaphas, the word of God came to John son of Zechariah in the wilderness" (Luke 3:1–2). Here we have a chronological statement that contrasts with the much less precise setting in Luke 1:5, which refers only to the days of Herod, king of Judea. The two statements also contrast in terms of the geographical settings involved. In Luke 1:5 only Judea is mentioned, in contrast to the inclusion in 3:1 of Galilee, Ituraea, Trachonitis, Abilene, and, by virtue of the reference to Tiberius, the entire Roman Empire. Roman officials, Herodians, and priests are brought together in a single statement. Clearly Luke 3:1–2 is intended to describe the setting of the narrative on a world stage without neglecting the more particular Jewish elements.

The case for regarding Luke 3:1 as the original beginning of Luke's gospel was perhaps most persuasively argued by the early proponents of the Proto-Luke hypothesis.[57] This theory, which depends directly on an assumption that the two-document hypothesis is the correct fundamental solution to the Synoptic Problem, states that in its earliest form the Gospel of Luke consisted of the non-Markan sections of canonical Luke, that is, those sections that are usually designated as coming from Q and L. Only at a later point did the author of the Third Gospel discover Mark, and when he did he supplemented his own earlier version with those sections of Mark that appeared to him to be useful. Thus in this theory the Gospel of Luke grew in at least two stages, a Proto-Luke and a second version that included material from Mark. Actually, however, there was a third stage. As Streeter understood it, the later author, who combined Proto-Luke with Mark, also added the preface and the infancy narratives in Luke 1–2.[58] Streeter claimed that Luke originally started with Luke 3:1. He also noted that the genealogy is appropriate in Luke 3:23–38 only if 3:1 is the beginning of the gospel.

Vincent Taylor developed many of these Streeterian contentions.[59] He classified Luke 1:5–2:52 as a non-Markan section that appears to stand apart from everything else in the gospel.[60] He noted that the carefully composed setting of time in Luke 3:1–2 is an appropriate beginning of a historical or biographical account and that John the Baptist is introduced here as if for the first time.[61]

Other scholars, who do not accept the Proto-Luke hypothesis, are nevertheless convinced that the Gospel of Luke at one time began at 3:1. Brown and others have observed that the requirements for apostleship set forth in Acts 1:22 appear to designate the beginning of the gospel as the baptism of Jesus. Thus a gospel that begins at Luke 3:1 is consistent with this view.[62] Further, if there are good reasons to claim that Mark was a source for Luke, it is not unreasonable to conclude that Luke began his gospel as did his predecessor. We must not, however, overlook the fact that yet another gospel began with something like Luke 3:1. Marcion's gospel apparently did not have the more elaborate coordination of political leaders that canonical Luke has, but it did begin with the reference to the "fifteenth year of Tiberius." For Marcion these words do not serve to introduce John the Baptist but rather to designate the first earthly appearance of Jesus, who "came down to Capernaum" (Luke 4:31).[63]

Without embracing the Proto-Luke hypothesis we may reasonably conclude that Luke 3:1 was the beginning of the pre-Marcionite version of Luke, as it is also the beginning of Marcion's gospel. Several additional considerations may be cited to support the conclusion that Luke 1:5–2:52 was a late addition to a text that started with the introduction of John the Baptist. Among these considerations are certain disjunctions of narrative and character and some differences in linguistic style and ideology that may be observed between Luke 1:5–2:52 and the body of Luke.

Disjunctions of narrative and character. The integrity of Luke's narrative has been accepted as a given among recent scholars of Luke-Acts. Robert Tannehill has produced what is perhaps the most important study that is based on this assumption.[64] In his two-volume study of Luke-Acts, Tannehill emphasized the unity of the narrative. He announced his intention at the beginning of the first volume: "The following study will emphasize the unity of Luke-Acts. This unity is the result of a single author working within a persistent theological perspective, but it is something more. It is a *narrative* unity, the unity appropriate to a well-formed narrative. Change and development are expected in such a narrative, yet unity is maintained because the scenes and characters contribute to a larger story that determines the significance of each part."[65] Tannehill consistently applied this principle throughout the two volumes, and the results are impressive. It is important to observe that Tannehill was working as a narrative critic. He did not deny that Luke-Acts was built on earlier sources or that it was written in stages, but for his purposes these factors are irrelevant. Tannehill's effort was to explore the meaning of the narrative as it stands, the "larger story" that reveals itself in the act of reading.[66]

The present writer has also attempted to work through particular aspects of Luke's story. In this effort I contended that it is necessary to explore canonical Luke and Acts as a unity, with a story that begins in Luke 1 and ends in Acts 28. I acknowledged that there were good reasons to think that Luke originally began at 3:1, but then I wrote: "But compelling reasons can be given for including the birth narratives in an attempt to interpret the Gospel of Luke in its present form and thus for regarding these narratives as integrally related to the rest of the gospel. Moreover, as an interpretative strategy for canonical Luke, the exclusion of the birth narratives is indefensible. Whatever the prehistory may have been, some conscious mind has put this book together in its canonical form, and the task of interpretation surely includes that of interpreting this finally achieved form."[67] I continue to embrace this position in regard to canonical Luke. There are good reasons for analyzing the narrative of canonical Luke as it now stands, and doing so requires an assumption of narrative unity.

But as I have continued to ponder Luke-Acts and ask about the context of its composition, I have reluctantly concluded that the assessment of narrative unity must be reconsidered. Although some editor/author brought the component parts of Luke-Acts together and consciously created a meaningful narrative, it is useful to examine the entire process of composition. Scholars universally acknowledge that, in both the gospel and Acts, this editor/author made use of existing material written by others. Further, as we have already seen, it is certain that the Gospel of Luke appeared in more than one edition, and since the first two editions probably began with what is now Luke 3:1, it would not be unreasonable to find some subtle but significant narrative disjunctions in canonical Luke between the first two chapters and the rest of the gospel.

Hans Conzelmann is probably the most prominent scholar to have questioned the relation between Luke 1–2 and the rest of the gospel.[68] In his pioneering redaction-critical study Conzelmann ignored Luke 1–2 and began with Luke 3:1. He so much took this procedure for granted that he felt no need to explain it until much later, actually on page 172 of the English translation. This explanation is brief enough to be quoted in full: "The introductory chapters of the Gospel present a special problem. It is strange that the characteristic features they contain do not occur again either in the Gospel or in Acts. In certain passages there is a direct contradiction, as for example in the analogy between the Baptist and Jesus, which is emphasized in the early chapters, but deliberately avoided in the rest of the Gospel. Special motifs in these chapters, apart from the typology of John, are the part played by Mary and the virgin conception, the Davidic descent and Bethlehem. On the other hand there is agreement in the fact that the idea of pre-existence is missing."[69] In a footnote Conzelmann adds that in the body of Luke-Acts Mary disappears even more than she does in Mark or Matthew and that nothing in the later chapters draws a connection to Jesus' birth.[70]

To be sure Conzelmann has been roundly condemned for ignoring Luke 1–2. The intention he expressed at the beginning of the book, to examine the theology of "the whole of Luke's writings as they stand," was obviously not fulfilled.[71] His reasons for omitting consideration of Luke 1–2 are rather cursorily expressed, and his mention of the disjunctions is challengeable. In his critique of Conzelmann Paul S. Minear pointed to a number of elements that connect the birth accounts with the rest of the gospel.[72] He included an impressive list of phrases "which appear both in the birth narratives and in the rest of Luke-Acts, and which are found more often in these two books than in the rest of the New Testament."[73] There are pervasive interests and themes as well, such as the use of the historiographical style, the use of speeches, citations and hymns, common ecclesiological conceptions, allusions to liturgical usage, reliance on epiphany and angels, the theme of promise and fulfillment, and other themes found both in the birth narratives and in the gospel and Acts as a whole. Minear concluded that "if Conzelmann had taken full account of the nativity stories, I believe his position would have been changed at several major points."[74]

Indeed there are themes that may be found in the birth and infancy narratives that reappear in other parts of the Lukan corpus. Elsewhere I have called attention to the theme of conflict.[75] There is a great deal of material in both Luke and Acts that is devoted to the description of situations of conflict between Jesus and Pharisees, Jesus and priests, the apostles and Jewish leaders, and between Paul and his various opponents. Although the birth narratives do not contain explicit descriptions of conflict situations and although their dominant tone is pacific, the narratives are not without anticipations of conflict. The Magnificat speaks of a reversal of social conditions, a reversal that implies conflict. Here, in Luke 1:52–54, the powerful and the rich are pitted against the lowly and the hungry. The expectation of aid for Israel has nuances of anticipated conflict in which social positions are to be changed. One could almost speak of expected political revolution in these verses:

> He has put down powerful people from thrones
> And lifted up lowly ones.
> The hungry he has filled with good things,
> And the rich he has sent away empty.
> He has come to the aid of Israel his child,
> To remember mercy.
> (Luke 1:52–54, my translation).

In the Benedictus Zechariah speaks of deliverance "from our enemies and from the hand of all who hate us" (Luke 1:71). And in Luke 2:34–35, Simeon describes Jesus as a controversial sign, "destined for the falling and the rising of many in Israel," and to the mother he says, "A sword will pierce your own soul too." Not only do these verses contain notes of social reversal and conflict, but they also connect with themes that work themselves out in the later parts of the gospel and Acts. Simeon's words, for example, anticipate the crucifixion of Jesus as well as the division among those who accept and those who reject him.[76]

Despite these connections with the body of Luke, there is still a disjunction between the birth narratives and the body of Luke. Although the birth narratives display themes that guide the reader's expectations, there is a profound sense that something new has begun in Luke 3:1. The abrupt change of time (from the time of Herod, Luke 1:5, to the time of Tiberius, 3:1) and the silent interval, encompassing some eighteen years (from Jesus at age twelve, Luke 2:42, to Jesus at age thirty, Luke 3:23), encourage the reader to reflect on the contrast between the tones in the birth narratives and in what follows. These include the contrasts between infancy and adulthood, between miraculous births and wilderness preaching, between prophetic blessings and demonic temptations, between good will and imprisonment. There is at this point a sense of a rudely abrupt change from a comfortable, idyllic, semimythical world to the cold cruel world of political and social reality.

Nor have the issues raised by Conzelmann been fully addressed. Although his *Theology of St. Luke* only noted these issues with little comment, they nevertheless have merit. It was important for Conzelmann's argument that he stress certain inconsistencies in the characterization of John the Baptist in Luke 1:5–2:52 and the rest of the gospel. He was guided by Luke 16:16, which, in his interpretation, located John in the age of Israel and separated him from the age of Jesus. Thus he called attention to the contrast between the closeness of Jesus and John that is described in Luke 1:5–2:52 and the distancing of the two characters in the rest of the gospel. The parallelism between Jesus and John that runs through the birth and infancy narratives is impressive.[77] Brown's excellent treatment of what he calls a "diptych" is a convincing analysis of these narratives, which shows both the similarities and the differences between John and Jesus.[78]

But in the body of Luke the relations between the two characters are different. Conzelmann rightly calls attention to several passages in the body of Luke where the distancing between John and Jesus is evident. The two occupy different geographical areas.[79] John actually completes his preaching mission before the baptism of Jesus, and he is imprisoned (Luke 3:20) before Jesus begins his ministry in Galilee (Luke 4:16). At this point the Lukan order of events is quite different from that in both Matthew and Mark, where John stays on the scene much longer. But Luke's narrative order places the imprisonment of John before Jesus' baptism, and by separating the two in this way he avoids the problem that Matthew has in explaining how Jesus could have been baptized by an inferior (Matt 3:13–17). Both Matthew and Mark say that Jesus was baptized in the Jordan *by John* (Matt 3:13; Mark 1:9), but Luke has, "Now when all the people were baptized, and when Jesus also had been baptized and was praying, the heaven was opened" (Luke 3:21). The agent of Jesus' baptism is not specified, and, indeed, the emphasis is placed by Luke on the descent of the Holy Spirit and the voice from heaven (Luke 3:22) rather than on the act of baptism.

Conzelmann has probably overstressed these differences by claiming that, while in the infancy narrative John is regarded as the returned Elijah, in the body of Luke this is not so. Clearly the Elijah link is present in the infancy narratives. It is explicit in Luke 1:17: "With the spirit and power of Elijah he will go before him, to turn the hearts of parents to their children, and the disobedient to the wisdom of the righteous, to make ready a people prepared for the Lord." John's function as the one to make the people ready is restated in Luke 1:76. It is true that in the body of the gospel Luke does not have the explicit statement of Matt 11:14, in which Jesus identifies the Baptist as Elijah, nor the allusion of Mark 9:13 (cf. Matt 17:12). Although he avoids these explicit statements about John, there are places in the body of the gospel where a link with the infancy narratives is evident. Luke 3:4 identifies John as the one shouting in the desert (cf. Luke 1:80) and fulfilling the prophecy to prepare the way (cf. Luke 1:17, 76). John's task of preparation is again indicated in Luke 7:27; his location in the desert is affirmed in Luke 7:24; his avoidance of wine is stated in Luke 7:33 (cf. Luke 1:15).

Conzelmann also calls attention to differences between Luke 1:5–2:52 and the body of Luke in the treatment of the parents of Jesus. Mary, who played such a leading role in the birth and infancy narratives, almost disappears in the rest of the gospel. One may say the same about other characters in the infancy narratives—Zechariah,

Elizabeth, Simeon, Anna. John the Baptist is the only character other than Jesus who has a major role after Luke 3:1. Of course these characters are like many others in Luke-Acts who appear only once—Simon the Pharisee (Luke 7:36–50); Zacchaeus (Luke 19:1–9); and numerous characters in Acts. But the disappearance of Jesus' parents is more significant. Joseph is referred to five times in the infancy narratives, three times by name. But after Luke 3:1 he is mentioned only twice (Luke 3:23; 4:22). The case with Jesus' mother is even more striking. She, to whom the angel Gabriel announced a miraculous birth and promised great things, and who, according to Simeon, would experience great pain, almost totally disappears from the rest of the narrative. Mary is mentioned by name eleven times and referred to five additional times in Luke 1:5–2:52. But in the rest of the gospel she appears only in one curious episode, Luke 8:19–21:[80] "Then his mother and his brothers came to him, but they could not reach him because of the crowd. And he was told, 'Your mother and your brothers are standing outside, wanting to see you.' But he said to them, 'My mother and my brothers are those who hear the word of God and do it.'"[81] The inclusion of "brothers" here is especially curious, since Luke had given the reader no information about Jesus' siblings up to this point, but it is probably owing to his use of Mark, which includes among the visitors Jesus' mother, brothers, and sisters (Mark 3:31–35). In view, however, of the near-sacred characterization of Mary in the Lukan infancy narratives, the episode in Luke 8 is strange indeed. For here it is implied that Jesus refused to see her and her other sons and rejected them in favor of those who made up his audience.

Two additional references in Luke contain similar attitudes about family. In Luke 12:53 Jesus speaks of creating division within families and in 14:26 says, "Whoever comes to me and does not hate father and mother, wife and children, brothers and sisters, yes, and even life itself, cannot be my disciple." To be sure Luke has Jesus quote from the commandment about honoring one's parents (Luke 18:20), but he does not have the condemnation of the practice of Corban, whereby children may abandon the support of parents, which we find in Mark 7:11–13 (cf. Matt 15:4–6). All in all it is necessary to say that the attitude toward family is exceedingly negative in the body of Luke and that it contrasts sharply with what is conveyed in the birth and infancy narratives. The contrast is striking between the reverential treatment of Jesus' parents in 1:5–2:52 and their rejection in the rest of the gospel. The contrast in the characterization of Mary (and Joseph) would support the hypothesis that the birth and infancy narratives of Luke 1:5–2:52 were added to a primitive version of Luke that did not contain these incidents.

In this connection we should also note that, except for the parenthetical comment, ὡς ἐνομίζετο, in Luke 3:23, Jesus' genealogy does not cohere with the narrative of Luke 1:5–2:52. Although the infancy narrative maintains that Jesus is to be a descendant of David (Luke 1:32) and that Joseph is "of the house of David" (Luke 1:27), the annunciation scene (Luke 1:26–38) involves a birth without participation from Joseph.[82] The organization of the narratives requires Jesus' conception and birth

The Composition of Canonical Luke 97

to be more miraculous than that of the Baptist, who was born from aged parents and a hitherto barren mother. The angel Gabriel alludes to this necessity in Luke 1:36–37, which calls attention to the advanced age of Elizabeth and ends with, "For nothing will be impossible with God" (Luke 1:37). As Brown says, since Jesus is clearly portrayed in Luke 1:5–2:52 as superior to John, his birth must be more spectacular, and the virgin birth satisfies this condition.[83] The genealogy in Luke 3:23–38, however, requires that Joseph be the father of Jesus; it works only if Jesus' ancestry is traced through him.

It should be clear that the disjunction of narrative and characterization is not total. There is much that ties Luke 1:5–2:52 to the rest of the gospel. But the disjunctions noted here—contrast of narrative tone, different treatment of prominent characters—together with the indications that Luke 3:1 was originally the beginning of the gospel, are sufficient to raise questions about the status of the first two chapters. In my judgment Fitzmyer adequately explained the linkages between the infancy narratives and the rest of the gospel by noting that the author of the later material had access to the earlier. He wrote: "Again, it should be noted that in both Matthew and Luke the infancy narratives function as a sort of overture to the Gospels proper, striking the chords that will be heard again and again in the coming narratives. This is, indeed, more evident in the Lucan Gospel than in the Matthean, since . . . the Lucan infancy narrative was composed with the hindsight not only of the gospel tradition prior to Luke but also of the Lucan Gospel proper."[84]

Differences of linguistic style and ideology. Certain notable differences in linguistic style and ideology add to the likelihood that Luke 1:5–2:52 did not belong to the pre-Marcionite edition of the gospel. In the infancy narratives of canonical Luke we find a multitude of quotations from and allusions to a wide range of texts from the Hebrew Scriptures in Greek translation. Furthermore, the narrative style here appears to be an intentional imitation of Septuagintal language.[85] The Septuagintal style has influenced the writing throughout Luke and Acts, but it is most prominent in the first two chapters. Cadbury wrote: "The style and even the subject matter [of Luke 1:5–2:52] are evidently affected by the Old Testament in the narrative, while the Canticles are reminiscent in grammar and poetic structure, as well as in phraseology, of the older psalmody."[86] Fitzmyer agrees that the influence of the LXX may be seen throughout but is strongest in Luke 1:5–2:52. Commenting on the "heavy Semitic flavor to the Greek of the infancy narrative," Fitzmyer says: "This characteristic of the first two chapters likewise stands in contrast to that of the rest of the Gospel and Acts, although there is some Semitizing Greek in Acts too."[87] It is worthwhile to note that the Septuagintal language and tone of Luke 1:5–2:52 would be subtle but effective antidotes to Marcionite claims about the separation of Jesus from Hebrew prophecy and would serve to provide links between the reader and the Hebrew Scriptures. As I wrote in my *Images of Judaism in Luke-Acts,* "In these chapters the implied author transports the implied reader back into the world of the ancient Hebrew writers and prophets. The characters in this part of the narrative are portrayed against this background, and their lives are governed by the values of the Hebrew Scriptures. Their piety is pictured in nearly idyllic terms."[88]

Some ideological differences have already been noted, especially in terms of attitudes toward family. Another ideological feature of the infancy narratives that contrasts with the body of Luke (and Acts) is the treatment of Jews and Judaism. Images of Jews in these chapters are strikingly positive, in contrast with those in the rest of Luke as well as in Acts. In my *Images of Judaism,* I was interested in exploring the narrative unity of the Lukan writing. I nevertheless was compelled to acknowledge that the portrayals in the infancy narratives were not consonant with those in the rest of Luke-Acts:

> The infancy narratives in Luke 1–2 present us with images of Jewish piety unlike any other descriptions in early Christian literature. Indeed, although, as we have seen, these chapters contain themes that connect with the rest of Luke-Acts, the portrait of Jewish religious life to be found here contrasts markedly with material to be encountered later. . . . Here we have a description of Jewish piety as the author sees it working apart from the Christian message. We learn of the importance of the Jewish Temple, about its ritual and priesthood, and the significance of sacrifices. Here are angelic messengers, miraculous births, and predictions of future greatness. Here are righteous people living lives of quiet devotion and hopeful expectation.[89]

The birth narratives function to connect Jesus and the Baptist with the Hebrew prophets and ongoing Jewish piety and expectation. For the most part the narratives are colored by hope and optimism. The only departure from such positive sentiments is to be found in the prophecy of Simeon in Luke 2:34b–35.

Considerations about narrative and character disjunctions, linguistic style, and ideology confirm the view that Luke 3:1 was once the beginning of the gospel we know as Luke and that the birth narratives of Luke 1:5–2:52 were added at a later date. I conclude that this large block of material is post-Marcionite, added by the canonical author, who may have had a number of intentions in mind, among them an intention to support the church in its battle against Marcionite Christianity.[90]

The infancy narratives and Marcion. As we saw earlier, Knox called attention to the appropriateness of the birth narratives as a reaction against Marcion. A number of elements in these narratives highlight this appropriateness. Above all, the narratives maintain that Jesus was born of a woman; he did not suddenly descend from heaven to Capernaum. As we know, Marcion thought that the process of human birth would be degrading for Jesus, and it would bring him into too close contact with human beings.[91] For the author of canonical Luke, although Jesus was born without the agency of Joseph and is called "son of the most high" (Luke 1:32) and "son of God" (1:35), his is nevertheless a human birth. The language that the angel Gabriel uses in addressing Mary in Luke 1:31 seems to have been selected specifically to offend the Marcionites—Mary is to conceive in her womb and produce a son (καὶ ἰδοὺ συλλήμψῃ ἐν γαστρὶ καὶ τέξῃ υἱὸν καὶ καλέσεις τὸ ὄνομα αὐτοῦ Ἰησοῦν; Luke 1:31; see also 2:21). Anatomical references are also stressed in the meeting between Elizabeth and Mary (Luke 1:39–45), when the child of Elizabeth leaps in her womb (Luke 1:41, 44).[92] Throughout the infancy narratives Jesus is referred to as a baby (Βρέφος, Luke 2:12, 16) or a child (παιδίον, Luke 2:17, 27, 40; παῖς, Luke 2:43; τέκνον, Luke 2:48). Two of the same terms are used of John the Baptist (Βρέφος, Luke 1:41, 44; παιδίον, Luke 1:59, 66, 76, 80). The language throughout Luke 1:5–2:52 emphasizes the humanity of Jesus, his proximity to his family, and his similarities with John.

We have already noted the close relationship between Jesus and John the Baptist that is maintained in Luke 1:5–2:52. The parallelism between the two makes use of a literary technique that we saw in Acts, where the author draws parallels between Peter and Paul.[93] The author of these narratives leaves no doubt about the superiority of Jesus to John, but no reader could miss the strong parallels between them. Angelic announcements predict the conception and birth of both (Luke 1:5–23; 1:26–38); there are narratives about the birth, naming, and circumcision of both (Luke 1:57–66; 2:1–27, 34–39); similar summary statements conclude the narratives of both (1:80; 2:40, 52).

The Lukan infancy narratives also stress the relationship of Jesus to Israel, the prophetic anticipation of his coming, and the fulfillment of Jewish expectation. Jesus' relationship to the Jewish people is made clear in the references to Joseph and Jesus as of the house of David (Luke 1:27; 1:69; 2:4) and to David as Jesus' father (Luke 1:32). Jesus is even born in the "city of David" (Luke 2:11). The fidelity of the family to Jewish practices is shown in Luke 2:22–24, the stories of the presentation of Jesus and of Mary's purification. Here Luke probably misunderstood passages in the Hebrew Scriptures, as well as Jewish practices, since he conflated two different religious duties and failed to mention the practice of redeeming the first-born son.[94] But the point to stress is that Luke's narrative portrays Jesus' family as pious Jews, who faithfully observe Torah (Luke 2:22), support the Jerusalem temple (Luke 2:22–38, 41–52), engage in sacrificial practices (Luke 2:24), and observe Jewish festivals (Luke 2:41). The author also implies that Jesus himself incorporated these practices, noting that as a child he was obedient to his parents (Luke 2:51). But Jesus' Jewishness is nowhere more emphatically signified than in the story of his circumcision (Luke 2:21).[95] Although there are a number of similarities between Luke's infancy accounts and Matthew's, only in Luke is Jesus circumcised.[96] Jacob Jervell is quite right to insist that "Luke 2:21 is scarcely a happenstance; it is not a 'subordinate clause.' Together with others, this passage indicates that the legitimacy and right of Jesus to speak and act in the name of the God of Israel for salvation on behalf of the people and the nations is beyond doubt."[97] For our purposes it is important to observe that the vital link with Judaism signified by Jesus' circumcision would have been highly offensive to Marcion and his followers.

The pervasive influence of the Hebrew Scriptures is notable in Luke 1:5–2:52. Allusions to a number of books may be found throughout the narratives, but the author makes prominent use of Daniel and Malachi. Clearly, in the announcement of the birth of John in Luke 1:17, the author is thinking of Mal 3:1: "See, I am sending my messenger to prepare the way before me, and the Lord whom you seek will suddenly come to his temple." The verse in Malachi may also govern the appearances of Jesus in the temple in Luke 2:22, 46. No fewer than eight characters from the Hebrew Bible are mentioned in the Lukan infancy narratives—Aaron (Luke 1:5); Abijah (1:5); Abraham (1:55, 73); Asher (2:36); David (1:27, 32, 69; 2:4, 11); Elijah (1:17); Jacob (1:33); and Moses (2:22). Also notable is the reference to the "holy prophets" in Luke 1:70, in a context that expresses the expectation of their fulfillment in Jesus. Not only are there specific quotations and allusions to biblical texts in these narratives, but certain biblical stories have provided models for our author as well. For example, 1 Sam 1:24–28, the presentation of the child Samuel, is probably the model for the story of the presentation of Jesus in the temple (Luke 2:22–38).[98]

These considerations make it highly probable, in my judgment, that the Lukan birth narratives were added in reaction to the challenges of Marcionite Christianity. It would be very difficult to explain why Marcion would choose a gospel with these, to him, highly offensive chapters at the beginning only to eliminate them. Further, it would be difficult to imagine a more directly anti-Marcionite narrative than what we have in Luke 1:5–2:52. As an addition to an existing gospel which began at Luke 3:1, the infancy narratives form what movie buffs would today call a prequel, a narrative that extends the story back in time. This one goes back thirty years (as judged from Luke 3:23), and it takes the reader back into the administrations of Herod the Great (Luke 1:5) and Caesar Augustus (Luke 2:1), as if to deny the Marcionite claim that Jesus' first appearance was in the time of Tiberius (Luke 3:1). The narrative stresses Jesus' birth, his connection with human beings, and his Jewishness. It cites the Hebrew prophets and other Scriptures and their connection with Jesus in ways directly counter to Marcionite interpretations. The author of Luke 1:5–2:52 wants his readers to know that Marcion is wrong in denying the human birth of Jesus, his Jewish connections, his fulfillment of Jewish expectations, and the role of the prophets in predicting his coming. In a relatively short span our author has succeeded in challenging and rejecting major Marcionite claims.

The Postresurrection Accounts—Luke 24

The strongest evidence that an anti-Marcionite author has added material to an earlier gospel is to be found in the Lukan infancy narratives. But this evidence creates a presumption that traces of this author's work may be found elsewhere, especially in Sondergut material. One such place is the closing chapter of canonical Luke.

Although one might presume that, if an author intended to add material to an earlier document, he would find it easiest to add that material at the beginning and at the end, there is no trace of a break before Luke 24 as there is at Luke 3:1. Furthermore, although Luke 24 is composed almost entirely of material unique to the Third

Gospel, there is evidence that Marcion's gospel had some material that resembled it. We discussed this part of Marcion's gospel in chapter 2, in which we faced some of the difficulties with the task of reconstructing his gospel.[99] Many questions remain about the exact contents of Marcion's resurrection account, but there are some things to be said about it with a relatively high degree of confidence. Our analysis of this material, which drew on Harnack's reconstruction, showed that the following details of the narrative in canonical Luke were missing in Marcion's gospel:

Luke 24:2: The stone rolled away from the tomb.
Luke 24:10: The names of the women at the tomb.
Luke 24:12: Peter's visit to the tomb.
Luke 24:25–27: References to the Scriptures, prophets, and Moses.
Luke 24:34: Report of Peter's visit to the tomb.
Luke 24:42–43: The story of Jesus eating fish (?). [Harnack's reconstruction
   has only: "fish . . . he ate."].[100]
Luke 24:44–46: References to the Scriptures and prophets.
Luke 24:49: Jesus' command to remain in the city.
Luke 24:50–53: Jesus' ascension.

A variation of Jesus' saying in Luke 24:39 is included in Marcion's gospel, despite Marcion's rejection of a physical resurrection. The resurrected Jesus affirms that he has bones, in a statement that perplexed Tertullian.[101] Some of the omissions listed above may be explained as deletions that Marcion made to avoid conflicts with his own theology; others may be understood as additions made by our canonical author for the purpose of denying Marcionite theology. The analysis of Luke 24 that follows will explore the likelihood that an anti-Marcionite author, perhaps drawing on earlier oral or written material, composed the greater part of the chapter.

Although there is no evidence of an original break before Luke 24:1, there is an apparent change in literary procedure that should not be overlooked. If we accept the usual hypothesis of synoptic relations and observe the ways in which the author of the body of Luke (that is, Luke 3–23) followed his sources, we should note the following. For the most part our author followed his sources faithfully, inserting L material from time to time but returning to the other source or sources after doing so. In the material he used from Mark his tendency to agree with Mark's wording varied from pericope to pericope, but for the most part he made good use of his source. It is true that, in the scenes of Jesus' trial, there are departures that suggest to some scholars that Luke preferred some other source to Mark. But even here Mark's influence is not absent. When we come to the closing chapter of canonical Luke, traces of Mark, which appear in 24:1–11, totally disappear in the last 42 verses. Almost all of the material in Luke 24 is Sondergut material, constituting the most extensive stretch of such material outside of Luke 1–2.[102] This apparent change in the use of sources suggests that something worthy of our attention is going on in this chapter.[103] It is important to examine it with respect to its distinctive viewpoints.

Only Luke 24:1–11 has traces of synoptic parallels, but here our author has actually used the Markan source to weave his own narrative. Luke's story in these verses is certainly reminiscent of Mark 16:1–8 but with significant differences. The canonical author of Luke prepares for the visit of the women to the tomb in Luke 23:55–56, in which he identifies women who had come with Jesus from Galilee and notes their purchase of spices and their observance of the Sabbath. Thus the reader knows that those who went to the tomb at dawn on Sunday were those women followers from Galilee, although they are not named until Luke 24:10. Luke's story also agrees with Mark's in saying that the stone sealing the tomb had been rolled away before the women arrived. There is further agreement in part of the message given to the women: "He is not here, but has been raised" (Luke 24:6). The names of the women who came to the tomb are probably drawn from Mark's version, but they are not identical with it. Mark 16:1 refers to three women by name: Mary Magdalene, Mary of James, and Salome. Luke 24:10 has the first two, but instead of Salome we have Joanna, who may be the same as the wife of Herod's steward, named in Luke 8:3.[104] In addition Luke refers to an indefinite number of unnamed women who also visited the tomb.

Although Luke 24:1–11 probably makes use of Mark, verbal resemblances are few, and the narrative departs from Mark's at a number of points. While Mark 16:5 makes no reference to Jesus' body, Luke 24:3 states explicitly that the women did not find the body of "the Lord Jesus."[105] The expression, which brings together the name Ἰησοῦς with the title κύριος, appears nowhere else in canonical Luke, although Jesus is frequently addressed as Lord in this gospel. But in Acts the expression "the Lord Jesus" appears with great frequency (see Acts 1:21; 4:33; 8:16; 9:17 (?); 11:20; 15:11; 16:31; 19:5, 13, 17; 20:21, 24, 35; 21:13), three times in the form, "the Lord Jesus Christ" (Acts 11:17; 15:26; 28:31).[106] Other details create a narrative that is very different from Mark's. The women who went to the tomb met two men (Luke 24:3) instead of a "young man" (Mark 16:5). Luke's women were confused and frightened and bowed to the ground (Luke 24:5). The two men at the tomb asked the women, "Why do you seek the living among the dead?" (Luke 24:5).

Probably the most significant divergences from the Markan narrative are to be seen in the message of the two men and in the response of the women to it. In Mark 16:7 the women are told to report to the disciples and Peter and tell them that Jesus will meet them in Galilee. In Luke, however, there is no mention of a postresurrection appearance in Galilee, and instead, the two men tell the women to remember what Jesus had said while they were in Galilee (Luke 24:6–7), an allusion to the passion predictions of Jesus in Luke 9:22, 44; 18:31–34.[107] The change in the reference to Galilee seems to have been dictated by the canonical author's intent to highlight Jerusalem as the center of Christian activity. While Mark alludes to a postresurrection appearance in Galilee and Matthew narrates it, Luke moves all such appearances to Jerusalem and its environs. Conzelmann rightly noted that Luke made this move deliberately,[108] and Fitzmyer stressed Luke's intention: "Having come from Galilee to Jerusalem, Jesus does not return there in the Lucan story, for the geographical perspective takes over. Jerusalem will become the focal point for the rest of the chapter and then function in an important way at the beginning of Acts (especially in its programmatic verse, 1:8). Luke undoubtedly knew of the appearances of Christ in other areas; but he has chosen to eliminate them in the interest of his overarching literary perspective."[109] The "overarching literary perspective" is one that ties Luke 24 to Acts. The final author / editor of Luke can have no resurrection appearances in Galilee, because for him Jerusalem is central to the Christian movement as a whole. Thus the apostles are told to remain in Jerusalem until they receive power (Luke 24:49), and so they return to Jerusalem and its temple at the end of the gospel (Luke 24:52–53). The reader is reminded of Jesus' order in Acts 1:4, and, as Fitzmyer and many others have observed, Acts 1:8 specifies that the beginning of apostolic activity is to be in Jerusalem. The "overarching literary perspective" also ties the narrative of Luke 24 to the infancy accounts in Luke 1:5–2:52. The Jerusalem setting forms an inclusion for the canonical gospel, which now begins and ends in Jerusalem, specifically in the temple.

Another major difference between Luke 24:1–11 and its probable Markan source is to be seen in the response of the women to the message they heard at Jesus' tomb. In Mark 16:7 they are told to report to the disciples and Peter but they do not do so (Mark 16:8). In Luke there is no similar command, but we are told that the women remembered what Jesus had said in Galilee and reported their experience at the tomb to the eleven and the others (Luke 24:9). Again in Luke 24:10–11 we read that the women, now named, spoke to the apostles but that the apostles did not believe—"but these words seemed to them an idle tale, and they did not believe them" (Luke 24:11). Luke 24:1–11, although based on Mark, is, therefore, a thorough rewriting of his source by the canonical author.

In the rest of Luke 24, which is extensive, we have Sondergut material. The only suggestion of a parallel is to be found in the so-called longer ending of Mark, at 16:12–13, a brief note that is similar to what was probably in Marcion's gospel and that may reflect knowledge of the Emmaus story. The remainder of the canonical Gospel of Luke appears to be quite independent of the synoptic tradition. It includes an account of a visit of Peter to the tomb (Luke 24:12), a postresurrection appearance on the way to Emmaus (Luke 24:13–35), an appearance to the apostles in Jerusalem (Luke 24:36–43), and Jesus' final words and ascension (Luke 24:44–53).

The account of Peter's visit to the tomb (Luke 24:12) is one of the most difficult verses in canonical Luke. Westcott and Hort, noting the absence of this verse in Codex Bezae, declared it to be one of nine "Western Non-Interpolations."[110] It is, however, included in p[75], a text dated at the end of the second or beginning of the third century, and most textual critics now accept it. Despite this early attestation, some recent critics have re-opened the issue that was introduced by Westcott and Hort. Mikeal Parsons examined all of the so-called western non-interpolations in Luke 24 and argued for their originality.[111] Parsons maintained that Luke 24:12, as well as the other non-interpolations in Luke's postresurrection account, was added by the scribe of p[75] in order to support an elevated Christology. In this way Parsons accounts for all the non-interpolations, and about Luke 24:12 he says it was added "to provide apostolic confirmation of the empty tomb."[112] Similarly, Bart Ehrman, pointing out the non-Lukan elements in the verse, maintains that Luke 24:12 was added "by an orthodox scribe as a hermeneutical lens through which the stories of Jesus' post-resurrection appearances in the rest of Luke's account could be read."[113] Michael Wade Martin argues that all the non-interpolations in Luke 24 were added by a single proto-orthodox scribe.[114] He points out that Luke 24:12, as well as 24:36b and 40, bear similarities to John 20, and he stresses the improbability that a text written by Luke would have been borrowed by John and then omitted by a Western scribe.[115] He thinks it far more probable that these verses were Alexandrian additions.

The last word about Western non-interpolations has almost certainly not been written, but in view of the work of Parsons, Ehrman, and Martin, it seems unwise to place much confidence in the authenticity of Luke 24:12 and the other "non-interpolations." Furthermore, from a literary, as distinguished from a textual, perspective, Luke 24:12 seems out of place in the narrative as we have it. It fits uncomfortably between Luke 24:11, the women reporting to the unbelieving apostles, and the introduction to the story of Emmaus (Luke 24:13). In Luke 24:12 Peter neither receives a message such as the one delivered to the women, nor is there an appearance to him. He sees the clothing, about which nothing had previously been said, and he leaves in confusion, even though presumably he was among those who had heard the report of the women. Nothing follows from the incident, and Luke later reports, through one of the Emmaus travelers (Luke 24:24), that some apostles—note the plural—visited the tomb and found it as the women had reported, but nothing more is said about Peter specifically until we get to Luke 24:34. Luke 24:22–24 is a brief summary of 24:1–11, which omits many details but makes it clear that it was women who went to the tomb early that day and that they did not find Jesus' body but saw a "vision of angels" (ὀπτασίαν ἀγγέλων). Verse 24 adds, "Some of those who were with us went to the tomb and found it just as the women had said; but they did not see him." This does not appear to be a reference to Luke 24:12, for there only Peter goes to the tomb, and his experience is not one about which it would be appropriate to write that he "found it just as the women had said." Neither can Luke 24:34 ("the Lord has risen indeed, and he has appeared to Simon!") be a reflection of Luke 24:12, in which no appearance occurred.[116] Despite its inclusion in p[75] it is difficult to avoid the conclusion that Luke 24:12 is a later interpolation into the text of Luke. It would appear to be a rather clumsy attempt to provide apostolic authentication of the empty tomb.[117]

It is important to take note of the major emphases in the Emmaus narrative (Luke 24:13–35), a section that is unique to canonical Luke. At one level this is a postresurrection narrative but a rather detailed one. In it the risen Jesus appears to two followers, one of whom is named Cleopas. But they do not recognize him until he breaks and blesses bread in a shared meal. The identification of the travelers is indefinite. In Luke 24:13 it is simply "two of them," apparently referring to persons in addition to the apostles in 24:9 to whom the women reported. In Luke 24:33 they are distinguished from the "eleven," to whom they report. The Emmaus story does not, therefore, involve an appearance to apostles, and the naming of the nonapostolic Cleopas confirms this. When we observe this we learn why Luke 24:34 is so important: it constitutes an allusion to the first postresurrection apostolic appearance. At this point our author has apparently been influenced by 1 Cor 15:5, in which Paul insists that the first postresurrection appearance of Jesus was to Cephas. Apparently no description of such an appearance was available, but the canonical author must have felt compelled to include an allusion to it and to make it chronologically prior to all other appearances.[118]

On another level, the Emmaus narrative seems intended to explicate some important theological teachings. In his important study of Luke 24 Paul Schubert showed that the various appearances in the chapter were used by Luke as settings for the elucidation of his major theological claim, which Schubert called proof-from-prophecy.[119] It is what the risen Jesus says on these occasions that must be stressed. In the Emmaus story Jesus' sayings revolve around his fulfillment of prophetic Scripture. When he first falls in with the two travelers and asks them about their conversation, they tell him that they had hoped that Jesus would be the one to redeem Israel (Luke 24:21). The response of Jesus is addressed to this concern, and he shows them from the Scriptures that, despite their doubts, he is the fulfillment of Jewish messianic expectation. He rebukes them for being slow to believe the prophets and the correspondence of the prophetic words with the events that have just transpired (Luke 24:24). The crucifixion of Jesus is said to have been necessary in order to fulfill Scripture (Luke 24:26). Then Jesus explains all the prophets, beginning with Moses, making it clear that these Scriptures pertained to his own life and death (Luke 24:27). Later, reflecting on their experience, the travelers "said to each other, 'Were not our hearts burning within us while he was talking to us on the road, while he was opening the scriptures to us?'" (Luke 24:32).

Commenting on Luke 24:26, Fitzmyer notes, "This is the first occurrence of the specifically Lucan christologoumenon that the Messiah must suffer."[120] He lists the subsequent occurrences of the theme in Luke 24:46; Acts 3:18; 17:3; 26:23 but stresses its absence from Old Testament or contemporary Jewish thought. One is reminded of the comment by the editors of *The Beginnings of Christianity* on Acts 3:18: "None of the prophets, rather than all of them, made this prophecy, if we confine ourselves to (a) Messianic prophecies, (b) the original meaning of these prophecies, or (c) Jewish interpretation of these prophecies. But Christian interpretation applied to Jesus all passages in the Psalms and Isaiah which refer to suffering."[121] In this connection it is important to note that Luke nowhere cites a scriptural reference to back up the contention about messianic suffering.

After the return of Cleopas and the other follower, there is an appearance of Jesus to the apostles and others in Jerusalem (Luke 24:36–43). In this pericope the major concern seems to be to certify Jesus' physical resurrection. Luke notes that the apostles and the others thought they were seeing a πνεῦμα, and that Jesus attempted to correct this impression, first by showing his body and then by eating in their presence. In Luke 24:39 he invites the apostles to touch and examine his hands and feet and to verify that he has flesh and bones (σάρκα καὶ ὀστέα).[122] As if to drive home the point that this is a physical resurrection, Jesus then asks for something to eat, and he takes and eats a piece of broiled fish (Luke 24:41–43).[123]

This Jerusalem appearance is followed by the final instructions of Jesus to the apostles and then by the ascension (Luke 24:44–53). The instructions are replete with themes that dominated the Emmaus narrative: Jesus' life and death are fulfillments of Scripture; Jesus is the suffering Messiah predicted in the Scriptures; through Jesus the apostles are led to understand the Scriptures. In Luke 24:44 Jesus announces that "everything written about me in the law of Moses, the prophets, and the psalms must be fulfilled." This particular combination of Hebrew Scriptures is unique. The phrase "Moses and the prophets" was used in the Emmaus narrative (Luke 24:27) and earlier in the parable of the rich and the poor men (Luke 16:29, 31). It occurs again in Acts 26:22 and 28:23 but nowhere else in the New Testament, except for a variation of the phrase in John 1:45. But the combination—Moses, Prophets, Psalms—occurs only in Luke 24:44. In fact, references to the Psalms as a book of the Hebrew Bible are confined to the Lukan corpus (Luke 20:42; Acts 1:20; 13:33). Evidently the combination—Moses, Prophets, Psalms—is meant to refer to the entirety of those writings that were regarded as biblical, and the phrase may suggest an awareness of canon, a not-inappropriate concept if Luke 24 comes from the first quarter of the second century.

In addition these final verses of Luke's gospel stress the centrality of Jerusalem. Jesus asserts that the Scriptures require that repentance be proclaimed in his name, beginning in Jerusalem (Luke 24:47). He appoints the apostles as witnesses and orders them to remain in Jerusalem until they have "been clothed with power from on high" (Luke 24:49). After his departure from them at Bethany, the apostles return to Jerusalem and to the temple (Luke 24:52–53). Thus the gospel ends where it began, in the temple of Jerusalem.

Several things seem to be going on in Luke 24. For one thing, in this chapter the author not only brings the gospel to a conclusion but prepares the way for Acts as well. Schubert observed that the sources for this chapter consist only of "a miscellany of data," but that in Luke 24 "not only a noticeable degree of literary coherence and effectiveness is achieved but also a substantial massive program is set forth which is no less than a summary of volume I and the skeleton of volume II."[124] Anticipations of Acts may be observed in the several references to those who were with the eleven (Luke 24:9, 24, 33). These small notes prepare the reader to understand the selection of Matthias to replace Judas among the apostles. The replacement must be "one of the men who have accompanied us during all the time that the Lord Jesus went in and out among us, beginning from the baptism of John until the day when he was taken up from us—one of these must become a witness with us to his resurrection" (Acts 1:21–22). Several things are notable when we compare these words with the material in Luke 24. First, the references in Luke 24:9, 33 to the "eleven" suggest to the reader that the apostolic group is at this point incomplete, and Acts 1:26 makes the point explicitly. Second, references to those with the eleven (Luke 24:9, 24, 33), even without attaching names to these persons, let us know that there was a pool of possible replacements for Judas. Third, the requirements establish that the person chosen must have been with the eleven "until the day when he was taken up from us," likely a reference to either Luke 24:51 or Acts 1:9–11.[125] Fourth, Acts says that this person must be a "witness with us to his resurrection," words that recall Jesus' appointment of witnesses in Luke 24:48. Thus one of the functions of Luke 24 is to prepare the apostles and their companions for the work they will do in Acts. By the end of this chapter their minds are opened to understand the Scriptures, they are witnesses to the resurrection, and they have received their appointments.

Luke 24 also functions to prepare for Acts by stressing the centrality of Jerusalem. Jesus' command for his followers to remain in Jerusalem (Luke 24:49) is repeated in Acts 1:4, and the narrative in the first several chapters of Acts underlines the apostolic adherence to this command. They initially gather in Jerusalem and remain close to the temple. The spiritual endowment for which they are to wait apparently occurs in Acts 2:1–2, when they begin to speak in other tongues. It would seem that they would have been free to leave Jerusalem after this incident, but Acts 8:1 makes a point of saying that the apostles remained in the city for some time afterward. They remain there even after a persecution brings about a scattering of other believers, and they are still headquartered there as late as Acts 15.

Luke 24:51 makes a connection with the ascension of Jesus narrated in Acts 1:9–11, but it also creates a problem that has long perplexed students of Luke-Acts. If both volumes were written by the same author, why did he include two reports of the ascension of Jesus, reports that conflict with one another in terms of temporal and geographic settings? In terms of time the ascension in the gospel is apparently to be understood as occurring on the same day as the discovery of the empty tomb, but the one in Acts is set forty days later (see Acts 1:3).[126] Further, the ascension in the gospel is set at or near Bethany, and the one in Acts is at the Mount of Olives. Several solutions have been proposed. One solution claims that Luke 24:51 describes a disappearance of Jesus but not an ascension. This view relies on the omission of the words "καὶ ἀνεφέρετο εἰς τὸν οὐρανόν" from the end of Luke 24:51.[127] The verse then would be translated "While he was blessing them, he withdrew from them." This is the reading of Western and other texts of Luke, and the phrase "καὶ ἀνεφέρετο εἰς τὸν οὐρανόν" is one of Westcott and Hort's Western non-interpolations. Bruce Metzger, however, points out that Acts 1:2 appears to make an explicit reference to Luke 24 and includes mention of Jesus as being taken up.[128] Alfred Plummer maintained that Luke 24:51 refers to an ascension, "whatever view we take of the disputed words which follow."[129] On the setting in time, Plummer wrote: "It is not improbable that, at the time when he wrote his Gospel, Lk. did not know the exact amount of interval between the Resurrection and the Ascension. That was a piece of information which he may easily have gained between the publication of the Gospel and of the Acts. . . . Being without knowledge, or not considering the matter of importance, he says nothing about the interval."[130]

Other solutions have been proposed, but none is completely satisfactory. It may seem best to regard the non-interpolations in Luke 24:51–52 as doubtful and to account for them as efforts to enhance and elevate Lukan Christology, as Parsons has suggested.[131] Otherwise we have little recourse but to agree with Fitzmyer, who says, "Why Luke has dated the ascension of Jesus in these two different ways no one will ever know."[132]

Not only does Luke 24 create links with the book of Acts; it also puts great stress on themes that connect not only with Acts but also with Luke 1:5–2:52. Schubert is quite right to say that, for the author of Luke 24, the importance of Jesus' resurrection lay not in the empty tomb or even the appearances, but rather in the message that he imparts to his followers. In Schubert's view the discovery of the empty tomb and the appearances are, for Luke, appropriate "settings for his proof-from-prophecy theology."[133] Certainly, "proof-from-prophecy" is an important aspect of Luke 24, as we may see in the various statements of Jesus. The themes of fulfillment of the prophets and of Jewish messianic expectation link these verses with Luke 1:5–2:52 and Acts, in which, as we have seen, the same themes are stressed. Although references to Moses, the prophets, and the Scriptures are not absent from the body of Luke's gospel, they are most prominently treated in Luke 1–2, 24, and Acts. In addition, however, the physicality of Jesus' resurrection, his appointment of the apostles as witnesses, and the centrality of Jerusalem are of special importance.

Once we recognize the importance of these themes in the composition of Luke 24, we may also recognize what a powerful objection this chapter makes against Marcionite theology. These are precisely themes that address issues raised by Marcion. Indeed the entire chapter may be read as an explicit rejection of the theological convictions of the Marcionites. The following exchange, although fictional, highlights the differences between Marcion and the author of Luke 24.

Marcion: The appearance of Jesus in the world was totally unanticipated.

Luke 24: Jesus, after his resurrection, explained that the prophets, and indeed the entire Hebrew Scriptures, foretold his life and death.

Marcion: Peter and the other apostles were false apostles.

Luke 24: The apostles were commissioned by Jesus as witnesses to his resurrection, and they were commanded to preach repentance.

Marcion: The resurrection of Jesus was a spiritual phenomenon.

Luke 24: After his resurrection Jesus asserted that he was not a spirit, he showed himself bodily to his apostles, and he ate food in their presence.

Marcion: The religion of the Jews has nothing to do with the religion of Jesus.

Luke 24: After his resurrection Jesus ordered his disciples to remain in Jerusalem, and they adhered closely to the temple.

I readily concede that these observations about Luke 24 do not prove that the chapter in its present form was written later than the body of Luke or that it was written as a response to Marcion. It is not difficult to read Marcion's gospel as a reaction to Luke 24. But the analysis of Luke 24 here should not be judged in isolation. If convincing reasons can be given for taking the birth and infancy narratives in canonical Luke as anti-Marcionite additions to a more primitive gospel text, as I hope to have demonstrated above, and if some of the same themes occur in both the beginning and the ending of canonical Luke, as well as in Acts, it is legitimate to suppose—in the absence of arguments to the contrary—that both the birth narratives and the postresurrection accounts, as we now have them, were composed by the same author and for many of the same purposes.

The Preface—Luke 1:1–4

It is appropriate to treat Luke's preface at this point, not only because—then and now—prefaces are usually composed last, but also because our understanding of these verses depends largely on a reading of the texts that follow them.[134] Our contention will be that the preface to Luke, which is unique to this gospel, forms an appropriate introduction to Luke-Acts when conceived as an anti-Marcionite text.

Cadbury once observed that "in the study of the earliest Christian history no passage has had more emphasis laid upon it than the brief preface of Luke."[135] The forty-two words that make up the first four verses of canonical Luke have received a remarkable amount of attention among critical scholars.

Cadbury called attention to the affinities between the preface to Luke and other contemporary prefaces. He described Luke's as "a single long sentence, well balanced, periodic, with some choice Greek words and inflections."[136] Cadbury also cautioned against interpreting Luke's preface in overly strict terms and neglecting its conventional aspects: "Even the specific purpose expressed in the preface—apparently that of defending Christianity from possible misunderstanding and odium on the part of the secular authorities—must not be applied too seriously to the work as a whole. The subjects discussed in prefaces were limited both naturally and by tradition, and several of the conventional *motifs* appear in this brief one."[137] Many scholars agree with Cadbury, but his cautious approach has been questioned by some recent scholars. Günter Klein, for example, has maintained that attention to the conventional aspects should not cause us to overlook the particular meanings that Luke wished to convey.[138]

The most recent exhaustive studies of Luke's preface are those of Loveday Alexander, especially her monograph that appeared in 1993.[139] Alexander is especially interested in challenging the widespread view that Luke's preface was modeled on those used by ancient Greek and Roman historians. These prefaces are noted for their attempts to impress audiences with high levels of literary expression. She points out a number of differences between Luke's preface and those of the historians, the following among them: "Luke's preface is one sentence long where Thucydides' consists of 23 chapters, each at least four times the length of Luke 1:1–4; Luke does not contain any of the general moral reflections which are a mark of the Hellenistic historians; the Greek historians by convention speak of themselves in the third person rather than the first; and they never open with a second-person address."[140]

Alternatively Alexander sees major affinities between Luke's preface and those in what she calls the scientific tradition. By this she means Greco-Roman writers on philosophy, math, engineering, "astrological herbals and books on dream-interpretation as well as what we would call 'scientific' medicine; and it includes even rhetorical schools."[141] These writers were more interested in the content of their writing than in the audiences. Consequently "there is little overt concern for presentation beyond what is necessary to make the subject clear."[142] Alexander claims that almost everything in Luke's preface has parallels in ancient scientific texts and that Luke's affinities with this tradition extend to structure, content, and style. Luke's adherence to this tradition may be most clearly seen in terms of structure and content. Alexander says that the "topics most common in the prefaces may be summarized under seven heads."[143] She lists these headings as follows:

(1) the author's decision to write
(2) the subject and contents of the book, with explanation where necessary of particular aspects of the presentation (e.g., illustrations)
(3) dedication: the second-person address, and topics related to the dedicatee
(4) the nature of the subject-matter
(5) others who have written on the subject or who have opinions on it, whether predecessors or rivals
(6) the author's qualifications
(7) general remarks on methodology.[144]

Anyone familiar with Luke's preface will easily see that our author includes these topics, although he gives them very brief treatments. Alexander also notes some of the particularities in Luke's preface, that is, elements that have no parallels with Greco-Roman scientific literature, and she notes that these elements probably come from the author's Christian context.

Informed by Alexander's masterful treatment of Luke's preface, I should like now to examine it in terms of the context that we have previously suggested for the composition of canonical Luke. A number of elements in the preface point to this context. It will be useful at this point to have before us a translation of the Lukan preface. The following is taken from Loveday Alexander's translation.

[1]Inasmuch as many have undertaken the task of compiling an account of the matters which have come to fruition in our midst [2]just as the tradition was

handed down to us by the original eyewitnesses and ministers of the word, [3]it seemed good to me also, having followed everything carefully and thoroughly, to write it all up for you in an orderly fashion, most excellent Theophilus, [4]so that you may have assured knowledge about the things in which you have been instructed.[145]

Instead of approaching the preface verse by verse I prefer to raise three questions, drawn from the list of topics which, according to Alexander, are usually included in scientific prefaces. Luke's use of literary conventions leads us not to expect explicit references, named predecessors or rivals, or revealing descriptions. Alexander has appropriately described the preface as "obscure and ambiguous, overburdened with heavy compounds imprecisely used; the difficulty of interpreting it should in itself warn us against placing it on too high a level of literary competence."[146] My questions are these: Who were the "others" who had written on the subject and what was Luke's attitude toward them (see Alexander's topic 5, above)? What is the nature of the subject matter (topic 4, above)? What methods does the author claim to employ and what does he hope to accomplish (topic 7, above)?

Who were the "others" who had written on the subject and what was Luke's attitude toward them? In Luke 1:1 we have a reference to those who had attempted to compile narratives on the subject. The characterization of the others as "many" has caused serious problems for interpreters of this passage. If, as the dominant solution to the Synoptic Problem maintains, Luke drew only on Mark and Q, there is no reason to think that he knew other such texts and no explanation for his counting these two as "many."[147] The problem is intensified for those who suspect that Q was not a written text but a collection of oral sayings. J. Bauer designates the term "many" as a cliché that did not involve any particular stress on the number of predecessors. He says that Luke used it simply to indicate that he belongs to this group, and so we cannot draw any meaningful conclusions from his use.[148] Similarly, in his commentary on Luke Joel Green writes: "Luke's use of the word 'many' here follows a widespread practice both in oral and in written beginnings, where 'many' is used for its rhetorical effect without necessarily implying 'a great number.' Its value here is rhetorical: to vouch for the value of Luke's enterprise by its association with the tradition."[149] Klein, however, objects and refers to Bauer's article as demonstrating the meaninglessness of such emphasis on literary convention. He says that the real question to ask is, "Why did Luke adopt this convention?"[150]

Alexander puts her finger on the root of our problem at this point. After rehearsing the problems in interpreting Luke 1:1, she writes: "It is simplest, then, to conclude, short of positive indications to the contrary, that Luke meant what he said. If this causes problems for our views on Gospel sources or chronology, perhaps we need to look more closely at those views and their assumptions."[151] Alexander goes on to challenge the assumption that Luke's reference was to written accounts, but in my judgment a challenge of the usual chronology of the composition of the Lukan preface is more appropriate. If the preface is part of the addition made by the canonical author of Luke and if this author wrote in the first quarter of the second century, his use of "many" to designate his predecessors is appropriate. Indeed under this scenario the predecessors would include not only Mark and Q, but also the pre-Marcionite version of Luke and perhaps Marcion's gospel and other gospel texts. Locating canonical Luke in the second century provides a reasonable basis for explaining his reference to the predecessors and avoids the problems that adhere to an earlier dating.

It is more difficult to perceive Luke's attitude toward the predecessors. About them he writes that they have "undertaken the task of compiling an account" (Luke 1:1). The verb translated here as "undertaken," ἐπιχειρεῖν, has received a good deal of attention. Many scholars think that the verb carries no negative connotation about the work of Luke's predecessors. Alexander, for example, stresses the conventional aspect of the preface at this point and thinks that Luke is only distinguishing between the accounts of the predecessors and his own in the sense that the former were oral and his is written. She writes: "Using the conventional language of any school treatise, he says merely that they had tried to 'put together an account'—a splendidly ambiguous phrase which could be interpreted in a number of historically plausible ways."[152] In addition we should note that Luke, in referring to his decision to write, says simply, "It seemed good to me also . . . to write" (Luke 1:3). He implies that his own work is to be seen as continuing the practices of the predecessors. Luke 1:2 seems also to express approval of the work of Luke's predecessors. The basis of their work is said to be tradition and eyewitness testimony, and this is surely a basis that Luke shared.

Klein, however, is convinced that the verb could not have been used in a value-free way. It must indicate some kind of inadequacy on the part of the predecessors.[153] He notes that in 1:4 Luke speaks of providing "assured knowledge" for his reader, and he sees this as something that distinguishes Luke's work from that of the predecessors. Klein stresses the audacity of Luke's claim in 1:4, namely, that the assurance of salvation was unavailable until the time of this very writing. Previous attempts to compile narratives, although based on tradition and eyewitness testimony, are therefore inadequate. Their inadequacy is seen in their incompleteness: among other things, they lack the story of the apostles, as our author tells this in Acts. Klein says that the preface claims that it is only through the apostolic tradition that assurance of faith can be given.

I conclude that Luke's attitude toward his predecessors is ambivalent. He seems to have no reluctance in associating himself with their writing, and he grants that their work is based on eyewitness testimony and tradition that has been handed on. Nevertheless there is in the preface a subtle hint that the attempts of the predecessors were in some ways inadequate. They probably have provided Theophilus with things about which he has been instructed (Luke 1:4) but have been unable to provide the assured knowledge that Luke intends. If Luke's predecessors include not only Mark and Q but also a pre-Marcionite Luke and possibly the Gospel of Marcion, the preface may be understood as a meaningful, if gentle, expression of the inferiority and inadequacy of these earlier texts.

What is the nature of the subject matter? Luke 1:2 indicates that the subject treated by the predecessors is "the matters which have come to fruition in our midst," matters based on tradition and eyewitness testimony. Apparently this is Luke's subject matter as well. The verb translated here as "come to fruition" is πεπληροφορημένων, the perfect passive participle of πληόω, which means to fulfill, bring about, or accomplish. Cadbury denied that the fulfillment of Scripture is intended here. "The suggestion that the fulfillment of Scripture is what Luke means need hardly to be taken seriously, though of course πληόω is so used."[154] But it is difficult to know why this may not be taken seriously, and some recent scholars have done so. Richard J. Dillon, for example, noted that Luke frequently uses the verb πληόω to express the idea of the fulfillment of Scripture. He noted in particular the stress on the concept of fulfillment of Scripture in Luke 24 and wrote: "Through the continuity of his story, Luke shows that Jesus' own instruction in the meaning of all the Scriptures became the content of the apostolic kerygma which assembled and increased the nascent Christian church."[155]

Dillon's study shows the important link that exists between Luke 24 and the preface. We have already noted the stress in Luke 24 on the proper interpretation of Scripture and Jesus' fulfillment of the prophets. Further, it is in this chapter that the apostles and those with them are appointed as witnesses and charged to preach repentance and forgiveness. Dillon translates Luke 1:2 to say that the eyewitnesses *became* servants of the word, and he adds: "Our version of v. 2 thus finds in the prologue an anticipation of the two moments of 'witness' formation which we observed in Luke's composition of the Easter story—viz., the phases of empirical observation and dominical instruction. Only when the resurrected Christ demonstrated the fulfillment of prophecy in himself did puzzled Easter onlookers become prospective Easter witnesses (Luke 24:45–48)."[156] It would seem hard to avoid the conclusion that the fulfillment of Scripture is intended in Luke's preface and that this very fulfillment is based on tradition handed down from those who were commissioned by Jesus to be his witnesses. It is not difficult to learn, from Luke, who these original witnesses were: they were Peter, the apostles, and their companions, who had been with Jesus from the time of his baptism to his ascension (Luke 24:48; Acts 1:22).

Given the connection with Luke 24, the allusion to the fulfillment of Scripture, and the appointment of witnesses, the anti-Marcionite aspects of Luke's preface become clear. Over against Marcionite claims the canonical author wishes to say that the subject matter that he will address has to do with the fulfillment of Scripture and that it was Peter and the apostles who were appointed by Jesus to be his witnesses and to hand down the tradition.

What methods does the author claim to employ and what does he hope to accomplish? The only reference the author of the preface makes to his literary methods is in Luke

1:3. There he claims to write "in an orderly fashion." One might think that this implies the order that would come with a written account as distinguished from a variety of oral accounts.[157] Or Luke's claim may be to place the material in correct chronological or geographical order. But a close examination of the word used here, "καθεξῆς," shows that something more is at stake. David P. Moessner studied Luke's use of the word in the preface and in other sections of Luke-Acts, especially the story of Cornelius in Acts 10:1–11:18.[158] Moessner pointed out that in the preface to Peter's report to the apostles in Jerusalem Luke says that "Peter began to explain it to them in order" (καθεξῆς, Acts 11:4). But what is curious is that Peter's report in Jerusalem (Acts 11:4–18) is different from the narrator's story of the same series of events in Acts 10:1–48. The accounts differ in order, and some events are given less space in Peter's account than in the narrator's. More important, "the material re-description of particular incidents is in some cases significantly different."[159] For example, Moessner asks, "Whose account is correct? Did the angel tell Cornelius that Peter would proclaim a message of salvation, as Peter's version says, or did Cornelius await with great expectation the message Peter would bring but not knowing the exact import of the visit, as the narrator's account suggests?"[160] Moessner concludes, that "καθεξῆς in Acts 11,4 therefore appears neither to be primarily chronological or geographical in its 'ordering' *sense.* Rather, it suggests an ordering or sequencing of Peter's account in which the 'logic' of the Cornelius encounter is illuminated for the larger narrative development or story."[161] Moessner suggests that the same idea is intended in Luke's preface, which does not suggest that the following account will be in chronological order but that it will stress the significance of the events being reported. Thus, as Moessner says, "To read Luke's two-volumes καθεξῆς is to 'get his story straight!'—'to gain a firmer grasp of the true significance of those events of which you have been instructed' (Lk 1,4)."[162]

The dedication to Theophilus reveals what the author of the Lukan preface wishes to accomplish. He writes so that the reader "may have assured knowledge about the things in which you have been instructed" (Luke 1:4). The key term in verse 4 is κατηχήθης, a form of the verb meaning to inform or instruct. As Alexander says, the interpretation of the verse must take into consideration the meaning of the verb, but vocabulary study alone will not decide the major issue.[163] The major issue is whether Theophilus is to be regarded as an outsider or an insider in relation to the Jesus movement.[164] Cadbury regarded him as an outsider, who had been supplied with information about the movement, some of it inaccurate.[165] Thus he regarded Luke 1:4 as introducing an apology to an official who had received hostile reports about Christianity. Luke's purpose is hence to correct the inaccuracies in these reports. W. C. van Unnik is unsure of Theophilus' relation to the Jesus movement, but he thinks he did not "have direct access to what the many had produced and to the testimony of eyewitnesses and preachers of the Word."[166] In van Unnik's view Luke wrote "so Theophilus may discover the unshakable truth of what he had heard."[167] Alexander leans toward the view that Luke wrote to provide written confirmation of what Theophilus had only heard, to provide "a written 'reminder' of oral teaching with which the reader is already familiar."[168] But she also cautions against taking Luke 1:4 as a definite statement of purpose. In most prefaces from the scientific tradition a statement of purpose "was little more than a flourish, a conventional afterthought designed to complete the balance of the sentence rather than to add anything of substance to the sense."[169]

In the case of the Lukan preface, however, brief as it is, it seems prudent to take the statement of purpose seriously. Luke 1:4 does not appear to be a "conventional afterthought" or a "flourish." Further, if it is appropriate to consider a second-century setting for the preface, the words take on a definite significance. I suggest that Theophilus is best seen here as one who has received some Christian instruction but that he is also aware of and perhaps unsettled by some challenges to this teaching. The canonical author writes in order to equip Theophilus with assured knowledge about this teaching, that is, to give him confidence that the information he has received is true. Thus equipped, Theophilus may be able to meet the challenges of which he had become aware. Van Unnik considered the possibility that Luke 1:4 implied some kind of "crisis of tradition," but he discarded this possibility as too rash.[170] His reasons for doing so are unclear. Since we know that Marcionite Christianity posed just such a challenge in the early second century and since there are good reasons for dating the preface to Luke, along with the infancy narratives, the resurrection accounts, and the Acts of the Apostles, at this time, it seems probable that the canonical author dedicated his writing to Theophilus in the expectation that, equipped with assured knowledge, he would be able to stand up against Marcionite challenges.[171]

I conclude this section on Luke's preface by quoting again Alexander's translation of these verses and adding in brackets a few interpretive notes that are intended to show how this pericope might be read within the context of the Marcionite challenge.

[1]Inasmuch as many [for example, Mark, Q, pre-Marcionite Luke, possibly Marcion and others] have undertaken the task of compiling an account of the matters which have come to fruition [that is, those things predicted by the Hebrew prophets and the Scriptures that have been fulfilled in the life, death, and resurrection of Jesus and in the preaching of the apostles] in our midst [2]just as the tradition was handed down to us by the original eyewitnesses and ministers of the word [that is, Peter and the other apostles, who were appointed by Jesus to witness his resurrection and preach the gospel of repentance] [3]it seemed good to me also, having followed everything carefully and thoroughly, to write it all up for you in an orderly fashion [that is, in a fashion that conveys its true significance], most excellent Theophilus, [4]so that you may have assured knowledge about the things in which you have been instructed [and not be misled by challenges coming especially from the Marcionites].

An examination of the Lukan preface by itself does not permit a definite conclusion about the context in which it was written. But together with the evidence that has previously been brought to bear on the context within which Acts and canonical Luke were written, the preface may plausibly be read as introducing a text that responds to "heretical" challenges, especially those of the Marcionites.

The Body of Luke—Luke 3–23

Thus far we have found that there are good reasons for regarding Luke 1–2 and most of 24 as additions by a post-Marcionite author to an earlier text. It is not likely that we will ever know just what was in the more primitive text, which in our theory was also the source document for Marcion. The difficulties we encountered with attempts to reconstruct the Gospel of Marcion caution against any attempt to reconstruct the hypothetical text on which he and the author of canonical Luke must have drawn. No such reconstruction will be attempted here. But we would not be far wrong in assuming that it was something like Luke 3–23, plus a brief postresurrection narrative. In this case it would not be difficult to understand and appreciate the canonical author's addition of Sondergut material at the beginning and end of his source gospel.

Additionally, if the same Luke 3–23 was the basic source for Marcion, his adoption of this gospel and his method of composition would not be mysterious. We observed earlier that, if Marcion used canonical Luke as a basis for his own gospel, he omitted from that gospel a much larger proportion of unique material than of common synoptic material. But on the supposition that his source was substantially Luke 3–23 the difference between Marcion's appropriation of unique and common material is much less dramatic, as we may see from tables 3 and 4, below. These tables follow the model used in tables 1 and 2, where the division into classes designates use or nonuse of the material by Marcion.[172]

TABLE 3. Luke 3–23 & Marcion: Verses

Source	Class	# Verses	% Verses
Synoptic Parallels	A	478.5	71.2
Synoptic Parallels	B	83.5	12.4
Synoptic Parallels	C	110	16.4
	Total	672	100.0
Peculiar to Luke	A	170.5	58
Peculiar to Luke	B	69	23.5
Peculiar to Luke	C	54.5	18.5
	Total	294	100.0

Tables 3 and 4 consider only the material in Luke 3–23 and its relation to Mark, Q, and Marcion. They show that the difference between Marcion's use of Sondergut material in Luke 3–23 and his use of material with synoptic parallels is substantially less than is the case when we assume he used canonical Luke as his source. Tables 1

TABLE 4. Luke 3–23 & Marcion: Words

Source	Class	# Words	% Words
Synoptic Parallels	A	8,318	71.9
Synoptic Parallels	B	1,460	12.6
Synoptic Parallels	C	1,783	15.4
	Total	**11,561**	**99.9**
Peculiar to Luke	A	3,017	60.2
Peculiar to Luke	B	1,094	21.8
Peculiar to Luke	C	897	18.0
	Total	**5,008**	**100.0**

and 2 show that, on the assumption that canonical Luke was available to Marcion, he omitted about 12 percent of the material with synoptic parallels and 42 percent of the material peculiar to Luke. But if Marcion had only Luke 3–23 at his disposal, the rate of omission, although still about 12 percent for material with synoptic parallels, is only about 22 percent for material peculiar to Luke. Although there is still a difference to be noted, the difference is about half of what we saw in tables 1 and 2.

Further, on the assumption that Luke 3–23 plus a brief postresurrection account was substantially the source used by Marcion in composing his gospel, it is not difficult to account for his omissions from this text. On this assumption he omitted some pericopes from the material with synoptic parallels and some from the nonparallel material. Among the major omissions from the material with synoptic parallels is the section on John the Baptist and the baptism of Jesus in Luke 3:2–22 (including an L pericope, 3:10–14), the temptation of Jesus (Luke 4:1–13), the triumphal entry of Jesus (Luke 19:29–40), and his cleansing of the temple (Luke 19:45–46). Apparently Marcion could not conceive of John as a predecessor or baptizer of Jesus, and the temptation story would almost certainly have been anathema to him. If he regarded the city of Jerusalem and its temple as belonging to the God who chose the Jewish people, he surely would not have included Jesus' entry into the city and the temple among his gospel stories.

The same is true of Marcion's alleged omissions from the Lukan Sondergut material that is in Luke 3–23. We have already indicated that it is not difficult to account for Marcion's neglect of a number of the pericopes in this group. He would, for example, have found the theme of judgment in Luke 13:1–9 objectionable. Jesus' weeping over Jerusalem (Luke 19:41–44) stresses his Jewish sympathies in a way that would have offended Marcion. Luke 22:35–38, the two swords, suggests a degree of violence that also would have been offensive. But we probably must plead ignorance in the case of the parable of the prodigal son (Luke 15:11–32) and the narrative of the two thieves (Luke 23:39–43).[173] Nothing we know of Marcion would give us reason to think he would have omitted these narratives for theological reasons.

A number of scattered comments in Luke 3–23 may also have been omitted by Marcion for doctrinal reasons. Luke 12:6–7, 28, speaks of God's regard for sparrows, human hair, and the grass of the field. Since, in Marcion's view, the God of Jesus is not the Creator-God, he would have considered it inappropriate for Jesus to have made statements such as these.

Turning now to the author of canonical Luke, we should not assume that his sole contribution was the addition of a beginning and an ending to Luke 3–23. We may be able to identify a few verses in the body of Luke as notes added by our canonical author. For example, Luke 5:39, a verse peculiar to Luke, appears to have been added to an earlier pericope about old and new wine (Luke 5:36–38). Without verse 39 the saying is straightforward and makes the point that new and old do not mix. As we saw in chapter 2, Epiphanius reported that there was vigorous discussion of these verses in a meeting between Marcion and the leaders of the church at Rome.[174] Marcion argued that these Lukan verses (Luke 5:36–38) supported his position that with the appearance of Jesus something thoroughly new had occurred and that the gospel could not be adjoined to older material coming from the God of the Jews. Luke 5:39, however ("And no one after drinking old wine desires new wine, but says, 'The old is good'"), does not cohere with Luke 5:36–38 and may well have been added by the canonical author in an effort to neutralize a Marcionite interpretation of the previous verses.[175]

I am inclined to think that the canonical version of Luke 16:17 also represents an alteration of an earlier text, although it is drawn from Q rather than from the Lukan Sondergut. As we have learned, the Gospel of Marcion at this point had: "But it is easier for heaven and earth to go away than for one of my words to fall."[176] Canonical Luke, however, reads: "But it is easier for heaven and earth to pass away, than for one stroke of a letter in the law to be dropped (εὐκοπώτερον δέ ἐστιν τὸν οὐρανὸν καὶ τὴν γῆν παρελθεῖν ἢ τοῦ νόμου μίαν κεραίαν πεσεῖν)." In its canonical context, Luke 16:17 presents difficulties, since the previous verse maintained that the age of Torah and prophets had concluded with John the Baptist. Further, a similar saying in Luke 21:33, probably drawn from Mark, upholds the Marcionite position and affirms that it is Jesus' words that are eternal: "Heaven and earth will pass away, but my words will not pass away (ὁ οὐρανὸς καὶ ἡ γῆ παρελεύσονται, οἱ δὲ λόγοι μου οὐ μὴ παρελεύσονται)." In Luke 16:17 the canonical author probably has altered an earlier saying of Jesus in order to make an anti-Marcionite claim about Torah.

It is tempting to think of the genealogy (Luke 3:23–38) as post-Marcionite, since it performs some of the same functions that the infancy narratives perform, namely emphasizing the humanity of Jesus and linking him biologically with the Jewish people. But we have already observed that there are fundamental differences of viewpoint between the genealogy and Luke 1:5–2:52. While the genealogy requires that Joseph be the father of Jesus, he is excluded from playing this role in the Lukan infancy narratives. Only the parenthetical comment in Luke 3:23 ("as was thought") casts doubt on Joseph's role as father, and it is plausible that these words were added by the canonical author or a later copyist. Further, we have seen good reason to think that Luke 3:23–38 formed a part of the pre-Marcionite edition of Luke, since it fits well in a gospel that begins with Luke 3:1. If this is the case, it is not difficult to see why Marcion would have omitted this section.[177]

Speculation about other pericopes and verses in Luke 3–23 is possible but hazardous. It is difficult to go beyond these few observations in identifying verses and pericopes that may have been either omitted by Marcion or added by the canonical author. If some or all of the material in Luke 3–23 had been in a primitive version of Luke that was available to Marcion and if he used it as a source but omitted certain pericopes and sayings, some ground would be provided for the charges leveled by Irenaeus and Tertullian that Marcion "mutilated" Luke. In this scenario Marcion omitted material from a primitive gospel version but not from canonical Luke, which was not available to him.

None of these observations is sufficient to compel the conclusion that Luke 3–23 was the exact text that Marcion and the author of canonical Luke used. It is doubtful that we will ever know just what was in this source gospel, but it is not imprudent to suggest that it was a text that bears substantial similarities to what we now have in Luke 3–23. Having said this, it is most important to stress our fundamental conclusion: *Whatever text lies behind the Gospel of Marcion and canonical Luke, it almost certainly did not contain the birth narratives or the preface, and it probably had only a trace of the resurrection account that now appears in canonical Luke.*

Conclusion

Without texts of the Gospel of Marcion or the pre-Marcionite edition of Luke, contentions about the composition of canonical Luke cannot be proven beyond a reasonable doubt. Any hypothesis is just that. But hypotheses carry conviction in the degree to which they answer questions and solve problems. In my judgment more problems are solved and fewer new ones created by a theory that understands canonical Luke to be the end of a rather long process of composition.

The first stage in this process would be the composition of a pre-Marcionite gospel. It probably began with Luke 3:1, and it would have contained material its author obtained, assuming the two-document hypothesis of synoptic relationships, from Mark and Q.[178] This gospel probably also contained a brief narrative of Jesus' resurrection, perhaps similar to what is now in Mark 16:1–8. Some material from the Lukan Sondergut was also used, but this early text almost certainly did not have the preface or the infancy narratives that now stand at the beginning of canonical Luke, and it probably did not contain the narratives of Jesus' postresurrection appearances that we find in Luke 24. Without being precise about its actual contents, we may think of the pre-Marcionite gospel as similar to our Luke 3–23. This text, coming after Mark and before Marcion, probably dates from ca. 70–90 C.E.

The second stage would be the composition of the Gospel of Marcion. This gospel was probably based on the pre-Marcionite gospel but with significant omissions, and so Marcion's opponents could claim that he had "mutilated" the Gospel of Luke. We cannot be certain when this text first appeared, but a date of ca. 115–120 C.E. would probably not be far off the mark.

The third stage would be the composition of canonical Luke. This gospel was almost certainly based on the pre-Marcionite gospel, but its author added a number of new pericopes. He appended a preface (Luke 1:1–4) and the infancy narratives (Luke 1:5–2:52); he rewrote the Markan story of the empty tomb (Luke 24:1–11) and added the postresurrection narratives (Luke 24:13–53). Undoubtedly this author also worked through his source and gave it his own stamp, thus creating the sense of literary unity that the work has. One of the purposes of this author was to publish a gospel that would clearly and forcefully respond to the claims of the Marcionites. The author of canonical Luke was also the author of Acts, and it is likely that he brought out the complete work about 120–125 C.E., just when Marcion's views were becoming widely known. The author of these volumes almost certainly did not make use of Marcion's gospel, which may well have appeared at about the same time. The work as a whole, Luke-Acts as we know it, surely served as a formidable anti-Marcionite text.

CHAPTER 5

The Lukan Achievement

It is no exaggeration to say that the author of Acts and canonical Luke participated in a defining struggle—a struggle over the very meaning of Christian faith. At the heart of this definition is the relation of the new faith to the old. For Luke-Acts the God of Israel is also the God of Christian believers, the Scriptures of the Jews presage the coming of Jesus, who is the fulfillment of Jewish expectation, and the followers of Jesus preached nothing that would challenge Moses or the prophets.

The canonical author's achievement may best be assessed by characterizing his primary target as Marcion and Marcionite Christianity, and the previous chapters have presented a series of arguments to show that such a characterization is valid. The book of Acts was composed, at least in part, to demonstrate the intimate connection of the apostolic tradition with Jesus: Jesus himself appoints the apostles and prepares them for their mission of preaching the gospel of repentance. The author also stresses the unity of the apostolic tradition and allows no disagreements to disturb the unanimity among the early believers, led by the apostles. He shows that Paul, although not an apostle himself, was accepted by the Jerusalem apostles and acted together with them. Thus he undermines any attempt to regard Paul as the only apostle. In this composition Peter, Paul, and all the apostles are shown to be faithful Jews, who are obedient to Torah and observant of Jewish practices. In particular the Paul of Acts preaches that Jesus is the fulfillment of long-held Jewish expectations, and Paul's Pharisaic beliefs are shown to be consistent with what Moses and the prophets had long ago asserted.

The same author who wrote Acts produced canonical Luke by adding significant materials—chiefly Luke 1-2, 24—to an earlier gospel that Marcion himself had also used. In these materials, most of which are found only in the Lukan gospel, Jesus is shown to be intimately, even biologically, related to the Jewish people. The author makes it clear that the coming of Jesus was announced ahead of time by the Hebrew prophets, and Jesus himself explained the Scriptures to his disciples, who became his apostolic witnesses only after he had opened their minds to the meaning of these texts.

Our discussion of the Lukan achievement will include a brief mention of his literary and theological achievements, but more attention will be devoted to the role of Luke-Acts in the history of second-century Christianity. Finally, we shall attempt an assessment of the canonical author's contribution to Christian-Jewish relations.

Luke's Literary Achievement

In the course of our study of the composition of Acts and canonical Luke, we had occasion to point out the literary connections that link Acts with the particular additions made by the canonical author. As Paul Schubert has shown, Luke 24 serves as a bridge between Luke and Acts and prepares readers for the role the apostles will play in the latter.[1] Luke 1:1–4, especially in its reference to the "original eyewitnesses and ministers of the word" (Luke 1:2), encompasses not only the gospel but also the Acts. The parallelism of Jesus and John the Baptist in Luke 1–2 employs a literary technique that also appears in Acts, where it is used to great effect for Peter and Paul.

Not only did the canonical author compose Acts and add new material to the gospel, but he also imposed a consistent literary style on the entirety of the work. He created a narrative that may still be read meaningfully from beginning to end. Henry J. Cadbury called attention to this unity when he gave us the title "Luke-Acts" for the work as a whole,[2] and Robert C. Tannehill's stress on the literary and narrative unity of Luke-Acts testifies to our author's literary achievement.[3] But neither Cadbury nor Tannehill claimed that the author created these texts without making use of earlier sources. They would accept the consensus of modern critical scholars that the author of Acts made use of a number of earlier traditions in compiling his narrative. The same is the case with the Gospel of Luke, which is usually said to have been composed by an author who brought together materials from Mark, Q, and the Lukan Sondergut. Chapter 3, above, accepted the consensus about Acts, while stressing the final author's work in shaping his materials to express his anti-Marcionite theology. Chapter 4 attempted to show that the major contribution of the canonical author to the Gospel of Luke was the addition of the first two chapters and the last, and this claim was based partly on the recognition that almost all of this material is from the Lukan Sondergut.[4]

The task of bringing together these various strands of material, only some of which can be reliably identified, was an immense one. Even more impressive, however, is the author's accomplishment in weaving these materials together into the kind of literary composition that we can now comfortably call "Luke-Acts." Here indeed is a narrative unity, which in our hypothesis is the achievement of the author of Acts and canonical Luke.

Luke's Theological Achievement

Impressive as is our author's literary accomplishment, of greater weight is his theological achievement. I have contended that the canonical version of Luke-Acts was composed in the early days of a major theological controversy that involved a conflict between proto-orthodox Christians and Marcionite Christians. This was not a one-issue controversy. It involved concepts of God, creation, and history, as well as the work of Christ. It involved the beliefs of the earliest Christians, the role of the first followers of Jesus, and interpretations of the writings of Paul. It involved questions about authority and the source for the authentic truth of Christian faith. The Marcionite controversy posed the question: Is authority only in Jesus and Paul, or is it to be found in the teachings of Moses, the prophets, and the apostolic tradition as a whole? The canonical edition of Luke-Acts provided answers to such questions. It provided for the proto-orthodox Christians a portrait of Jesus and his early followers that was accessible, persuasive, and meaningful.

Our author's task was a complex one, which included rescuing Paul from the Marcionites. The difficulty may be seen by examining the heated controversies that even today continue to engage critical scholars, controversies about the Paul of the letters and the Paul of Acts. The fact that to many scholars there appears to be a significant gulf between the two Pauls illustrates the possibility that the Marcionite interpretation of Paul, based on Galatians and other Pauline epistles, may not be too wide of the mark. The author of Acts, who knew some of the Pauline letters and was aware of the Marcionite interpretation of them, undertook the enterprise of reinterpreting Paul to show that he was not a maverick and that Pauline theology was not to be distinguished from Petrine. Paul, for Luke, was a faithful Jew and a devout Pharisee, whose core belief was that Jesus, who rose from the dead, was the fulfillment of Jewish expectation. Nothing that Paul said or did implied any modification of his Jewish beliefs or practices. It would be appropriate to say that one of Luke's major theological achievements was to rescue Paul from the "heretics" and preserve his legacy for proto-orthodox Christians.

Luke's Historical Achievement

In my judgment the author of Acts and canonical Luke discerned the dangers of Marcionite Christianity at an early point in its development. But these documents also played a major role in the controversies that took place later in the second century. In a recent monograph Christopher Mount has called attention to the power that Acts had in late-second-century conflicts with nonorthodox forms of Christian faith.[5] He notes that Irenaeus was the first writer to make explicit use of the text of Acts and that "what is particularly remarkable, indeed unprecedented, in Irenaeus's intellectual defense of his construction of a fourfold gospel canon and a normative ecclesiastical tradition as a weapon against heretics is the importance the Acts of the Apostles takes as a part of scripture."[6] Mount also claims that the text of Luke-Acts "became the focal point in intellectually defining Christian scripture and tradition in the dispute between Marcion and Irenaeus."[7] Mount adds: "Apparently, Irenaeus has pulled Acts off the shelf (so to speak), dusted it off, and put it to use to establish his construction of the standard for the Gospel—a unified constellation of apostolic witnesses in scripture and tradition."[8]

To say that Irenaeus dusted off Acts may obscure its relation to the ongoing controversy. Although it is true that we have only vague and ambiguous allusions from writers before Irenaeus, Acts probably was composed during the lifetime of Marcion himself. It may be better to say that the author of Acts became aware of the threat posed by Marcionite Christianity long before Irenaeus took up his pen. Nevertheless Mount is quite right to emphasize the role of Luke-Acts in establishing the apostolic tradition as the source of authority for second-century Christianity.

Yet another aspect of Luke's role in the history of Christianity is the relationship of his writings to the development of the New Testament canon. In the concluding chapter of his *Marcion and the New Testament* John Knox proposed that the publication of Luke-Acts constituted a significant step in the development of the canon.[9] He noted that from earliest times most Christian churches accepted only the LXX as Scripture. The "words of the Lord" had authority, but only as Jesus' sayings, not as parts of written documents. But just after the middle of the second century there appears "a New Testament, regarded as having the full status and authority of Scripture."[10] How can we account for this dramatic change? Knox accepts the view that the establishment of a specific body of Christian writings was part of the proto-orthodox "response to various forms of Gnosticism current in the second century, and especially to Marcionism."[11] The response might take the form simply of rejecting Marcion's canon as heretical, or the church might appropriate it and add to it. The latter was the church's choice. "'Orthodox' churchmen would not let it appear that Marcion had a monopoly on reverence for the apostolic Christian documents."[12]

The hypothesis that Marcion's canon impelled his opponents to respond with a specific collection of authoritative Christian writings is widely, if not universally, accepted among scholars of the early church. But Knox adds that Marcion's canon and Luke-Acts served as models for the New Testament canon as it developed. Marcion's canon was made up of two parts: "Gospel" and "Apostle." Knox writes: "Indeed, one of the most convincing reasons for finding in Marcion the original occasion of the New Testament lies in the predominating position of Paul in the New Testament canon, a position apparently out of proportion to his influence in the church of the early second century."[13] Thus, according to Knox, the church retained the Marcionite division of "Gospel" and "Apostle" but enlarged it at both points. In the "Apostle" section it kept the ten letters of Paul that Marcion had but added the Pastorals and other presumably apostolic writings—James; 1, 2, 3 John; Jude; 1, 2 Peter. In addition the Acts of the Apostles was "canonized and made the beginning book of the 'Apostle.'"[14] The church also added to the Marcionite "Gospel" section by including an enlarged Luke plus three other gospels. Knox is struck by the fact that the New Testament takes the two-part form of "Gospel" and "Apostle," the same form as the canon of Marcion, and he stresses the point that Luke-Acts also has this form.

> Now it is a strange fact that when our New Testament took form as "Gospel and Apostle," there should lie at hand for use in it another two-part work and that this other two-part work should also have been in the form, "Gospel and Apostle." We have seen reasons for believing that the Gospel-Apostle pattern of the New Testament was derived from Marcion; is it not natural to account for

the Gospel-Apostle pattern of Luke-Acts in the same way? The plausibility of that explanation of the occasion of Luke-Acts as a single work is increased by the observation that the Luke-Acts Apostle is Paul—but a catholic Paul—and that the Gospel section of Luke-Acts is an enlarged form of Marcion's Gospel. This latter is really a quite remarkable fact and appears more remarkable the more one reflects on it. Here are two two-part works—Marcion's canon and Luke-Acts—making their appearance at approximately the same time. Both are organized as "Gospel and Apostle," and the *Gospel section is largely the same.* That there is no connection between these two sets of acts seems to me highly improbable.[15]

Knox was aware that these suggestions went beyond the possibility of proof, but his presentation forms a compelling hypothesis. He does not claim that the author of Acts and canonical Luke was responsible for the formation of the New Testament canon, but he argues persuasively that the model of "Gospel" and "Apostle," used both by Marcion and Luke, served the later church in the shaping of its New Testament canon.

Luke-Acts and Christian-Jewish Relations

Partly due to the influence of Luke-Acts, proto-orthodox writers of the late second century were able to argue for the inclusion of documents from the Hebrew Scriptures. Thus the Christian Bible not only includes these texts, but in fact begins with them. It is generally conceded that the Scripture of the earliest Christians was the LXX. If so Marcion was, as far as we know, the first Christian to issue an explicit challenge to the authority of these documents, and in our judgment it was Luke who prepared a formidable defense against their being jettisoned. Since Luke showed that the God of Israel was the God of Jesus and his followers, that the Hebrew Scriptures predicted the coming of Jesus, and that his followers were truly devout Jews, it may seem that his views would have prepared the way for a form of Christian faith that was not hostile to Jews and Judaism. We know, however, that this was not the result, and so when considering the achievement of Luke, we cannot overlook his contribution to Christian-Jewish relations. Luke's contribution at this point may best be assessed by comparing and contrasting his approach with Marcion's.

In his recent study of early Christian theological diversity Bart D. Ehrman entertains the possibility that things might have turned out differently and Marcionite Christianity might have prevailed over all other movements of the second century.[16] He regards its victory as plausible because "it took what most people in the empire found most attractive about Christianity—love, mercy, grace, wonder, opposition to this harsh, material world and salvation from it—and pushed it to an extreme, while taking Christianity's less attractive sides—law, guilt, judgment, eternal punishment, and, above all, association and close ties with Jews and Judaism—and getting rid of them."[17] Then he projects two possible results: "This may have opened the doors to heightened hostilities, since Marcion seems to have hated Jews and everything Jewish; or possibly even more likely, it may have led simply to benign neglect as Jews and their religion would have been considered to be of no relevance and certainly no competition for Christians. The entire history of anti-Semitism might have been avoided, ironically, by an anti-Jewish religion."[18] Ehrman finally, however, abandons the scenario of a Marcionite victory on the grounds that second- and third-century Greco-Romans would not have embraced a religion that stressed its own novelty.

Ehrman adopts the customary judgment that Marcion "hated Jews and everything Jewish" and that his form of Christianity was "anti-Jewish." Our own study of Marcion shows that this characterization of his views needs to be more carefully nuanced. Further, Marcion's theology should be assessed in the light of views expressed by his opponents, those who did in fact win the day. How, in other words, does the issue of anti-Judaism play out in Marcion on the one side and proto-orthodox Christian writings, chiefly Luke-Acts, on the other?

As we have seen, Marcion took his inspiration from the letters of Paul, most notably Galatians. He was deeply impressed with Paul's contrast of law and grace and concluded that these must be the domains of two Gods. One God is revealed in the Hebrew Bible as the Creator, law-giver, and judge of humankind. This God thus is identified with the created order, Torah, and the Jews, his chosen people. The second God is the Father of Jesus Christ, the God of grace, love, and mercy, who was completely unknown in this world before the appearance of Jesus. The work of Jesus was to release people from the Creator-God and deliver them into the domain of the God of grace.

Our ancient sources agree that Marcion made a complete separation between the religion that Jesus and Paul espoused and that of the Hebrew Scriptures. Consonant with his conviction that the God of Jesus had been totally unknown before the appearance of Jesus, he concluded that there could be no connection between Jesus and the Hebrew Scriptures. Thus Marcion's canon did not include these writings, and his theology completely separated the God of Jesus from the God revealed in them. Evidently he stressed a nonallegorical, nonfigurative interpretation of the prophets and, indeed, of all the Hebrew Scriptures. Tertullian condemned him for this because it meant that he was in agreement with Jews, who likewise denied that the prophets predicted the coming of Jesus.[19] Despite their exclusion from his canon Marcion accepted the Hebrew Scriptures as containing accurate history and prophecy. For him the creation stories of Genesis, indeed the Torah as a whole, were not to be challenged on the grounds of their accuracy but rather in terms of the God portrayed in them. Moreover, Isaiah and the other prophets were trustworthy predictors of the future. But Marcion insisted that the figure predicted by these prophets was not Jesus and that such a one had not yet come. That coming was still to be anticipated as a future event, as Jews believed.[20] Marcion's critique of the Hebrew Bible thus was not directed to its authority but to its theology and morality. He saw in these writings, especially in Torah, something that fell beneath the teachings of Jesus and Paul, and the contrasts were so extreme that, although he accepted a divine origin for the Hebrew Bible, he concluded that the God who inspired these Scriptures was not the God revealed in Jesus Christ.

These considerations strongly suggest that it is not sufficient to judge Marcion strictly as anti-Jewish on the grounds of his attitude toward the Hebrew Bible. Apparently he agreed both with Jews and proto-orthodox Christians that the books in this collection were divinely inspired, while differing with both about the inspiring deity. Nor did Marcion question the historical accuracy of these writings or their prophetic power. On these points Marcion's interpretation of the Hebrew Scriptures would be consonant with Jewish interpretations. He would agree that the Hebrew prophets predicted the coming of the Messiah and that this figure was not Jesus. Key to Marcion's interpretation is his insistence on the literal meaning: Isaiah, for example, was addressing the people of his own time about the threats from foreign kingdoms; he was not speaking of the coming of Jesus. Thus although they are irrelevant for Christian faith, Isaiah and all the prophets are historically trustworthy and authoritative for the people of Israel.

Marcion's attitude toward Jews and Judaism was more complex than it is usually described to be. It is not sufficient simply to say that he was anti-Jewish, although he was certain that the morality he saw in the Hebrew Bible was deficient. Inevitably he would judge the religion that was based on these writings as inferior to his own. But apparently he would not question its legitimacy or its right to continue after the appearance of Jesus. He would pity Jews as being kept under the control of the God of creation, but he would regard their expectation of a Messiah as fully conforming to the writings of the Hebrew prophets. Further, his insistence on literal interpretation would, as Tertullian himself observed, create a significant basis for agreement with major Jewish beliefs.[21] Marcion's decision to exclude the Hebrew Bible from the Christian canon creates a clear demarcation between Christianity and Judaism, and in this sense he would probably have encouraged his followers to regard the survival of Judaism after the time of Jesus as legitimate but theologically irrelevant. Whether this would have led to a diminished degree of anti-Judaism on the part of his followers is, of course, impossible to say, but Ehrman is probably correct to observe that "benign neglect" is at least consistent with Marcionite principles.

In reacting against Marcion the author of Acts and canonical Luke seems to be drawing the church back toward a more intimate relationship with Judaism. In stressing the validity of Moses and the prophets the canonical author would also imply that there is an underlying unity between the Hebrew Scriptures and Christian faith. His portrayal of the birth, life, death, and resurrection of Jesus, followed by the preaching of his followers, fortified the proto-orthodox Christian retention of these writings and their canonization as the Christian Old Testament. This meant that Christians would continue to hear readings from the Hebrew Scriptures and thus be led to understand the story of ancient Israel as part of their own history, as

Luke-Acts showed. It meant that they would be able to see Jesus as part of an ongoing history and as a participant in an ancient and vibrant Jewish culture. By insisting on the role of Jesus and the apostles in fulfilling prophetic promises the canonical author must have paved the way for the Hebrew Scriptures to become a part of the Christian Bible, as the Old Testament.[22] This is not an issue that the author of Luke-Acts faced directly, but it is plausible to suggest that without his contribution the canonical status of the Christian Old Testament would have been far more questionable than it in fact was.

But the connection between Moses, the prophets, and Jesus on which the canonical author of Luke-Acts insisted did not assure a positive relation between Christians and Jews. On the contrary this author walks a line carefully separating Marcionite Christians on the one side and Jews on the other. While he elevates Moses and the prophets to a high status for Christians, he simultaneously denigrates most ancient and contemporary Jews. For the most part the Jewish people in Luke-Acts are cast in the role of opponents of Jesus and his followers. Both Peter and Paul accuse them of putting Jesus to death. Not only do Jews reject the message that ostensibly was meant for them, but they also frequently oppose the preachers in violent ways. They engage in plots; they incite riots; they bring accusations in Roman courts and call for executions. The Paul of Acts affirms that Jews hear the Scriptures read to them every Sabbath, but they do not understand them (Acts 13:27). Although the early chapters of Acts show that Jews responded heartily and in large numbers to the Christian preachers, much-more-negative images increase as the narrative progresses. At the end of the book Paul quotes from Isaiah to condemn the Jews of Rome and, by implication, all Jews, for their imperceptiveness and disobedience (Acts 28:25–28).[23]

In addition the proto-orthodox victory over Marcionite Christianity had the potential to bring Jews and Christians into conflict over the interpretation of the same texts. If Christians believe that the same God who sent Jesus Christ also inspired the Hebrew Scriptures, they must develop some ways to address the apparent differences between their teachings, and at this point our canonical author provides a few hints. We would judge from Luke-Acts that interpretation of the Hebrew Bible must be guided by two principles: it must show the continuity of the Hebrew Scriptures with the events surrounding Jesus and the early Christian community, and it must show the infidelity of the Jewish people. Although lacking in specific and explicit commentary on the cited texts, Luke-Acts makes these two points quite clearly. Our author insisted that the Hebrew prophets predicted the suffering and death of the Messiah but did not specify the texts that would support this contention (see Luke 24:25–26; Acts 3:18; 17:3; 26:22–23). Although the speeches of Peter, Stephen, and Paul do not directly address questions about apparent differences between Christian teachings and those in the Hebrew Scriptures, they nevertheless make it clear that it is Christians, and not Jews, who are faithful to the God of Israel. For example, the speech of Stephen in Acts 7:2–53 contains a long recitation of the history of Israel

from Abraham to Solomon with abundant references to the Scriptures, and the citations serve mainly to highlight the rebelliousness of the Hebrew people, which, in
Stephen's view, culminated in their murder of Jesus. Without citing specific incidents Stephen charges that the ancient Hebrews murdered all the prophets, and he
concludes by identifying his present audience with the rebellious Hebrews of the past
(Acts 7:52). The speech connects contemporary Jewish opposition to the early Christians with historic Jewish disobedience to God and Torah. In other respects
Stephen's speech contains little that would help later Christians in their efforts to
interpret the Hebrew Bible.[24] Paul's speech in Pisidian Antioch (Acts 13:16–41) may
be more helpful. Here Paul quotes several texts and provides a christological interpretation, but even here the main thrust is the use of ancient Hebrew history to connect
Jesus with David. The canonical author, therefore, provides hints about the interpretation of the Hebrew Scriptures—quoting it to condemn contemporary Jews and
justify Christian convictions—but has neither an extended commentary on the texts
nor a discussion of methods of interpretation. The point is not that we should expect
such commentary or discussion in writings such as Luke-Acts but that their omission
created a lacuna that later Christian writers must struggle to fill.

It is essential to note that the rejection of Marcion meant that proto-orthodox
Christians would rarely be able to make use of literal interpretations of texts from the
Hebrew Scriptures. Writing only a few decades after Luke, Justin Martyr illustrates
the ways in which Christian writers might interpret these texts. In his *Dialogue with
Trypho* he categorizes the commandments in Torah in three groups. First there are
those ethical commands that are universal. Justin says: "God shows every race of
man that which is always and in all places just, and every type of man knows that
adultery, fornication, murder, and so on are evil. Though they all commit such acts,
they cannot escape the knowledge that they sin whenever they do so."[25] Thus for
commands in this category Torah may be interpreted literally, but it adds nothing
that human beings may not obtain from a variety of other sources. Second are the
historical, that is, those commands that are intended only for Jews. Justin admits
that circumcision is a practice that is deeply rooted in the Scriptures, but he insists
that God intended it for Jews alone in order to mark them for punishment. He later
makes specific mention of the prohibition that followed upon the second Jewish
rebellion against Rome (132–135 C.E.) and says that circumcision provides a means
of identification, so that Jews can be barred from entering the city of Jerusalem.[26]
These requirements—circumcision, Sabbath, festivals—were imposed upon Jews
because of their hardness of heart.[27] Third there are the prophetic passages, that is,
those that typologically refer to Jesus the Christ. Justin says that some of these passages
have been misunderstood by Jews. He claims that this is the case with the practice of
using unleavened bread at Passover. Although Jews understand this commandment in
a literal, material fashion, it really refers, says Justin, to a command to repent,
"to practice other deeds, not to repeat your old ones."[28] Many prescriptions in the
Hebrew Bible have a typological purpose and so were not understood by Jews. The

Passover lamb, for example, is a type of the crucified Christ.[29] The flour offering for a cleansed leper is a type of the eucharistic bread.[30] Circumcision on the eighth day is a type of the resurrection of Jesus on the first day of the week (which is both first day and eighth day).[31] The twelve bells on the high priest's robe are types of the twelve apostles.[32]

Justin is an early representative of a developing Christian tradition of denigrating literal interpretations of texts from the Hebrew Scriptures. He identifies such interpretation as Jewish, and his method of interpretation is an implicit admission that literal interpretation does not produce an understanding of the underlying unity of Old Testament and New Testament. He and other opponents of Marcion were thus compelled to find different ways to interpret the Hebrew Scriptures. At the beginning of the third century Tertullian is explicit in attacking Marcionite and Jewish literalism. He makes a special effort to describe a nonliteral method of interpretation: "So from now on I demand that our opponents acknowledge two special cases of prophetic diction. The first is that by which things future are sometimes set down as if they had already taken place."[33] "Another form of speech will be that by which not a few things are set forth figuratively by means of enigmas and allegories and parables, and are to be understood otherwise than as they are written."[34] And Tertullian cites the example of Paul, who

> interprets as concerning not oxen but ourselves that law which grants an unmuzzled mouth to the oxen that tread out the corn [cf. 1 Cor 9:9], and affirms that the rock that followed them to provide drink was Christ [cf. 1 Cor 10:4], in the same way as he instructs the Galatians that the two narratives of the sons of Abraham took their course as an allegory [cf. Gal 4:22ff.], and advises the Ephesians that that which was foretold in the beginning, that a man would leave his father and mother, and that he and his wife would become one flesh, is seen by him to refer to Christ and the Church [cf. Eph 5:31ff.].[35]

For Tertullian, literal interpretation of the Scriptures is to be regarded as Jewish and hence deficient.[36]

Marcion was one of the first Christians to see that the effort to ground the new faith in the old was beset with problems. He certainly was the first known to us to propose a simple if draconian solution to the problems, a solution that would continue to regard the Hebrew Scriptures as valid, accurate, authoritative, and divinely inspired but irrelevant for Christian faith. In a sense this solution liberated Marcion and allowed him to interpret these Scriptures literally. He admitted no obligation to see a pattern of prophecy and fulfillment that would relate Christian faith to the Hebrew Scriptures.

Marcion's opponents, however, were convinced not only that the Hebrew Scriptures were divinely inspired but also that there was an underlying unity between them and the story of Jesus and the church. The author of Acts and canonical Luke maintained that the promises of the Hebrew Scriptures were fulfilled by Jesus and the early church. He also made it clear that for the most part contemporary Jews, because of their rejection of the gospel, were no longer heirs of the promises. The conviction of an underlying unity between the Hebrew Scriptures and the early Christians, together with the defeat of Marcion, meant that interpreters such as Justin and Tertullian were rarely able to interpret the Scriptures literally. It was by way of nonliteral interpretation that one could see the underlying unity. [37]

Conclusion

I do not wish to project what might have been the course of history if Marcion had been victorious over his opponents. I do think, however, that it is a misreading of history to think of him as the arch-anti-Semite of the early church. On the contrary Marcion's insistence on the literal interpretation of the Hebrew Scriptures potentially created a bond of understanding between him and at least some Jews that his opponents could not have achieved. Nor did they attempt to do so. Although they may have been aware of some Jewish interpretations, as Justin and Tertullian exhibit, they were confident that their own methods of nonliteral interpretation supported Christian faith.[38]

The work of the author of Acts and canonical Luke should be appreciated as a major literary and theological achievement. We must also stress the role that these texts played in the history of second-century Christianity, especially in the defeat of Marcionite Christianity and in the development of the New Testament canon. In its own time and in its legacy Luke-Acts participated in a defining struggle. It drew Christian believers to reflect on the close relation of their faith to the Hebrew Scriptures and to see their lives in Christ as the fulfillment of long-held Jewish expectation and ancient prophecy. But in regard to Christian-Jewish relations the proto-orthodox victory, in which Luke-Acts played such an important part, was a two-edged sword. On the one side it secured the retention of the Hebrew Scriptures for Christian use. On the other it opened the way to a Christian interpretive strategy that supported virulent and frequently disastrous forms of anti-Judaism.

APPENDIX

John Knox's Classifications of Material in Marcion and Canonical Luke

The tabulations in chapter 4, pages 87, 116, and 117, are based on those of John Knox, *Marcion and the New Testament* (Chicago: University of Chicago Press, 1942). Because of some variance in classifying material the raw numbers in my chapter 4 are not identical to those of Knox, although the percentage calculations are comparable. For this reason I include here a display of Knox's calculations in tabular form. Knox worked only with verses, not with numbers of words. The design of table 5, below, is the same as that of tables 1–4, in chapter 4. The column headed "Source" represents the issue of parallelism in canonical Luke, i.e., the first group ("synoptic parallels") is composed of material in canonical Luke that appears to have a parallel in either Mark or Matthew or both. The column headed "Class" represents the issue of Marcionite or non-Marcionite use. Material marked "A" is material that seems to have been included in the Gospel of Marcion. Material marked "B" is material that is known not to have been included in the Gospel of Marcion. Material marked "C" is material about which we cannot be certain whether or not it was included in the Gospel of Marcion. In each case the number of verses and the percentage of verses are noted in the third and fourth columns.

TABLE 5: Canonical Luke and Marcion: Verses

Source	Class	# of Verses	% of Verses
Synoptic Parallels	A	419.5	73.7
Synoptic Parallels	B	57.5	10.1
Synoptic Parallels	C	92	16.2
	Total	**569**	**100.0**
Peculiar to Luke	A	262.5	45.3
Peculiar to Luke	B	225.5	38.9
Peculiar to Luke	C	91	15.8
	Total	**579**	**100.0**

The table shows that canonical Luke has 569 verses that have parallels in Matthew or Mark or both and 579 that have no parallels in either of the other two Synoptic

Gospels. Of the verses with parallels 73.7 percent of them probably appeared in the Gospel of Marcion. Of the verses peculiar to Luke only 45.3 percent probably appeared in Marcion. The percentage figures in my chapter 4, table 1, above, are comparable: 71.7 percent of the verses in canonical Luke that have parallels and 40.9 percent of the nonparallel material probably appeared in the Gospel of Marcion. Note also should be taken of the verses in Class B. In Knox's count 10.1 percent of the verses with parallels were omitted in Marcion, while 38.9 percent of the non-parallel materials were so omitted. My figures for these two categories are slightly higher: 12.5 percent and 43 percent, respectively. See table 1, page 87.

ABBREVIATIONS

AB   Anchor Bible
ABD   *Anchor Bible Dictionary*. Edited by D. N. Freedman. 6 vols. New York, 1992.
ACW   Ancient Christian Writers, 1946–
AnBib   Analecta biblica
ANF   *Ante-Nicene Fathers*
BETL   Bibliotheca ephemeridum theologicarum louvaniensium
BibInt   Biblical Interpretation
BJRL   *Bulletin of the John Rylands University Library in Manchester*
BZ   *Biblische Zeitschrift*
BZNW   Beihefte zur Zeitschrift f ür die neuentestamentliche Wissenschaft
CBQ   *Catholic Biblical Quarterly*
EBib   Etudes biblique
ETL   *Ephemerides theologicae lovanienses*
EvT   *Evangelische Theologie*
ExpTim   *Expository Times*
FC   Fathers of the Church. Washington, D.C., 1947–
FF   Foundations and Facets
HibJ   *Hibbert Journal*
HTKNT   Herders theologischer Kommentar zum Neuen Testament
HTB   Histoire du Texte Biblique. Lausanne, 1996–
HTR   *Harvard Theological Review*
ICC   International Critical Commentary
JAOS   *Journal of the American Oriental Society*
JBL   *Journal of Biblical Literature*
JRS   *Journal of Roman Studies*
JSNT   *Journal for the Study of the New Testament*
JSNTSup   Journal for the Study of the New Testament: Supplement Series
JTS   *Journal of Theological Studies*
KEK   Kritisch-exegetischer Kommentar über das Neue Testament (Meyer-Kommentar)
LCC   Library of Christian Classics. Philadelphia, 1953–
LCL   Loeb Classical Library
Neot   *Neotestamentica*
NHS   Nag Hammadi Studies

NICNT	New International Commentary on the New Testament
NIGTC	New International Greek Testament Commentary
NovT	*Novum Testamentum*
NovTSup	Novum Testamentum Supplements
NRSV	New Revised Standard Version Bible
NTS	*New Testament Studies*
OECT	Oxford Early Christian Texts. Edited by H. Chadwick. Oxford, 1970–
OTP	*Old Testament Pseudepigrapha.* Edited by J. H. Charlesworth. 2 vols. New York, 1983
PRSt	*Perspectives in Religious Studies*
RB	*Revue biblique*
SANT	Studien zum Alten und Neuen Testaments
SBL	Society of Biblical Literature
SBLCP	Society of Biblical Literature Centennial Publications
SBLDS	Society of Biblical Literature Dissertation Series
SBLMS	Society of Biblical Literature Monograph Series
SBLSBS	Society of Biblical Literature Sources for Biblical Study
SBLSymS	Society of Biblical Literature Symposium Series
SecCent	*Second Century*
SNTSMS	Society for New Testament Studies Monograph Series
SP	Sacra Pagina
SPCK	Society for the Promotion of Christian Knowledge
ST	*Studia Theologica*
THKNT	Theologischer Handkommentar zum Neuen Testament
TRu	*Theologische Rundschau*
TU	Texte und Untersuchungen
TUGAL	Texte und Untersuchungen zur Geschichte der altchristlichen Literatur
TynBul	*Tyndale Bulletin*
TZ	*Theologische Zeitschrift*
VC	*Vigiliae Christianae*
WC	Westminster Commentaries
WUNT	Wissenschaftliche Untersuchungen zum Neuen Testament
ZNW	*Zeitschrift für die neutestamentliche Wissenschaft und die Kunde der älteren Kirche*
ZTK	*Zeitschrift für Theologie und Kirche*

NOTES

Preface

1. See Richard I. Pervo, *Dating Acts: Between the Evangelists and the Apologists* (Santa Rosa, Calif.: Polebridge Press, 2006).

2. See John Knox, *Marcion and the New Testament: An Essay in the Early History of the Canon* (Chicago: University of Chicago Press, 1942).

3. See Patrick H. Alexander, et al., eds., *The SBL Handbook of Style for Ancient Near Eastern, Biblical, and Early Christian Studies* (Peabody, Mass.: Hendrickson, 1999).

Chapter 1: The Date of Acts

1. John A. T. Robinson, *Redating the New Testament* (Philadelphia: Westminster Press, 1976), 9.

2. Joseph A. Fitzmyer, *The Acts of the Apostles: A New Translation with Introduction and Commentary*, AB 31 (New York: Doubleday, 1998), 54.

3. Fitzmyer, *Acts*, 55.

4. James D. G. Dunn, *The Acts of the Apostles*, Narrative Commentaries (Valley Forge, Pa.: Trinity Press International, 1996), xi.

5. F. Scott Spencer, *Acts* (Sheffield: Sheffield Academic Press, 1997), 16.

6. Ben Witherington III, *The Acts of the Apostles: A Socio-Rhetorical Commentary* (Grand Rapids: Wm. B. Eerdmans, 1998), 62.

7. Jacob Jervell, *Die Apostelgeschichte*, 17th ed., KEK 3 (Göttingen: Vandenhoeck & Ruprecht, 1998), 86.

8. Luke Timothy Johnson, *The Gospel of Luke*, SP 3 (Collegeville, Minn.: Liturgical Press, 1991), 2. See also Johnson, *The Acts of the Apostles*, SP 5 (Collegeville, Minn.: Liturgical Press, 1992), and Johnson, "Luke-Acts, Book of," *ABD*, 6 vols., ed. David N. Freedman (New York: Doubleday, 1992), 4:403–20.

9. C. K. Barrett, *A Critical and Exegetical Commentary on the Acts of the Apostles*, ICC (Edinburgh: T & T Clark, 1998), 2:lxiii.

10. Barrett, *Acts*, 2:xlii.

11. Henry J. Cadbury called attention to this range of dates in "Subsidiary Points," in *The Beginnings of Christianity*, ed. F. J. Foakes Jackson and Kirsopp Lake (London: Macmillan, 1920–1933; reprint, Grand Rapids: Baker Book House, 1979), 2:349–59. Cadbury set the probable limits at 70–115 but was hesitant to determine a more precise date. He commented: "If they [the editors of *Beginnings*] were obliged to choose a more specific

date they would take the last five years of the first century, thus leaving room for the proba- bility that Luke was acquainted with Josephus. Nevertheless, they would conclude by repeating that this view is based on a general balance of probabilities, on which wide differ- ence of opinion is possible and even desirable. Its truth cannot be demonstrated; but neither can that of any other view; the only wise course is, whenever a question is at issue involving the authorship or date of Acts, to leave a wide margin for possible error" (2:359).

12. Baur did not publish a commentary on Acts. His most extensive treatment is in *Paul, the Apostle of Jesus Christ, His Life and Work, His Epistles and His Doctrine: A Con- tribution to a Critical History of Primitive Christianity*, 2 vols., trans. Allan Menzies (Lon- don: Williams & Norgate, 1876). The English is a translation of the second German edition edited by Eduard Zeller, 1866–1867. Other comments are to be found in several of Baur's journal articles.

13. See A. J. Mattill, Jr., "The Purpose of Acts: Schneckenburger Reconsidered," in *Apostolic History and the Gospel: Biblical and Historical Essays Presented to F. F. Bruce on His 60th Birthday,* ed. W. Ward Gasque and Ralph P. Martin (Grand Rapids: Wm. B. Eerdmans, 1970), 108–22. See also Matthias Schneckenburger, *Über den Zweck der Apostel- geschichte* (Bern: Fischer, 1841).

14. A case can be made for the contention that Peter in Acts sounds like Paul. But how does one make the case that Paul is made to sound like Peter? To say that Paul in Acts does not sound like Paul in his own letters is one thing, but to say that Paul in Acts sounds like Peter is quite another. How does Baur know what the historical Peter should sound like, since he is not able to cite anything he has written? To be quite accurate we should say that Luke has made Paul speak and act in ways that Baur conceived to be appropriate for a first- generation Jewish Christian.

15. Baur, *Historisch-Kritische Untersuchungen zum Neuen Testament* (Stuttgart: Friedrich Frommann, 1963), 462. This is a reprint of selected writings by Baur. The quo- tation here is from "Über Zweck und Veranlassung des Römerbriefs und die damit zusammengehängenden der römischen Gemeinde," *Tübinger Zeitschrift für Theologie* 9 (1836): 59–178.

16. Baur, *Paul, the Apostle,* 1:6.

17. Baur, *Paul, the Apostle,* 1:132.

18. Baur, *Paul, the Apostle,* 1:135.

19. Baur, *Kritische Untersuchungen über die kanonischen Evangelien, iIhr Verhältnisz zu einander, ihren Charakter und Ursprung* (Tübingen: L. F. Fues, 1847), 607.

20. See Albrecht Ritschl, *Die Entstehung der altkatholischen Kirche: Eine kirchen- und dogmengeschichtliche Monographie,* 2d ed. (Bonn: Adolph Marcus, 1857).

21. The change in the solution to the Synoptic Problem from the Griesbach to the two-document hypothesis carries with it changes in the dating of the documents. Under the new hypothesis the key will be the date of Mark, with the other gospels following, but the relationship between the two-document hypothesis and the dating of the documents is more complex than one might expect. On the relationship of the Synoptic Problem to New Testament studies generally, see William R. Farmer, *The Synoptic Problem: A Criti- cal Analysis* (New York: Macmillan, 1964).

22. See J. B. Lightfoot, *The Apostolic Fathers,* part 2, 3 vols. (London: Macmillan, 1885).

23. See Adolf von Harnack, *Die Chronologie der Altchristlichen Litteratur bis Eusebius,* 2 vols. (Leipzig: J. C. Hinrichs, 1897).

24. Harnack, *Chronologie,* 1:247.

25. Harnack, *Chronologie,* 1:248.

26. Harnack, *Chronologie,* 1:248.

27. Harnack, *Chronologie,* 1:249.

28. Harnack, *Chronologie,* 1:250. Harnack adds a comment about the date of the composition of the Gospel of Luke: "If the work does come from this time, 93 is also the terminus ad quem for the conception of the Gospel of Luke, and we can date this important piece of gospel literature in c. 78–93 with probability. The chronology of gospel literature is the most difficult and at the same time the most important part of early Christian literature. So it is of the highest value to be able to date a gospel like Luke, which presupposes the Gospel of Mark and speaks expressly of countless other gospel books, to a range of c. 15 years. The gospel itself says nothing about its origin, apart from the unmistakable indications of the destruction of Jerusalem."

29. See Harnack, *Luke the Physician: The Author of the Third Gospel and the Acts of the Apostles,* trans. J. R. Wilkinson, New Testament Studies 1 (London: Williams & Norgate/ New York: G. P. Putnam's, 1908).

30. Harnack, *The Acts of the Apostles,* trans. J. R. Wilkinson, New Testament Studies 3 (London: Williams & Norgate/ New York: G. P. Putnam's, 1909), 293.

31. Harnack, *Acts,* 294.

32. Harnack, *Acts,* 293.

33. Harnack, *Acts,* 297, emphasis in original.

34. See Harnack, *The Date of Acts and of the Synoptic Gospels,* trans. J. R. Wilkinson, New Testament Studies 4 (London: Williams & Norgate/ New York: G. P. Putnam's, 1911).

35. Harnack, *Date of Acts,* 91.

36. Harnack, *Date of Acts,* 96–97.

37. Harnack, *Date of Acts,* 97.

38. Harnack, *Chronologie,* 1:248.

39. See Colin J. Hemer, *The Book of Acts in the Setting of Hellenistic History,* ed. Conrad H. Gempf (Winona Lake, Ind.: Eisenbrauns, 1990).

40. Hemer, *Book of Acts,* 365.

41. Hemer, *Book of Acts,* 384.

42. Hemer, *Book of Acts,* 401.

43. On the significance of rhetorical criticism for the study of early Christian texts, see, for example, Vernon K. Robbins, *The Tapestry of Early Christian Discourse: Rhetoric, Society, and Ideology* (New York: Routledge, 1996); see also Todd Penner and Caroline Vander Stichele, eds., *Contextualizing Acts: Lukan Narrative and Greco-Roman Discourse,* SBLSymS 20 (Atlanta: SBL, 2003).

44. See Ernst Haenchen, *The Acts of the Apostles: A Commentary,* trans. Bernard Noble and Gerald Shinn (Oxford: Basil Blackwell, 1971), 3–14.

45. See Hans Conzelmann, *Acts of the Apostles,* trans. James Limburg, A. Thomas Kraabel, and Donald H. Juel, Hermeneia Commentaries (Philadelphia: Fortress Press, 1987), xxvii–xxxiii.

46. Conzelmann, "Luke's Place in the Development of Early Christianity," in *Studies in Luke-Acts: Essays Presented in Honor of Paul Schubert*, ed. Leander E. Keck and J. Louis Martyn (Nashville and New York: Abingdon Press, 1966), 299. For the texts of the relevant documents see Cadbury, "The Tradition," in *Beginnings of Christianity*, 2:209–64.

47. See Haenchen, *Acts*, 8.

48. Haenchen, *Acts*, 8. On this issue see further Andrew Gregory, *The Reception of Luke and Acts in the Period before Irenaeus: Looking for Luke in the Second Century*, WUNT 2:169 (Tübingen: Mohr Siebeck, 2003), 211–92. Gregory shows that Justin's citations indicate that he had a version of Luke that differed from the canonical edition. See also the section on the date of canonical Luke below, pp. 80–83.

49. See John T. Townsend, "The Date of Luke-Acts," in *Luke-Acts: New Perspectives from the Society of Biblical Literature Seminar*, ed. Charles H. Talbert (New York: Crossroad, 1984), 47–62.

50. Townsend, "Date of Luke-Acts," 47, refers to Tertullian, *Adversus Marcionem*, 4, 42. See Tertullian, *Adversus Marcionem*, 2 vols., ed. and trans. Ernest Evans, OECT (Oxford: Clarendon Press, 1972).

51. Townsend, "Date of Luke-Acts," 48.

52. Townsend, "Date of Luke-Acts," 47. Townsend is concerned about the date of the Gospel of Luke as well as of Acts, but he devotes more attention to the latter. Although it is related to the present discussion, the date of the Gospel of Luke will be treated in greater detail in chapter 4.

53. See Haenchen, *Acts*, 9. Note, however, that stories about the apostles appear as early as Paul's letter to the Galatians. See pp. 50–51, below, for further consideration of Haenchen's view.

54. Robinson, *Redating*, 13.

55. *Sibylline Oracles*, 4:125–27 (*OTP* 1: 387).

56. Robinson, *Redating*, 21.

57. Hans Windisch, "The Case Against the Tradition," in *Beginnings of Christianity*, 2:310.

58. Witherington, *Acts*, 61. See also C. H. Dodd, "The Fall of Jerusalem and the 'Abomination of Desolation,'" *JRS* 37 (1947): 47–54. Dodd believes that the Lukan form of these oracles does not depend on Mark but is directly borrowed from the LXX.

59. See Harnack, *Chronologie*, 1:245–51.

60. *Pace* Robert L. Brawley, *Luke-Acts and the Jews: Conflict, Apology, and Conciliation*, SBLMS 33 (Atlanta: Scholars Press, 1987).

61. Classical scholars have shown that other ancient writings have ambiguous conclusions and that determining the sense of an ending is no easy task. See, e. g., the various essays in Deborah H. Roberts, Francis M. Dunn, and Don Fowler, eds., *Classical Closure: Reading the End in Greek and Latin Literature* (Princeton: Princeton University Press, 1997).

62. See Richard I. Pervo, *Dating Acts: Between the Evangelists and the Apologists* (Santa Rosa, Calif.: Polebridge Press, 2006).

63. Pervo, *Dating Acts*, 151.

64. Pervo, *Dating Acts*, 159.

65. Pervo, *Dating Acts*, 159, emphasis in original.

66. Pervo, *Dating Acts*, 198.

67. See Edgar J. Goodspeed, *An Introduction to the New Testament* (Chicago: University of Chicago Press, 1937). For a critical review of various proposals on the collection of the Pauline letters, see Robert M. Price, "The Evolution of the Pauline Canon," *Hervormde Teologiese Studies* 53 (1997): 36-67. Price concludes, with Walter Bauer and others, that Marcion was the first systematic collector of the Pauline letters.

68. Witherington, *Acts*, 62.

69. See, for example, F. F. Bruce, *The Acts of the Apostles* (Grand Rapids: Wm. B. Eerdmans, 1951). Bruce writes: "Luke may have seen Paul's letters, but if he did, he has successfully concealed all knowledge of them" (p. 9).This is a sentiment with which John Knox would agree, but Knox was able to explain Luke's concealing his knowledge of the letters. See note 70.

70. See John Knox, "Acts and the Pauline Letter Corpus," in *Studies in Luke-Acts*, 279-87.

71. Knox, "Acts and the Pauline Letter Corpus," 284.

72. We shall devote attention to this view of the intent of Acts in chapter 3, below.

73. See John C. O'Neill, *The Theology of Acts in its Historical Setting* (London: SPCK, 1961).

74. O'Neill, *Theology of Acts*, 25.

75. O'Neill, *Theology of Acts*, 26.

76. Baur and his associates had confidently affirmed that Luke was acquainted with some Pauline letters, but this point of view fell out of favor along with the rejection of the Tübingen School.

77. Morton S. Enslin, "'Luke' and Paul," *JAOS* 58 (1938): 84.

78. Enslin, "'Luke' and Paul," 84.

79. More recent text critics lean toward accepting the longer text of Luke 22. Bruce M. Metzger notes the division among critics on these verses but explains that the majority of members of the editorial committee for the third edition of the United Bible Societies New Testament was impressed with "the overwhelming preponderance of external evidence supporting the longer form." Metzger adds: "The similarity between verses 19b–20 [in Luke 22] and 1 Cor 11:24b–25 arises from the familiarity of the evangelist with the liturgical practice among Pauline churches, a circumstance that accounts also for the presence of non-Lukan expressions in verses 19b–20" (Metzger, *A Textual Commentary on the Greek New Testament* [London and New York: United Bible Societies, 1971], 176–77).

80. Enslin, "'Luke' and Paul," 89.

81. Enslin, "Once Again, Luke and Paul," *ZNW* 61 (1970): 253–71.

82. See Knox, "Acts and the Pauline Letter Corpus."

83. Enslin, "Once Again," 271.

84. Enslin, "Once Again," 271.

85. C. K. Barrett, "Acts and the Pauline Corpus," *ExpTim* 88 (1976–1977): 4.

86. See William O. Walker, Jr., "Acts and the Pauline Corpus Reconsidered," *JSNT* 24 (1985): 3–23.

87. Walker, "Acts and the Pauline Corpus," 11.

88. Walker, "Acts and the Pauline Corpus," 17.

89. See Walker, "Acts and the Pauline Corpus Revisited: Peter's Speech at the Jerusalem Conference," in *Literary Studies in Luke-Acts: Essays in Honor of Joseph B. Tyson*, ed.

Richard P. Thompson and Thomas E. Phillips (Macon, Ga.: Mercer University Press, 1998), 77–86.

90. Comparisons with Schneckenburger are inevitable.

91. See Walker, "Acts and the Pauline Corpus Revisited," 80–82.

92. Walker, "Acts and the Pauline Corpus Revisited," 82.

93. See Heikki Leppä, "Luke's Critical Use of Galatians" (Ph. D. diss., University of Helsinki, 2002).

94. Leppä, "Luke's Critical Use," 35.

95. Leppä, "Luke's Critical Use," 45.

96. Leppä, "Luke's Critical Use," 56–57.

97. Leppä, "Luke's Critical Use," 113–14, emphasis in original.

98. See Lars Aejmelaeus, *Die Rezeption der Paulusbriefe in der Miletrede (Apg 20:18–35)* (Helsinki: Suomalainen Tiedeakatemia, 1987).

99. See Michael D. Goulder, "Did Luke Know Any of the Pauline Letters?" *PRSt* 13 (1986): 97–112.

100. See Pervo, *Dating Acts.*

101. Pervo, *Dating Acts,* 54–55.

102. Lightfoot, *St. Paul's Epistle to the Galatians* (London: Macmillan, 1890), 123–24, emphasis in original.

103. Pervo, *Dating Acts,* 90.

104. Pervo, *Dating Acts,* 94.

105. Here again one is reminded of Baur and his insistence on interpreting Acts as a consensus document, intended to make peace between the parties of Peter and Paul.

106. Pervo, *Dating Acts,* 92.

Chapter 2: The Challenge of Marcion and Marcionite Christianity

1. For a reconstruction of the *Antitheses,* see Adolf von Harnack, *Marcion: Das Evangelium vom Fremden Gott: Eine Monographie zur Geschichte der Grundlegung der Katholischen Kirche,* TU 45 (Leipzig: J. C. Hinrichs, 1921), 81–135. To distinguish it from the English translation this volume will hereafter be referred to as Harnack, *Marcion: Das Evangelium.*

2. See below for references to other anti-Marcionite texts.

3. See Tertullian, *Adversus Marcionem,* 2 vols., ed. and trans. Ernest Evans, OECT (Oxford: Clarendon Press, 1972) 1, 1:1.

4. Tertullian, *Adv. Marc.* 1, 1:3.

5. Tertullian, *Adv. Marc.* 1, 1:4.

6. Harnack, *Marcion: The Gospel of the Alien God,* trans. John E. Steely and Lyle D. Bierma (Durham, N. C.: Labyrinth Press, 1990), 18. To distinguish it from the German original, this volume will hereafter be referred to as Harnack, *Marcion: The Gospel.*

7. Walter Bauer, *Orthodoxy and Heresy in Earliest Christianity,* ed. Robert A. Kraft and Gerhard Krodel (Philadelphia: Fortress Press, 1971).

8. John Knox, *Marcion and the New Testament: An Essay in the Early History of the Canon* (Chicago: University of Chicago Press, 1942).

9. R. Joseph Hoffmann, *Marcion: On the Restitution of Christianity: An Essay on the Development of Radical Paulinist Theology in the Second Century,* American Academy of Religion Academy Series 46 (Chico, Calif.: Scholars Press, 1984).

10. Gerhard May and Katharina Greschat, eds., *Marcion und seine kirchengeschicht-liche Wirkung: Vorträge der Internationalen Fachkonferenz zu Marcion, gehalten vom 15.–18. August 2001 in Mainz*, TUGAL 150 (Berlin and New York: Walter de Gruyter, 2002).

11. See May, "Marcion ohne Harnack," in May and Greschat, *Marcion*, 1–7.

12. See Tertullian, *Adv. Marc.* 1, 18:4.

13. See Irenaeus, *Against the Heresies*, (Unger, ACW), 1, 27:2.

14. Tertullian, *Adv. Marc.* 1, 2:3.

15. See Tertullian, *Adv. Marc.* 1, 1:6; 4, 4:3.

16. See Hoffmann, *Marcion*, 39–44. Hoffmann, in turn, draws on Bauer, *Orthodoxy*, who provides greater detail. As Bauer expresses the orthodox concept, "where there is heresy, orthodoxy must have preceded" (p. xxiii).

17. Clement of Alexandria, *Stromateis* 7, 17 (*ANF edition* 2:554–555). The studies of Bauer, in *Orthodoxy*, show clearly that the situation was far more complex than Clement allowed.

18. See Irenaeus, *Heresies* 1, 27:1–2.

19. Tertullian, *Adv. Marc.* 1, 19:3.

20. Harnack, *Marcion: Das Evangelium*, 18*. Ernst Barnikol takes 144 c.e. to be the date of Marcion's death. See Barnikol, *Die Enstehung der Kirche im zweiten Jahrhundert und die Zeit Marcions*, 2d ed., Forschungen zur Enstehung des Urchristentums des Neuen Testaments und der Kirche 8 (Kiel: Walter G. Mühlau, 1933). Here and throughout the asterisk indicates another set of page numbers in the original.

21. Tertullian, *Adv. Marc.* 1, 19:2.

22. Hoffmann, *Marcion*, 70.

23. Clement of Alexandria, *Stromateis* 7, 17 (*ANF* 2:555).

24. Hoffmann, *Marcion*, 67–68.

25. See Harnack, *Marcion: Das Evangelium*, 1*–27*.

26. See Knox, *Marcion*, 12.

27. See Hoffmann, *Marcion*, 74.

28. Justin Martyr, *First Apology* 26 (Hardy, LCC 1:258).

29. See Justin, *First Apology* 58.

30. Hoffmann, *Marcion*, 45.

31. See Justin, *First Apology* 26.

32. There is much to support the contention that the Pastorals are basically antiheretical, perhaps specifically anti-Marcionite texts. See Hoffmann, *Marcion*, 281–305. See also Stephen G. Wilson, *Luke and the Pastoral Epistles* (London: SPCK, 1979). See also Martin Dibelius and Hans Conzelmann, *The Pastoral Epistles*, trans. Philip Buttolph and Adela Yarbro, Hermeneia Commentaries (Philadelphia: Fortress Press, 1972).

33. Hoffmann, *Marcion*, 36.

34. See Hoffmann, *Marcion*, 61.

35. Polycarp, *To the Philippians* 7:1(Lake, LCL).

36. See Harnack, *Marcion: Das Evangelium*, 3* n. 4.

37. See P. N. Harrison, *Polycarp's Two Epistles to the Philippians* (Cambridge: Cambridge University Press, 1936).

38. See Harnack, *Marcion: Das Evangelium*, 3* n. 4.

39. See Irenaeus, *Heresies* 3, 3:4 (*ANF*).

40. Irenaeus, *Heresies* 3, 3:4 (*ANF*).

41. Hoffmann, *Marcion,* 39.

42. Harnack, *Marcion: The Gospel,* 66.

43. Quoted by Harnack, *Marcion: The Gospel,* 59. The quotation comes originally from the fourth-century Syrian writer, Ephrem, *An Exposition of the Gospel,* 1. Ephrem locates the sentence at the beginning of what he calls Marcion's "Proevangelium," apparently indicating the location of the *Antitheses* in Marcion's canon. If authentic, this would constitute the longest surviving sentence composed by Marcion.

44. Harnack, *Marcion: The Gospel,* 21, emphasis in original.

45. Tertullian, *Adv. Marc.* 1, 19:4. Apparently Tertullian refers here to Marcion's *Antitheses.* Cf. Tertullian, *Adv. Marc.* 2, 2:5; 2, 11:1, 3; 2, 12:1; 2, 17:1.

46. The episode is reported in Epiphanius, *Panarion* 42, 2 (Frank Williams, *The Panarion of Epiphanius of Salamis,* NHS 35 [Leiden: Brill, 1987]). If this incident is historical, it is impossible to know what text Marcion would actually have used. Apparently the verses were included in Marcion's gospel, and they are in canonical Luke. But it does not seem likely that the Roman leaders would have acknowledged Marcion's gospel in a debate that involved his orthodoxy, and, in my judgment, canonical Luke is post-Marcionite. The only conclusion seems to be that the text in question here must have come from a gospel known both to Marcion and the Roman leaders. Such a text could have served as a source both for Marcion's gospel and canonical Luke. On this point see below, chapter 4, which treats the relationships between Marcion's gospel and canonical Luke in greater detail.

47. Harnack, speaking for Marcion, wrote: "When he [Jesus] spoke of the two trees, the corrupt and the good, which are able to produce only such fruits as are given by their very nature, he can mean thereby only the two great divine authors, the Old Testament God, who creates nothing but bad and worthless things, and the Father of Jesus Christ, who produces exclusively what is good" (Harnack, *Marcion: The Gospel,* 22).

48. See Tertullian, *Adv. Marc.* 1, 9:2.

49. See Tertullian, *Adv. Marc.* 3, 1:2; 3, 5:1.

50. See Irenaeus, *Heresies* 1, 27:3; 4, 8:1.

51. See, for example, Irenaeus, *Heresies* 4, 34:1

52. Harnack, *Marcion: The Gospel,* 67.

53. See Tertullian, *Adv. Marc.* 2, 21:2; 3, 5:4; 3, 12:1.

54. Tertullian, *Adv. Marc.* 3, 12:1.

55. See Tertullian, *Adv. Marc.* 3, 6:3; 3, 7:1–8; 3, 8:1–2; 3, 21:1.

56. Tertullian, *Adv. Marc.* 3, 21:1.

57. Harnack, *Marcion: The Gospel,* 23.

58. See Tertullian, *Adv. Marc.* 2, 18:1.

59. Tertullian, *Adv. Marc.* 2, 21:1.

60. See Tertullian, *Adv. Marc.* 2, 22:1–4.

61. See Tertullian, *Adv. Marc.* 2, 23:1.

62. See Tertullian, *Adv. Marc.* 2, 24:1–2.

63. See Tertullian, *Adv. Marc.* 2, 25:1, 3.

64. See Irenaeus, *Heresies* 2, 6:1.

65. Irenaeus, *Heresies* 3, 25:3 (*ANF* 1:459).

66. See Tertullian, *Adv. Marc.* 1, 2:1, 3.

67. See Tertullian, *Adv. Marc.* 1, 15:6.

68. Harnack, *Marcion: The Gospel,* 71, emphasis in original.

69. See Tertullian, *Adv. Marc.* 1, 11:8; 1, 24:3, 5, 6; 3, 8:1–2, 5; 3, 11:1, 7–8.

70. See Tertullian, *Adv. Marc.* 3, 11:7–8.

71. See Tertullian, *Adv. Marc.* 3, 11:7–8.

72. Markus Vinzent, "Der Schluss des Lukasevangelium bei Marcion," in May and Greschat, *Marcion,* 86.

73. See Tertullian, *Adv. Marc.* 1, 29:1, 5–6.

74. Alistair Steward-Sykes, "Bread and Fish, Water and Wine: The Marcionite Menu and the Maintenance of Purity," in May and Greschat, *Marcion,* 207-220.

75. Steward-Sykes, "Bread and Fish," 220.

76. Harnack, *Marcion: The Gospel,* 13–14.

77. Knox, *Marcion,* 72.

78. Harnack notes that Gal 2:6–9a is unattested, and he maintains that this section was either missing or greatly altered in Marcion's text. See Harnack, *Marcion: Das Evangelium,* 69*. The language here, which speaks of two gospels, would appear to Marcion to be contradictory to what Paul affirmed in Galatians 1. The phrase in Gal 2:9, which affirms that the Jerusalem leaders "recognized the grace that had been given to me," would suggest the superiority of these leaders to Paul. In this connection it should be noted that William O. Walker, Jr., has recently maintained that Gal 2:7b–8 is a non-Pauline interpolation. See Walker, "Galatians 2:7b–8 as a Non-Pauline Interpolation," *CBQ* 65 (2003): 568–87. See also Barnikol, *Der nichtpaulinische Ursprung des Parallelismus der Apostel Petrus und Paulus (Galater 2. 7–8),* Forschungen zur Enstehung des Urchristentums, des Neuen Testaments und der Kirche 5 (Kiel: Mühlau, 1931).

79. Cited in Knox, *Marcion,* 170.

80. Harnack, *Marcion: The Gospel,* 26.

81. Harnack, *Marcion: The Gospel,* 26.

82. For a reconstruction of Marcion's *Apostolikon,* see Harnack, *Marcion: Das Evangelium,* 65*–124*.

83. See Tertullian, *Adv. Marc.* 4, 2:3.

84. Irenaeus, *Heresies* 1, 27:2 (ACW); see also 3, 11:7; 3, 12:12; 3, 14:4.

85. See Tertullian, *Adv. Marc.* 4, 2:4.

86. Irenaeus, *Heresies* 3, 11:8 (*ANF*).

87. See Bauer, *Orthodoxy,* 194.

88. Andrew Gregory has recently shown that ancient commentators did not follow Irenaeus, Tertullian, and Epiphanius in claiming that Marcion altered the canonical Gospel of Luke. See his *Reception of Luke and Acts in the Period before Irenaeus: Looking for Luke in the Second Century,* WUNT 2:169 (Tübingen: Mohr Siebeck, 2003), 183–92.

89. See Irenaeus, *Heresies* 3, 1:1.

90. On local texts see B. H. Streeter, *The Four Gospels: A Study of Origins* (London: Macmillan, 1924), 27–50. Harnack accepted the contention that Marcion adapted the canonical Gospel of Luke to make his own gospel. But he believed that Luke may have originally been the only gospel available in the Pontic church: "The first Gospel to reach Pontus probably was the Gospel of Luke; Marcion would have been familiar with it before any others, if indeed it was not for some years his only gospel in his Pontic homeland. So he may have clung to the gospel book which he had first come to know" (Harnack, *Marcion: The Gospel,* 29).

91. See Harnack, *Marcion: Das Evangelium*, 165*–221*. These notes appear in one of the several appendixes, which were not included in the English translation of this volume.

92. Epiphanius complained that Marcion "falsifies some things, as I said, he adds others helter-skelter, and he does not go straight on but roams freely all over the material." (*Pan.* 42, 11:6). But in the 78 scholia that follow this comment Epiphanius takes up the various Marcionite "falsifications" in the Lukan order.

93. Paul-Louis Couchoud maintained that there were a few passages in Marcion's gospel that were not in Luke and that Harnack overlooked them. See Couchoud, "Is Marcion's Gospel One of the Synoptics?" *HibJ* 34 (1936): 265–77. For a response to Couchoud, see Alfred Loisy, "Marcion's Gospel: A Reply," *HibJ* 34 (1936): 378-87.

94. See Knox, *Marcion*, 86.

95. See David S. Williams, "Reconsidering Marcion's Gospel," *JBL* 108 (1989): 477–96. See also Gregory, *Reception*, 175–83.

96. Williams, "Reconsidering," 478.

97. Williams, "Reconsidering," 478.

98. Williams, "Reconsidering," 479.

99. Williams, "Reconsidering," 479.

100. Williams, "Reconsidering," 479–80.

101. Williams, "Reconsidering," 480.

102. Williams, "Reconsidering," 480.

103. Epiphanius, *Pan.* 42, 11:6; Scholion 1.

104. Tertullian, *Adv. Marc.* 4, 36:4.

105. Epiphanius, *Pan.* 42, 11:6; Scholion 50.

106. Note that two pericopes are reversed at this point. Canonical Luke has the narrative of Jesus at Nazareth (Luke 4:16–30) followed by Jesus at Capernaum (Luke 4:31–35). The Gospel of Marcion has the Capernaum episode before the Nazareth episode. See further on this issue, pp. 83–85, below.

107. Below, pp. 90–100, I will introduce evidence to show that Luke 1–2 was probably added to an original Lukan text by a post-Marcionite canonical author.

108. In line with the distancing of Jesus from birth and ancestors, Luke 8:19, which calls attention to his mother and brothers, is probably missing from the Gospel of Marcion. Epiphanius, *Pan.* 42, 11:6; Scholion 12, and Tertullian, *Adv. Marc.* 4, 19:6, show that the Gospel of Marcion had some of the pericope in question. In Gos. Mar. 8:20–21 it is simply stated that someone reported to Jesus that his relatives were standing outside, and this provides Jesus with the opportunity to say, "My mother and my brothers are they who hear and do the word of God" (Gos. Mar. 8:21). The newness that is so important in Marcion's theology is strongly supported by a saying of Jesus in Gos. Mar. 5:36–38, which concludes with the words "But new wine is to be put in new skins." Epiphanius, *Pan.* 42, 2, reports that Marcion used these verses as a test case in his confrontation with the leaders of the Roman church. Marcion would understand this to mean that what Jesus revealed cannot be contained within the limits of Judaism. Harnack believed that Luke 5:39 was absent from the Gospel of Marcion. The verse is a statement in praise of old wine, which appears to contradict the preceding verses.

109. Epiphanius, *Pan.* 42, 11:6; Scholion 8.

110. Harnack, *Marcion: Das Evangelium*, 178*.

111. See Harnack, *Marcion: Das Evangelium,* 211*.

112. See Harnack, *Marcion: Das Evangelium,* 202*; Tertullian, *Adv. Marc.* 4, 33:9.

113. Epiphanius, *Pan.* 42, 11:6; Scholion 1. Tertullian, *Adv. Marc.* 4, 9:10, quotes the verse with the reference "to you." Cf. Luke 17:14, which Harnack includes in the Gospel of Marcion.

114. Harnack, *Marcion: Das Evangelium,* 216*, says it is unattested, and Knox, *Marcion,* 86, classifies it as uncertain.

115. See Harnack, *Marcion: Das Evangelium,* 219*–21*.

116. See further on Luke 24:12, below, pp. 103–4.

117. Tertullian, *Adv. Marc.* 4, 43: 7.

118. Knox, *Marcion,* 115.

Chapter 3: A Context for the Composition of Acts

1. John Darr has argued vigorously against attempts to find a single purpose for the composition of Luke-Acts. See Darr, *On Character Building: The Reader and the Rhetoric of Characterization in Luke-Acts,* Literary Currents in Biblical Interpretation (Louisville, Ky.: Westminster/John Knox, 1992).

2. Ernst Haenchen, *The Acts of the Apostles: A Commentary,* trans. Bernard Noble and Gerald Shinn (Oxford: Basil Blackwell, 1971), 9.

3. Haenchen, *Acts,* 9.

4. See Haenchen, *Acts,* 9. Note that the major target of Irenaeus was Marcion. Although he does not say so explicitly, it is probable that Haenchen meant to include Marcion among the Gnostics whom Irenaeus attacked.

5. Haenchen's views about the neglect of Acts in the early second century are echoed by, among others, C. K. Barrett, *A Critical and Exegetical Commentary on the Acts of the Apostles,* 2 vols., ICC (Edinburgh: T & T Clark, 1994, 1998), 1:48. For a critique of Haenchen's contention that there was no interest in stories of the apostles in the late first century, see Jacob Jervell, *Luke and the People of God: A New Look at Luke-Acts* (Minneapolis: Augsburg, 1972), 19–39. The role that Luke-Acts played in the struggle against Marcionite Christianity has recently been highlighted by Christopher Mount, *Pauline Christianity: Luke-Acts and the Legacy of Paul,* NovTSup 104 (Leiden: Brill, 2002).

6. Robert J. Karris, *Luke: Artist and Theologian: Luke's Passion Account as Literature,* Theological Inquiries: Studies in Contemporary Biblical and Theological Problems (New York, Mahwah, N.J., and Toronto: Paulist Press, 1985), 5.

7. Karris, *Luke,* 1.

8. For an identification of the genre of Acts as general history, see Martin Hengel, *Acts and the History of Earliest Christianity,* trans. John Bowden (Philadelphia: Fortress Press, 1979). Jervell, *The Theology of the Acts of the Apostles,* New Testament Theology (Cambridge: Cambridge University Press, 1996), refers to Luke as a pragmatic historian, by which he means a historian who writes to solve specific problems in the church. Gregory E. Sterling, *Historiography and Self-Definition: Josephos, Luke-Acts and Apologetic Historiography,* NovTSup 64 (Leiden: Brill, 1992), argues for apologetic historiography as a generic classification for Luke-Acts that was widely acknowledged in the ancient world. He defines the genre as "*the story of a subgroup of people in an extended prose narrative written by a member of the group who follows the group's own traditions but Hellenizes them in*

an effort to establish the identity of the group within the setting of the larger world" (p. 17, emphasis in original). Daniel Marguerat, *The First Christian Historian: Writing the "Acts of the Apostles,"* SNTSMS 121 (Cambridge: Cambridge University Press, 2002), takes a similar approach but, drawing on Paul Ricoeur, prefers to designate Acts as "poetic history." See also Loveday Alexander, *The Preface to Luke's Gospel: Literary Convention and Social Context in Luke 1.1–4 and Acts 1.1*, SNTSMS 78 (Cambridge: Cambridge University Press, 1993), who regards the prefaces to Luke and Acts as standing within the scientific tradition.

9. See Richard I. Pervo, *Profit with Delight: The Literary Genre of the Acts of the Apostles* (Philadelphia: Fortress Press, 1987).

10. The issue of the genre of Luke-Acts will receive more extensive attention in our consideration of the preface to Luke, below, pp. 109–16.

11. In most cases determinations of genre and of intended readers are complementary. A political apology, for example, would likely be directed to Roman officials. An author intending to write an apologetic history would likely have in mind a mixed audience (see Sterling, *Historiography*, 374–78). In a previous study of Luke-Acts I tentatively designated the implied reader as one similar to a "God-fearer." See my *Images of Judaism in Luke-Acts* (Columbia: University of South Carolina Press, 1992), 19–41.

12. See Gerhard Lohfink, *Die Sammlung Israels: Eine Untersuchung zur lukanischen Ekklesiologie*, SANT 39 (Munich: Kösel, 1975), 55. Lohfink adds that Acts 5:42 is the end of any positive treatment of the people of Israel.

13. Barrett, *Acts,* 2:li.

14. Henry J. Cadbury, "The Summaries in Acts," in *The Beginnings of Christianity,* 5 vols. ed. F. J. Foakes Jackson and Kirsopp Lake (London: Macmillan, 1920–1933; reprint, Grand Rapids: Baker Book House, 1979), 5:401.

15. Cadbury, "Summaries," 5:396.

16. A strictly narratological approach would distinguish between the implied author of a text and the "flesh and blood" author. The implied author is the *persona* that the real author uses in the act of composition and so is the only author who might be revealed in the text. See, among others, Wayne Booth, *The Rhetoric of Fiction,* 2d ed. (Chicago: University of Chicago Press, 1983); John M. Ellis, *The Theory of Literary Criticism* (Berkeley: University of California Press, 1974); Wolfgang Iser, *The Implied Reader: Patterns of Communication in Prose Fiction from Bunyan to Beckett* (Baltimore: Johns Hopkins University Press, 1974). Since these approaches have been derived from the study of eighteenth- to twentieth-century fiction, their appropriateness for ancient potentially nonfiction compositions is questionable. In what follows the distinction between real author and implied author will play little role since our object is not to write a biography of the author but to determine the context of the composition.

17. For an exploration of this pattern see my "Acts 6:1–7 and Dietary Regulations in Early Christianity," *PRSt* 10 (1983): 145–61. C. K. Barrett, *Acts,* 2:xxxvi, recognizes this pattern, which he sees best exemplified in Acts 15. He writes: "It is one of Luke's ways of expressing the victory of the Gospel. A difficulty arises; it is addressed by the Christian community; a solution is found which not merely solves the difficulty but leads to a further expansion of the Christian movement. Acts 15 provides a crucial example of this pattern which may be said without exaggeration to constitute the pattern of the whole book."

18. The story of Cornelius is preceded in Acts by the story of the Ethiopian eunuch (Acts 8:26–40), and we are not told explicitly if this convert is Jewish or Gentile. He is identified as "a court official of the Candace, queen of the Ethiopians, in charge of her entire treasury" (Acts 8:27). But he has come to worship in Jerusalem and is reading from the Hebrew Scriptures; that is, he is engaging in activities that the narrative generally associates with Jews. In addition the narrative structure of Acts requires that no Gentile precede Cornelius into Christian faith. Haenchen, *Acts*, p. 315, regards the story of the eunuch as originally an account from the Hellenists of "the first conversion of a Gentile." But he insists that Luke cannot present the eunuch as a Gentile. "Otherwise Philip would have forestalled Peter, the legitimate founder of the Gentile mission! For that reason Luke leaves the eunuch's status in a doubtful light. . . . And so it remains uncertain what the eunuch really is; but it is precisely this screen of secrecy about his person which is best suited to the stage now reached in the history of the mission. Without permitting the emergence of all the problems which an explicit baptism of a Gentile must bring in its wake, Luke here leaves the reader with the feeling that with this new convert the mission has taken a step beyond the conversion of Jews and Samaritans" (Haenchen, *Acts*, 314). Robert C. Tannehill, *The Narrative Unity of Luke-Acts: A Literary Interpretation*, 2 vols., FF (Minneapolis: Fortress Press, 1986, 1990), 2:102–112, argues that in its context in Acts the eunuch is a Gentile, but he must then deal with the fact that the episode has no consequences in the narratives that follow. He thus refers to it as a private event.

19. For studies of rhetorical devices in Acts, see Todd Penner and Caroline Vander Stichele, eds., *Contextualizing Acts: Lukan Narrative and Greco-Roman Discourse*, SBLSymS 20 (Atlanta: SBL, 2003).

20. This suggestion was made over a century ago by R. B. Rackham, *The Acts of the Apostles*, WC (London: Methuen, 1901), xlviii.

21. For evidence that the author of Acts had access to Galatians, see pp. 15–22, above.

22. *1 Clem.* 5:4 (Lake, LCL).

23. See comments by Bruce M. Metzger, *A Textual Commentary on the Greek New Testament* (London and New York: United Bible Societies, 1971), 184, and especially the general discussion of "Western non-Interpolations," 191–93. See pp. 103–4, below, for a more extensive treatment of this verse.

24. Andrew C. Clark, *Parallel Lives: The Relation of Paul to the Apostles in the Lucan Perspective* (Carlisle, U.K.: Paternoster Press, 2001), 209.

25. See, for example, Charles H. Talbert, *Literary Patterns, Theological Themes and the Genre of Luke-Acts*, SBLMS 20 (Missoula, Mont.: Scholars Press, 1974), who treats parallelism as fundamental to the entire structure of Luke-Acts.

26. See Matthias Schneckenberger, *Über den Zweck der Apostelgeschichte* (Bern: Fischer, 1841).

27. See Clark, *Parallel Lives*.

28. Clark, *Parallel Lives*, 92–93.

29. Clark, *Parallel Lives*, 100.

30. Clark also deals with other characters in Acts, notably Stephen, Philip, and Barnabas.

31. Clark, *Parallel Lives*, 325.

32. For further discussion of Baur's views, see pp. 3–6, above.

33. For further discussion of Harnack's views, see pp. 6–9, above.

34. Adolf von Harnack, *Luke the Physician: The Author of the Third Gospel and the Acts of the Apostles,* trans. J. R. Wilkinson, New Testament Studies 1 (London: Williams & Norgate/ New York: G. P. Putnam's, 1908), 126–27.

35. Harnack, *The Date of Acts and of the Synoptic Gospels,* trans. J. R. Wilkinson, New Testament Studies 4 (London: Williams & Norgate/ New York: G. P. Putnam's, 1911), 43.

36. Harnack, *Date of Acts,* 49.

37. Harnack, *Date of Acts,* 60–61, emphasis in original.

38. *EvT* 10 (1950–51): 1–15. Translated as "On the 'Paulinism' of Acts," in *Studies in Luke-Acts: Essays Presented in Honor of Paul Schubert,* ed. Leander E. Keck and J. Louis Martyn, trans. William C. Robinson, Jr., and Victor P. Furnish (Nashville and New York: Abingdon Press, 1966), 33–50. References below are to the English translation.

39. Vielhauer, "Paulinism," 44.

40. Vielhauer, "Paulinism," 45.

41. Vielhauer, "Paulinism," 45.

42. Vielhauer, "Paulinism," 45.

43. Vielhauer, "Paulinism," 38.

44. The NRSV translation conceals the fact that Luke here uses a favorite Pauline term, δικαιόω. The Greek of Acts 13:38–39 reads γνωστὸν οὖν ἔστω ὑμῖν, ἄνδρες ἀδελφοί, ὅτι διὰ τούτου ὑμῖν ἄφεσις ἁμρτιῶν καταγγέλλεται, [καὶ] ἀπὸ πάντων ὧν οὐκ ἠδυνήθητε ἐν νόμῳ Μωϋσέως δικαιωθῆναι, ἐν τούτῳ πᾶς ὁ πιστεύων δικαιοῦται. The New King James translation makes the meaning clearer: "Therefore let it be known to you, brethren, that through this Man is preached to you the forgiveness of sins; and by Him everyone who believes is justified from all things from which you could not be justified by the law of Moses." Even if Luke uses a term we tend to identify with the Pauline letters, he seems to equate forgiveness and justification in a way that is not characteristic of Paul.

45. Haenchen, *Acts,* 112, emphasis in original.

46. Haenchen, *Acts,* 113.

47. Haenchen, *Acts,* 113.

48. Haenchen, *Acts,* 115.

49. Jervell, *The Unknown Paul: Essays on Luke-Acts and Early Christian History* (Minneapolis: Augsburg, 1984), 90.

50. Jervell, *Unknown Paul,* 70.

51. Jervell, *Unknown Paul,* 67.

52. Jervell, *Unknown Paul,* 75.

53. Stanley E. Porter, *The Paul of Acts,* WUNT 115 (Tübingen: Mohr Siebeck, 1999).

54. See below, pp. 70–72, for a fuller discussion of Acts 14:4, 14.

55. Porter, *Paul of Acts,* 199. Note, however, that the references to Paul's disobeying the law and instructing others to do so are regarded as false charges.

56. Porter, *Paul of Acts,* 205–6. On this topic see also Colin J. Hemer, *The Book of Acts in the Setting of Hellenistic History,* ed. Conrad H. Gempf (Winona Lake, Ind.: Eisenbrauns, 1990). In support of finding harmony between Acts and the Pauline letters is Hengel, *Acts and the History.* See also Luke Timothy Johnson, *The Acts of the Apostles,* SP 5 (Collegeville, Minn.: Liturgical Press, 1992). Johnson writes: "When Paul's movements in

Acts are compared to those reported in his letters, furthermore, it appears that despite his selection and shaping of materials, Luke provides a reliable if partial framework for reconstructing that portion of Paul's career. Indeed, Acts is indispensable for any attempt at such reconstruction. Where we can check him on details, Luke's factual accuracy in the latter part of Acts is impressive" (p. 5). Hemer, Hengel, and Johnson stress the historical and biographical details more than the theological.

57. See especially E. P. Sanders, *Paul and Palestinian Judaism: A Comparison of Patterns of Religion* (Philadelphia: Fortress Press, 1977).

58. See Mark D. Nanos, *The Irony of Galatians: Paul's Letter in First-Century Context* (Minneapolis: Fortress Press, 2002). See also Nanos, ed., *The Galatians Debate: Contemporary Issues in Rhetorical and Historical Interpretation* (Peabody, Mass.: Hendrickson, 2002).

59. Nanos, *Irony*, 3.

60. Marguerat, *The First Christian Historian*, has clearly perceived this issue. In reference to Vielhauer, Marguerat writes: "This view (which is correct) of the theological difference between the Paul of the epistles and the Paul of Acts must today be replaced in a historical paradigm which takes account of the reception of the Pauline tradition and the school phenomenon. In other words, we should stop repeating that Luke was a (bad) student of the apostle to the Gentiles and ask why and how the missionary figure of Paul was received along a narrative trajectory (Luke-Acts, *The Acts of Paul and Thecla*), while the pastoral and institutional dimension was retained in a discursive trajectory (deutero-Pauline epistles; the Pastoral Epistles; *Correspondence of Paul and Seneca*)" (p. 62 n. 46).

61. See p. 65, above.

62. It may be reasonably objected that the use of the terms *Judaism* and *Christianity* is anachronistic when dealing with the time of Paul. But in the second century the terms are appropriate to use, and the author of Acts is certainly familiar with the term *Christian* in the singular (Acts 26:28) and the plural (Acts 11:26).

63. These verses link with the pericope in Luke 6:12–16, in which Jesus himself chooses twelve of his disciples and grants them the title *apostle*. As if to remove any doubt the names of the apostles are given in both Luke 6:14–16 and Acts 1:13. The lists are identical except for slight changes in the order and for the omission of Judas Iscariot in the Acts list. One might object that even those listed in Luke 6 and Acts 1 did not meet the requirements set out in Acts 1:21–22, since none of them were present at Jesus' baptism, which is recounted in Luke 3:21–22. But in the face of the lists of named apostles in Luke and Acts, the objection seems trivial.

64. For a discussion of the textual problems see Günter Klein, *Die Zwölf Apostel: Ursprung und Gehalt einer Idee* (Göttingen: Vandenhoeck & Ruprecht, 1961), 212–13; see also Metzger, *Textual Commentary*, 423–24.

65. The translation in NRSV masks the problem at this point by including names, Paul and Barnabas, that are not present in the Greek.

66. For a helpful discussion of these verses, together with a summary of critical opinions about them, see Clark, *Parallel Lives*, 136–49.

67. See Klein, *Zwölf Apostel*, 212.

68. See Clark, *Parallel Lives*, 136–49.

69. Barrett's comment at this point is germane: "The drift of the section as a whole, especially when it is viewed in the setting provided for it by Luke, is that the event marks

a notable step in the extension of the Gospel to the world outside Judaism. . . . Yet within the narrative, Luke goes out of his way to show how close Cornelius was to Judaism" (Barrett, *Acts,* 1:493).

70. The contrast between the vision and its interpretation presents critics with a number of thorny issues. Martin Dibelius, *Studies in the Acts of the Apostles,* ed. Heinrich Greeven, trans. Mary Ling (New York: Charles Scribner's Sons, 1956), 109–22, concluded that Luke had access to a traditional conversion story similar to that of the Ethiopian and that he altered it so that it would serve as a precedent to be invoked in Acts 15. Dibelius's position is supported by Gerd Lüdemann, *Early Christianity According to the Traditions in Acts: A Commentary,* trans. John Bowden (Minneapolis: Fortress Press, 1989), 124–33, and by Jervell, *Die Apostelgeschichte,* 17th ed., KEK 3 (Göttingen: Vandenhoeck & Ruprecht, 1998), 299–320. See also Lüdemann, *The Acts of the Apostles: What Really Happened in the Earliest Days of the Church* (Amherst, N. Y.: Promethus Books, 2005), 138-49. François Bovon, "Tradition et redaction en Actes 10,1–11, 18," *TZ* 36 (1970): 22–45, has a similar approach. He concludes that "tradition gives a literal sense to the vision, redaction a figurative sense" (p. 34). Haenchen, however, rejects Dibelius's views on the grounds that such stories were inappropriate for Christians under the influence of their eschatological convictions. See Haenchen, *Acts,* 343–63. For a compelling critique of Dibelius see Klaus Haacker, "Dibelius und Cornelius: Ein Beispiel formgeschichtlicher Überlieferungskritik," *BZ* 24 (1980): 234–51. See also my "Gentile Mission and the Authority of Scripture in Acts," *NTS* 33 (1987): 619–31.

71. Note, however, that the terminal point in Acts 1 is the ascension, whereas in Acts 10 it is the resurrection appearances.

72. See pp. 15–22, above.

73. Dibelius, *Studies in Acts,* 93–101, regarded Acts 15 as literary theology rather than history. He noted that the reference to Cornelius in Acts 15 would have meaning only for readers of Acts and would not have stood independently of the story in Acts 10–11. Dibelius did, however, believe that the decree was not part of Luke's invention; Luke drew on a source for the four requirements, but it was a source that did not go back to the time of Paul and Peter. Philip F. Esler, *Community and Gospel in Luke-Acts: The Social and Political Motivations of Lucan Theology,* SNTSMS 57 (Cambridge: Cambridge University Press, 1987), 107, recognizes the contribution of Luke: "The particular method employed by Luke to legitimate Jewish-Gentile table-fellowship against the background of persistent opposition from the Jerusalem church in the period before the events of 67–70 C.E. is both simple and yet thoroughly audacious—he re-writes the history of early Christianity relating to this subject and assigns to Peter, James and the church in Jerusalem exactly the opposite roles to those which they played in fact."

74. Dibelius, in *Studies in Acts,* regards Paul's claims at his trials as part of Luke's political apologetic. "These themes are intended to emphasise the fact that Christians have not rebelled against the emperor, nor against the temple, nor against the law, but that the essential matter of dispute between them and the Jews is the question of the resurrection" (p. 213). Darr, in *Character Building,* recommends that we should not take Paul's claims at these points seriously. "Given Paul's desperate situation, the reader will take these words about his membership in the Pharisaic party with a grain of salt. In any event, the emphasis of Paul's claim seems to fall on his affiliation through heritage ('a son of Pharisees'), not on

the status of his present membership" (p. 213). Tannehill, in *Narrative Unity,* argues that Luke intends to present Paul "as a resourceful witness from whom other missionaries can learn" (2:290). As such, later Christians can learn how to address Jews. Tannehill adds: "This view does imply that there is a continuing concern in Acts with a mission to Jews, even though relations have been poisoned by controversy" (2:290).

75. In chapter 1 we noted the probable confusion of Timothy with Titus, who accompanied Paul at the meeting in Jerusalem described in Galatians 2, at which Paul stated that Titus, a Greek, was not compelled to be circumcised (Gal 2:3). See p. 21–22, above.

76. On the appropriateness of James's advice to Paul, see Jacob Neusner, "Vow-Taking, the Nazirites, and the Law: Does James' Advice to Paul Accord with Halakhah?" in *James the Just and Christian Origins,* ed. Bruce Chilton and Craig Evans (Leiden: Brill, 1999), 59–82.

77. 1 Cor 16:8 shows that Paul continued to think in terms of the Jewish calendar.

78. See John Knox, *Marcion and the New Testament: An Essay in the Early History of the Canon* (Chicago: University of Chicago Press, 1942).

79. Knox, *Marcion,* 115.

80. Knox, *Marcion,* 115.

81. Knox, *Marcion,* 117.

82. Knox, *Marcion,* 119.

83. See Knox, *Marcion,* 120.

Chapter 4: The Composition of Canonical Luke

1. See Irenaeus, *Against the Heresies* 3, 1:1; 14:2–3.

2. For text see Henry Bettenson, ed., *Documents of the Christian Church, 3rd* ed. edited by Chris Maunder (Oxford: Oxford University Press, 1999).

3. See Henry J. Cadbury, *The Making of Luke-Acts,* 2d ed. (London: SPCK, 1958), 11.

4. I do not here consider the Proto-Luke hypothesis, which is treated below.

5. Arthur J. Bellinzoni notes that another complicating factor results from the fact that the church fathers paid little attention to quoting texts accurately. He writes: "The second-century Christian writings that reflect knowledge and use of Luke freely adapted the gospel and made significant alterations and modifications, sometimes harmonizing Luke with Matthew or otherwise radically modifying the text of the gospel. There is nothing in the literature before Irenaeus to suggest that church fathers in the second century felt obliged to preserve the Gospel of Luke in its original form" ("The Gospel of Luke in the Second Century CE," in *Literary Studies in Luke-Acts: Essays in Honor of Joseph B. Tyson,* ed. Richard P. Thompson and Thomas E. Phillips [Macon, Ga.: Mercer University Press, 1998]), 75.

6. See pp. 10–11, above.

7. Martin Hengel, *The Four Gospels and the One Gospel of Jesus Christ: An Investigation of the Collection and Origin of the Canonical Gospels* (Harrisburg: Trinity Press International, 2000).

8. *2 Clem.* 8:5 (*ANF* 10:253).

9. Hengel, *The Four Gospels,* 63. But see, for example, Robert M. Grant, "Clement, Second Epistle of," *ABD,* 6 vols., ed. David N. Freedman (New York: Doubleday, 1992), 1:1061. It should also be noted that Luke 16:10 was probably in the version of Luke that

Marcion had, and so it is not necessary to claim that the author of *2 Clement* knew canonical Luke.

10. Hengel, *The Four Gospels*, 57–58.

11. Winrich Alfried Löhr, *Basilides und seine Schule: Eine Studie zur Theologie- und Kirchengeschichte des zweiten Jahrhunderts* (Tübingen: J. C. B. Mohr [Paul Siebeck], 1996).

12. Clement of Alexandria, *Stromateis* 1, 145:6–146:4 (*ANF* 2:333).

13. Clement also, in the same chapter of the *Stromateis*, accepted the same conclusion, based on Luke 4:19 (see *ANF* 2:333).

14. Löhr, *Basilides*, 48.

15. Löhr, *Basilides*, 219.

16. See Hegemonius, *Acta Archelai*, 41 (*ANF* 6:216). Unfortunately the divisions observed in *ANF* do not correspond to those used by Löhr.

17. Hegemonius, *Archelai*, 55 (*ANF* 6:233).

18. S. D. F. Salmond, *ANF* 6:233 n. 5.

19. Löhr, *Basilides*, 329.

20. Hengel, *The Four Gospels*, 57.

21. See Andrew Gregory, *The Reception of Luke and Acts in the Period before Irenaeus: Looking for Luke in the Second Century*, WUNT 2:169 (Tübingen: Mohr Siebeck, 2003).

22. See Gregory, *Reception of Luke*, 70–74; See also William R. Schoedel, *Ignatius of Antioch: A Commentary on the Letters of Ignatius of Antioch*, ed. Helmut Koester, Hermeneia Commentaries (Philadelphia: Fortress Press, 1985), 9; 225–29.

23. Gregory, *Reception of Luke*, 210.

24. Gregory, *Reception of Luke*, 190. The reference is to Irenaeus, *Heresies* 1, 27:3.

25. This conclusion is supported by John T. Townsend, who writes: "The earlier writer most likely to have used Luke-Acts is Justin Martyr, and the possible citation of Luke-Acts is in *Dial.* 105. There Justin cites words of Jesus from the cross that appear in no gospel except Luke (23:46)" ("The Date of Luke-Acts," in *Luke-Acts: New Perspectives from the Society of Biblical Literature Seminar*, ed. Charles H. Talbert [New York: Crossroad, 1984], 47). Even this quotation from Justin, like the alleged Basilidean uses of Luke 3:1; 16:19–31, may have come from the pre-Marcionite edition of Luke rather than the canonical version. See also Barbara Shellard, *New Light on Luke: Its Purpose, Sources and Literary Context*, JSNTSup 215 (Sheffield: Sheffield Academic Press, 2002). Shellard dates Luke-Acts ca. 100 C.E., basing this date partially on her conviction that the author of canonical Luke made use of Matthew, Mark, and John.

26. See Albrecht Ritschl, *Das Evangelium Marcions und das kanonische Evangelium des Lukas* (Tübingen: Osiander, 1846).

27. See Ferdinand Christian Baur, *Kritische Untersuchungen über die kanonischen Evangelien, ihr Verhältnisz zu einander, ihren Charakter und Ursprung* (Tübingen: L. F. Fues, 1847), 391–531. By 1851 Ritschl was convinced that he had erred in maintaining that canonical Luke was based on the Marcionite gospel, and he retracted his earlier views. See Ritschl, "Über den gegenwärtigen Stand der Kritik der synoptischen Evangelien," *Theologische Jahrbücher* 10 (1851):480–538.

28. Note that Baur made use of the Griesbach hypothesis, the prevailing theory of synoptic relations in his time. In this hypothesis Luke used Matthew as his main source, adding to it material available only to him.

29. Baur, *Kritische Untersuchungen,* 505.

30. See Adolf von Harnack, *Marcion: Das Evangelium vom Fremden Gott: Eine Monographie zur Geschichte der Grundlegung der Katholischen Kirche,* TU 45 (Leipzig: J. C. Hinrichs, 1921), 165*–168*.

31. See Adolf Hilgenfeld, *Kritische Untersuchungen über die Evangelien Justin's, der clementinischen Homilien und Marcion's* (Halle: Schwentschke & Sohn, 1850); Gustav Volckmar, "Über das Lukas-Evangelium nach seinem Verhältniss zu Marcion und seinem dogmatischen Character, mit besonderer Beziehung auf die kritischen Untersuchungen F. Ch. Baur's und A. Ritschl's," *Theologische Jahrbücher* 9 (1850): 110–38; 185–235.

32. See Volckmar, "Über das Lukas-Evangelium," 234.

33. See Volckmar, "Über das Lukas-Evangelium," 116–18.

34. John Knox, *Marcion and the New Testament: An Essay in the Early History of the Canon* (Chicago: University of Chicago Press, 1942), 81.

35. Knox, *Marcion,* 110. Note that long before Knox published this book, the two-document hypothesis had become the accepted solution to the Synoptic Problem.

36. Knox, *Marcion,* 110. The traditional view is, however, subject to challenge. It is likely that the source of the Marcionite gospel was the gospel that was in use in Pontus at the time and thus the only gospel that Marcion and his followers knew.

37. On the basis of the Griesbach hypothesis, one could make a similar claim. "Original Luke" used Matthew as the main source, and "canonical Luke" added to it materials from the Lukan Sondergut.

38. For a listing of passages in each category, see Knox, *Marcion,* 86. For the most part those pericopes in Knox's category C are designated by Harnack as *unbezeugt,* undocumented —that is, Harnack was not aware of a reference one way or the other regarding these sections.

39. See John C. Hawkins, *Horae Synopticae: Contributions to the Study of the Synoptic Problem,* 2d ed. (Oxford: Clarendon Press, 1909).

40. See Lloyd Gaston, *Horae Synopticae Electronicae: Word Statistics of the Synoptic Gospels,* SBLSBS 3 (Missoula, Mont.: SBL, 1973); Joseph B. Tyson and Thomas R. W. Longstaff, *Synoptic Abstract,* Computer Bible 15 (Wooster, Ohio: Biblical Research Associates, 1978).

41. See Tyson and Longstaff, *Synoptic Abstract;* Harnack, *Marcion: Das Evangelium.*

42. To compare my results with those of Knox, see the appendix.

43. It may be objected that, since we do not know what words were actually used in the Gospel of Marcion, it is inappropriate to make verbal comparisons. The objection would be valid if we were actually comparing Marcion and Luke word for word. Here, however, only the number of words is at stake, and these numbers are used only to provide approximate statistical comparisons. The same objection could be made to comparisons of verses, but in both cases our goal is to gain some sense of how the two gospels might be compared. The tables do not intend to imply anything about the actual verses or words that might have been included in the Gospel of Marcion.

44. Knox also included figures for the uncertain (class C) material by estimating that it would divide up in the same proportions as the other classes and concluded that "79.5 per cent of all the verses known to have been missing from Marcion would be verses peculiar to Luke; and, of all the verses of Luke peculiar to Luke, no less than 46.3 per cent would be missing from Marcion, whereas, of the common material of Luke, only 12 per

cent of the verses would be missing" (Knox, *Marcion*, 109). Knox's figure of 79.5 percent was arrived at by dividing the number of Lukan Sondergut verses not included in Marcion's gospel by the total number of Lukan verses not so included. I have left the uncertain (class C) material out of consideration and so would calculate that about 68–70 percent of the material missing from Marcion was from the Lukan Sondergut. In other respects my figures and Knox's are close, despite different judgments about parallelism.

45. Knox, *Marcion*, 109–110. Leland E. Wilshire, "Was Canonical Luke Written in the Second Century?—A Continuing Discussion," *NTS* 20 (1974): 246–53, raised serious questions about Knox's contentions. Assuming that Marcion's gospel drew on the three Synoptic Gospels, Wilshire noted that it was heavily influenced by synoptic parallels. As we have seen, there is no reason to suppose that Marcion knew more than one gospel. On the issue of Lukan Sondergut material in Marcion, he wrote: "Out of 718 verses that are found in Marcion (using Knox's analysis), 228 are verses peculiar to Luke. That is, 31.4 per cent of the verses in Marcion are verses peculiar to Luke. This is an exceedingly high percentage if those verses characteristic of Luke were written after Marcion" (Wilshire, "Canonical Luke," 250). This was not, however, Knox's point. Rather, Knox was comparing the number of Lukan Sondergut verses presumed to have been used by Marcion with the number not so used. Whether the number used by Marcion is a high proportion of the total number in his gospel is a different issue. Further, Knox never claimed that all of the Lukan Sondergut material was added after Marcion. On this issue see below, pp. 90–116.

46. See Knox, *Marcion*, 110.

47. See Volckmar, "Über das Lukas-Evangelium," 207, who regarded this objection as definitive.

48. Baur noted that the parable admirably fits the conditions of Paul's letter to the Romans, in which the jealousy of Jewish Christians is contrasted with the joy of receiving Gentile Christians. According to Baur, the parable cannot be about Jews and Christians, groups that are usually characterized by unbelief and belief respectively. It is about Jewish Christians and Gentile Christians, as portrayed in Paul's letter to the Romans. Baur believed that Marcion did not know this parable but that it was added by the canonical author of Luke, who understood it as relating to party struggles in the later church, that is, after the times of Paul and Peter. Baur commented: "Who does not see here the behavior, known from Romans, of Jewish Christians against Gentile Christians and Pauline Christianity?" (Baur, *Kritische Untersuchungen*, 510). Similar concerns may be addressed to the alleged Marcionite omission of the parable of the Good Samaritan, Luke 10:29–37, which does not appear to be incompatible with what we know of Marcionite theology. This parable is in group C of Knox's classifications and designated as *unbezeugt* by Harnack. However, Marcion apparently included the parable of the Pharisee and the publican, Luke 18:9–14. For a discussion of the parable of the Good Samaritan, see Riemer Roukema, "The Good Samaritan in Ancient Christianity," *VC* 58 (2004): 56–74. Roukema cites a seventh-century Syriac manuscript that appears to quote Marcion as saying, "Our Lord was not born from a woman, but stole the domain of the Creator and came down and appeared for the first time between Jerusalem and Jericho, like a human being in form and image and likeness, but without our body" (p. 57). The quotation would suggest that Marcion knew the parable of the Good Samaritan, but Roukema doubts the authenticity of the statement largely on the grounds that Marcion did not like

allegories, such as this saying which equates the Samaritan with Jesus. Thus Roukema doubts that Marcion knew the parable of the Good Samaritan.

49. See Tertullian, *Adversus Marcionem* 4, 43:7, and his explanation of Marcion's inclusion of a variant of Luke 24:39. Alfred Plummer, who was convinced that Marcion made use of canonical Luke, noted that it is easy to see why he omitted most things. But then he wrote: "It is less easy to see Marcion's objection to the Prodigal Son (xv. 11–32) and the massacre of Galileans, etc. (xiii. 1–9); but our knowledge of his strange tenets is imperfect, and these passages probably conflicted with some of them" (*A Critical and Exegetical Commentary on the Gospel According to S. Luke,* 5th ed., ICC [Edinburgh: T & T Clark, 1922], lxix). His comment sounds like a counsel of despair.

50. The material in Luke 1–2, 24 constitutes about 15 percent of canonical Luke in terms of word count and about 16 percent in terms of the number of verses.

51. Luke 1:5–2:52 constitutes about 57 percent of the verses, and 63 percent of the words not present in Marcion's gospel but in Luke's Sondergut.

52. Our ancient authorities are unanimous in claiming that Marcion's gospel omitted this material and began with what is now Luke 3:1. For a discussion of the witnesses, see Harnack, *Marcion: Das Evangelium,* 166*–67*.

53. Knox, *Marcion,* 87.

54. The reference to a census under Augustus and Quirinius in Luke 2:1–2 may have been derived from Josephus. If so it would serve as an additional indication of a late date for the infancy narratives. See p. 15, above, where the connection of the census of 6 C.E. with Josephus is discussed.

55. Raymond E. Brown, *The Birth of the Messiah: A Commentary on the Infancy Narratives in Matthew and Luke* (Garden City, N.Y.: Doubleday, 1977), 240. Note that Brown thought that the same author wrote both parts.

56. Joseph A. Fitzmyer, *The Gospel According to Luke (I–IX): Introduction, Translation, and Notes,* AB 28 (Garden City, N.Y.: Doubleday, 1981), 310.

57. See, for example, B. H. Streeter, *The Four Gospels: A Study of Origins* (London: Macmillan, 1924); Vincent Taylor, *Behind the Third Gospel: A Study of the Proto-Luke Hypothesis* (Oxford: Clarendon Press, 1926).

58. See Streeter, *Four Gospels,* 208.

59. See his *Behind the Third Gospel;* also Taylor's "Is the Proto-Luke Hypothesis Sound?" *JTS* 29 (1927–1928): 147–55.

60. See Taylor, *Behind the Third Gospel,* 164–66.

61. Thomas L. Brodie has continued advocating the cause of Proto-Luke, but he regards Luke 1:1–4:22a as a literary unity. See Brodie, "A New Temple and a New Law: The Unity and Chronicler-based Nature of Luke 1:1–4:22a," *JSNT* 5 (1979): 21–45; also Brodie, "The Unity of Proto-Luke," in *The Unity of Luke-Acts,* ed. J. Verheyden, BETL 142 (Leuven: University Press, 1999), 627–38. See also J. H. Davies, "The Lucan Prologue (1–3): An Attempt at Objective Redaction Criticism," in *Studia Evangelica,* ed. Elizabeth A. Livingstone; 6 vols., TU 112 (Berlin: Akademie-Verlag, 1973), 6:78–85, who maintains the unity of Luke 1–3. In the same volume J. M. Gibbs claims that the prologue to Luke runs from 1:1–4:30. See Gibbs, "Mark 1, 1–15, Matthew 1, 1–4, 16, Luke 1, 1–4,30, John 1, 1–51: The Gospel Prologues and Their Function," in *Studia Evangelica,* 6:154–88. A strong case that Luke 1:5–4:44 constitutes a literary unit is made by Fearghus Ó Fearghail,

The Introduction to Luke-Acts: A Study of the Role of Lk1,1–4,44 in the Composition of Luke's Two-Volume Work, AnBib 126 (Rome: Editrice Pontificio Instituto Biblico, 1991).

62. For objections see Charles H. Talbert, "Prophecies of Future Greatness: The Contribution of Greco-Roman Biographies to an Understanding of Luke 1:5–4:15," in *The Divine Helmsman: Studies on God's Control of Human Events, Presented to Lou H. Silberman,* ed. James L. Crenshaw and Samuel Sandmel (New York: KTAV Publishing House, 1980), 129–41. Talbert regards Luke1:5–4:15 as a literary unity. See also Harald Sahlin, *Der Messias und Das Gottesvolk: Studien zur Protolukanischen Theologie* (Uppsala: Almquist & Wiksells, 1945). Sahlin uses the term *Proto-Luke* to designate the entire section of Luke-Acts from Luke 1:5 to the end of Acts 15.

63. See Fred C. Conybeare, "Ein Zeugnis Ephräms über das Fehlen von c. 1 und 2 im Texte des Lucas," *ZNW* 3 (1902): 192–97. Conybeare announced that he had found evidence in two twelfth-century manuscripts of Ephraem on Tatian's *Diatessaron* that Luke did not originally include chapters 1 and 2. D. Volter, "Das angebliche Zeugnis Ephräms über das Fehlen von c. 1 und 2 im Texte des Lucas," *ZNW* 10 (1909): 177–80, however, rejected Conybeare's contentions, and his rejection has largely prevailed among critical scholars. Note, however, that, as we observed above, if Justin had a copy of the Gospel of Luke, it was a copy lacking the first two chapters. See Gregory, *Reception of Luke,* 211–92.

64. See Robert C. Tannehill, *The Narrative Unity of Luke-Acts: A Literary Interpretation,* 2 vols., FF (Philadelphia: Fortress Press, 1986, 1990).

65. Tannehill, *Narrative Unity,* 1:xiii.

66. In this connection see also the various essays in J. Verheyden, ed., *The Unity of Luke-Acts,* BETL 142 (Leuven: University Press, 1999).

67. Tyson, *Images of Judaism in Luke-Acts* (Columbia: University of South Carolina Press, 1992), 43.

68. See Hans Conzelmann, *The Theology of St. Luke,* trans. Geoffrey Buswell (New York: Harper & Brothers, 1960).

69. Conzelmann, *Theology,* 172. Earlier, in a comment on Luke 1:33, Conzelmann had written: "But as the objection might be raised, that the authenticity of these first two chapters is questionable, we have not taken into consideration the statements that are peculiar to them" (p. 118).

70. Conzelmann, *Theology,* 172 n. 1.

71. Conzelmann, *Theology,* 9.

72. Paul S. Minear, "Luke's Use of the Birth Stories," in *Studies in Luke-Acts: Essays Presented in Honor of Paul Schubert,* ed. Leander E. Keck and J. Louis Martyn (Nashville and New York: Abingdon Press, 1966), 111–30.

73. Minear, "Luke's Use," 113.

74. Minear, "Luke's Use," 121; see also H. H. Oliver, "The Lucan Birth Stories and the Purpose of Luke-Acts," *NTS* 10 (1964): 202–26.

75. See Tyson, "Conflict as a Literary Theme in the Gospel of Luke," in *New Synoptic Studies,* ed. William R. Farmer (Macon, Ga.: Mercer University Press, 1983), 303–27; see also Tyson, *The Death of Jesus in Luke-Acts* (Columbia: University of South Carolina Press, 1986), 48–83.

76. The significance of Simeon's oracle within the context of Luke-Acts as a whole is treated by David L. Tiede, "'Glory to Thy People Israel': Luke-Acts and the Jews," in

Luke-Acts and the Jewish People: Eight Critical Perspectives, ed. Tyson (Minneapolis: Augsburg, 1988), 21–34. J. K. Elliott ("Does Luke 2:41–52 Anticipate the Resurrection?" *ExpTim* 83 [1971–72]: 87–89) has called attention to an interesting parallel between the birth narratives and later sections of Luke. The narrative of Jesus in discussion with the leaders in the temple (Luke 2:41–52) appears to be a kind of foreshadowing of the longer section in Luke in which Jesus teaches for several days in the temple (Luke 20:1–21:38). That long section calls attention to the location of Jesus. At night he is at the Mount of Olives, and during the day he is in the temple (Luke 21:37–38). In the temple he is constantly engaged in teaching the people under the suspicious eyes of the priests, who watch for a chance to arrest him in the absence of the supporting populace (Luke 22:2). Luke 2:41–52 serves as a typical story of the precocious child, but it also foreshadows his future career as a teacher. The location of the discussions in the temple and the presence of the Jewish leaders are significant foreshadowing devices.

77. Recall the parallelization of Peter and Paul that we observed in Acts. See pp. 62–63, above.

78. See Brown, *Birth,* especially 250–53; 292–98.

79. See Conzelmann, *Theology,* 18–22.

80. Note, however, that Mary and Jesus' brothers are included among those gathered in Jerusalem in Acts 1:14.

81. On Marcion's use of this pericope, see ch. 2, n. 108, above.

82. Sahlin, *Messias,* 328, denies that virginal conception figures into the Lukan birth narratives. He maintains that Luke 1:34b is an interpolation and not originally a part of Luke or Proto-Luke. So Mary asks only how she can be the mother of the Messiah not how she can be a mother.

83. See Brown, *Birth,* 298–301.

84. Fitzmyer, *Luke (I–IX),* 306.

85. Luke Timothy Johnson observed that "Luke's intention of continuing the biblical narrative is shown by the dramatic shift from the balanced, complex sentence of the prologue (1:1–4) to the more plodding rhythms of the Greek Bible (LXX) in 1:5. His language suddenly is filled with Semitisms. These do not suggest that Luke was using Hebrew or Aramaic sources, but that he was imitating biblical language. So skillful is he that the reader is plunged into the world of Ruth, the Judges, and Samuel" (*The Gospel of Luke,* SP 3 [Collegeville, Minn.: Liturgical Press, 1991], 34–35).

86. Cadbury, *Making,* 223.

87. Fitzmyer, *Luke (I–IX),* 312.

88. Tyson, *Images,* 46.

89. Tyson, *Images,* 45–46.

90. Another scenario would be to suggest that there were four stages in the history of the composition of Luke. In the first stage we have a primitive gospel that started with what is now Luke 3:1. Somewhat later an anonymous author added the birth narratives, which Marcion deleted and the author of canonical Luke restored. It is, of course, likely that, if the birth narratives had been present in Marcion's source, he would have omitted them for theological reasons. But this scenario would violate the principle of Occam's razor by positing yet another hypothetical text.

91. See Tertullian, *Adv. Marc.* 3, 11:7–8.

92. See also Luke 1:42, in which the unborn Jesus is referred to as the fruit of Mary's womb.

93. See pp. 62–63, above.

94. See Brown, *Birth*, 447–51.

95. Note also the circumcision of John the Baptist, Luke 1:59, an incident that maintains the parallelism between him and Jesus.

96. On the parallels with Matthew, see especially Fitzmyer, *Luke (I–IX)*, 307.

97. Jacob Jervell, *The Unknown Paul: Essays on Luke-Acts and Early Christian History* (Minneapolis: Augsburg, 1984), 145.

98. See Brown, *Birth*, 450–51.

99. See pp. 45–48, above.

100. Harnack, *Marcion: Das Evangelium,* 221*.

101. See Tertullian, *Adv. Marc.* 4, 43:7.

102. The number of L verses in Luke 1–2 is 132; in Luke 24, at least 41 verses. Other lengthy sections are Luke 15:8–16:12, consisting of 37 verses, and Luke 10:29–11:8, which has 22 verses.

103. Another indication that Luke 24 may not have originally belonged to the body of Luke is the high incidence of Western non-interpolations to be found here. See B. F. Westcott and F. J. A. Hort, *The New Testament in the Original Greek* (New York: Macmillan, 1957). See also the discussion in Bruce M. Metzger, *A Textual Commentary on the Greek New Testament* (London and New York: United Bible Societies, 1971), 191–93. Westcott and Hort designated nine passages as Western non-interpolations, and seven of the nine are to be found in Luke 24 (24:3, 6, 12, 36, 40, 51, 52).

104. The grouping of women followers here is reminiscent of that in Luke 8:2–3, which has the Magdalene, Joanna, Susanna, and many others who accompanied Jesus. Both Luke 8:2–3 and 24:10 are unique to Luke.

105. The words τοῦ κυρίου Ἰησοῦ are missing in D and constitute the first of the Western non-interpolations in Luke 24.

106. If the phrase is authentic, the linguistic link between Luke 24 and Acts should not be overlooked. It is a small detail that confirms the view that these sections have the same author, who probably was not the author of the body of Luke.

107. It should be noted, however, that Luke 24:7 does not correspond exactly with any of the previous predictions. Luke 9:44 and 18:32 speak of Jesus as being "handed over," and 9:22 and 18:33 predict his killing and resurrection. But none of the passion predictions in the body of Luke uses the term for crucifixion that we have in Luke 24:7. On the differences between Luke 24:7 and the passion predictions, see Daryl D. Schmidt, "Remembering Jesus: Assessing the Oral Evidence" (paper presented at the annual meeting of the Southwestern Region of the SBL, Irving, Tex., 13 March 2005), 14–15.

108. See Conzelmann, *Theology*, 93.

109. Joseph A. Fitzmyer, *The Gospel According to Luke (X–XXIV): Introduction, Translation, and Notes,* AB 28A (Garden City, N.Y.: Doubleday, 1985), 1540.

110. See Westcott and Hort, *New Testament*, 184.

111. See Mikeal C. Parsons, "A Christological Tendency in P75," *JBL* 105 (1986): 463–79.

112. Parsons, "Christological Tendency," 476.

113. Bart D. Ehrman, *The Orthodox Corruption of Scripture: The Effect of Early Christological Controversies on the Text of the New Testament* (New York and Oxford: Oxford University Press, 1993), 217.

114. See Michael Wade Martin, "Defending the 'Western Non-Interpolations': The Case for an Anti-Separationist *Tendenz* in the Longer Alexandrian Readings," *JBL* 124 (2005): 269–94.

115. Shellard regards Luke 24:12, which she maintains is authentic, as crucial to her case that Luke used John. See Shellard, *New Light,* 254.

116. Raymond Brown, *The Gospel According to John (XIII–XXI): Introduction, Translation, and Notes,* AB 29a (Garden City, N.Y.: Doubleday, 1970), 1000, claimed that the verse is "obviously an addition to the narrative, but in our opinion a redactor's addition, not a scribe's." He added: "Much of the language of Luke xxiv 12 is non-Lucan in style, and the redactor may have borrowed it from an earlier form of the Johannine tradition (where Peter but not the Beloved Disciple was mentioned)." Fitzmyer, *Luke (X–XXIV),* 1542, likewise cites Luke 24:12 as evidence that Luke and John used a common source.

117. But for a defense of the authenticity of the verse see, among others, Franz Neirynck, "The Uncorrected Historic Present in Lk. xxiv. 12," *ETL* 48 (1972): 548–53. Neirynck here reconstructs the alleged source. See also Neirynck, "John and the Synoptics: The Empty Tomb Stories," *NTS* 30 (1984): 161–87. Against Neirynck, see A. Dauer, "Lk 24,12—Ein Produkt Lukanischer Redaktion?" in *The Four Gospels 1992: Festschrift F. Neirynck,* 3 vols., ed. F. van Segbroeck et al. (Leuven: University Press, 1992), 2:1697–1716. See also Bruce M. Metzger, "The Bodmer Papyrus of Luke and John." *ExpTim* 73 (1962): 201–3; George Rice, "Western Non-Interpolations: A Defense of the Apostolate," in *Luke-Acts: New Perspectives,* 1–16. See also Odette Mainville, "De Jésus à l'Église: Étude rédactionnelle de Luc 24," *NTS* 51 (2005): 192–211, who defends the authenticity of Luke 24:12 as a necessary component of Lukan redaction.

118. For a discussion of this verse as shaped under the influence of 1 Cor. 15:5, see Morton S. Enslin, "'Luke' and Paul," *JAOS* 58 (1938): 84. See also our discussion of the influence of Paul's letters on Acts, pp. 15–22, above.

119. See Paul Schubert, "The Structure and Significance of Luke 24," in *Neutestamentliche Studien für Rudolf Bultmann zu seinem 70. Geburtstag am 20. August 1954,* ed. Walther Eltester, BZNW 21 (Berlin: Alfred Töpelmann, 1954), 165–86.

120. Fitzmyer, *Luke (X–XXIV),* 1565.

121. F. J. Foakes Jackson and Kirsopp Lake, eds., *The Beginnings of Christianity,* 5 vols. (London: Macmillan, 1920–1933; reprint, Grand Rapids: Baker Book House, 1979), 4:37.

122. Luke 24:40 is another Western non-interpolation.

123. Acts 10:41 appears to refer back to this incident.

124. Schubert, "Structure and Significance," 173.

125. Note, however, that different verbs are used in the various references: ἀναφέρω in Luke 24:51; ἐπαίρω in Acts 1:9; πορεύομαι in 1:10; ἀναλαμβάνω in 1:11 and 1:22.

126. Enslin, "'Luke' and Paul," suggested that the forty-day duration of Jesus' appearances in Acts 1:3 was influenced by 1 Cor. 15:5. Luke must have felt that the longer period would have been required for the various appearances listed in Paul's letter.

127. This is the view of J. M. Creed, who said that the phrase in question was added at the time when Luke and Acts were separated. See Creed, *The Gospel According to St. Luke* (London: Macmillan, 1950), 302.

128. See Metzger, *Textual Commentary*, 189–90. But note the problems with the Western texts of Acts 1:2–3; see Metzger, *Textual Commentary*, 273–77.

129. Plummer, *S. Luke*, 565.

130. Plummer, *S. Luke*, 564.

131. See Parsons, "Christological Tendency," 476, who accounts for the Alexandrian addition of these verses as intended "to emphasize both the corporeal nature and the exalted state of the body of the risen Lord by making explicit reference to Christ's ascension into heaven (24:51); [and] to record the appropriate attitude of worship on the part of the disciples (24:52)."

132. Fitzmyer, *Luke (X–XXIV)*, 1588.

133. Schubert, "Structure and Significance," 176.

134. See Fitzmyer, *Luke (I–IX)*, 290.

135. Cadbury, "Commentary on the Preface of Luke," in *Beginnings of Christianity*, 2: 489.

136. Cadbury, *Making*, 223.

137. Cadbury, "Commentary on the Preface," 2:490.

138. See Günter Klein, "Lukas 1, 1–4 als Theologisches Programm," in *Zeit und Geschichte: Dankesgabe an Rudolf Bultmann zum 80. Geburtstag*, ed. Erich Dinkler (Tübingen: J. C. B. Mohr [Paul Siebeck], 1964), 193–216.

139. See Loveday Alexander, *The Preface to Luke's Gospel: Literary Convention and Social Context in Luke 1.1–4 and Acts 1.1*, SNTSMS 78 (Cambridge: Cambridge University Press, 1993); see also Alexander's "Luke's Preface in the Context of Greek Preface-Writing," *NovT* 28 (1986): 48–74.

140. Alexander, "Luke's Preface," 50.

141. Alexander, *Preface to Luke's Gospel*, 42.

142. Alexander, *Preface to Luke's Gospel*, 44.

143. Alexander, *Preface to Luke's Gospel*, 69.

144. Alexander, *Preface to Luke's Gospel*, 69.

145. Alexander, *Preface to Luke's Gospel*, 107; 116; 125; 136.

146. Alexander, "Luke's Preface," 50.

147. To be sure the author of canonical Luke drew on material that we have designated as coming from the Lukan Sondergut. But in view of the various problems associated with this material it seems best not to include it among those accounts that might be intended in Luke 1:1. In the scenario entertained here the Sondergut material should not be considered as composed by one of Luke's predecessors. Rather it supplies the material that he intends to introduce. Further, we should not exclude the possibility that the canonical author is the author of the Sondergut material.

148. See J. Bauer, "Πολλοι Luk 1, 1," *NovT* 4 (1960): 263–66.

149. Joel B. Green, *The Gospel of Luke*, NICNT (Grand Rapids: William B. Eerdmans, 1997), 38.

150. Klein, "Lukas 1, 1–4," 194.

151. Alexander, *Preface to Luke's Gospel*, 115.

152. Alexander, *Preface to Luke's Gospel,* 115

153. See Klein, "Lukas 1, 1–4."

154. Cadbury, "Commentary on the Preface," 2:496.

155. Richard J. Dillon, "Previewing Luke's Project from His Prologue (Luke 1:1–4)," *CBQ* 43 (1981): 212.

156. Dillon, "Previewing," 215.

157. Alexander, *Preface to Luke's Gospel,* 136, suggests this.

158. See David P. Moessner, "The Meaning of ΚΑΘΕΞΗΣ in the Lukan Prologue as a Key to the Distinctive Contribution of Luke's Narrative among the 'Many,'" in *The Four Gospels 1992,* 2:1513–1528.

159. Moessner, "Meaning of ΚΑΘΕΞΗΣ," 2:1516.

160. Moessner, "Meaning of ΚΑΘΕΞΗΣ," 2:1516.

161. Moessner, "Meaning of ΚΑΘΕΞΗΣ," 2:1517.

162. Moessner, "Meaning of ΚΑΘΕΞΗΣ," 2:1528.

163. See Alexander, *Preface to Luke's Gospel,* 141–42.

164. There is a wide scholarly consensus that Theophilus is a real person but not on the view of him as a government official of some sort. In any event it seems right to conclude that the author of the preface did not intend his document to be a private communication but expected a readership beyond the dedicatee.

165. See Cadbury, "Commentary on the Preface," 2:509-510.

166. W. C. van Unnik, "Once More St. Luke's Prologue," *Neot* 7 (1973): 18.

167. Van Unnik, "Once More," 18.

168. Alexander, *Preface to Luke's Gospel,* 142.

169. Alexander, *Preface to Luke's Gospel,* 142.

170. See van Unnik, "Once More," 18.

171. Although he does not date the preface to Luke in the second century or link it specifically with Marcion, I. Howard Marshall suggests a view of the purpose of the preface that is compatible with the one expressed here. See I. Howard Marshall, *The Gospel of Luke: A Commentary on the Greek Text,* NIGTC (Grand Rapids: William B. Eerdmans, 1978), 39–44.

172. See p. 87, above.

173. But on Luke 15:31 see the objection of Volckmar referred to in footnote 47, above.

174. See Epiphanius, *Panarion* 42, 2; see pp. 31–32, above. The date of this incident is unclear.

175. Note that Luke 5:39 is omitted by Codex D and other Western texts. Ulrich Schmid, however, objects to Harnack's omission of Luke 5:39 in the Gospel of Marcion. He maintains that Harnack omitted this verse simply because he thought it conflicted with Marcion's theological tendencies. See Schmid, "How Can We Access Second Century Gospel Texts? The Cases of Marcion and Tatian," in *The New Testament Text in Early Christianity: Proceedings of the Lille Colloquium, July 2000,* ed. Christian-B. Amphoux and J. Keith Elliott, HTB (Lausanne: Editions du Zebre, 2003), 139–50.

176. See Harnack, *Marcion: Das Evangelium,* 202*; see also Tertullian, *Adv. Marc.* 4, 33:9.

177. On the biblical genealogies see Marshall D. Johnson, *The Purpose of the Biblical Genealogies with Special Reference to the Setting of the Genealogies of Jesus,* SNTSMS 8 (Cambridge: Cambridge University Press, 1969).

178. In terms of the two-gospel hypothesis we would say that the author of this pre-Marcionite text obtained material from Matthew and added to it some material from his special source, usually designated as the Lukan Sondergut.

Chapter 5: The Lukan Achievement

1. See Paul Schubert, "The Structure and Significance of Luke 24," in *Neutestamentliche Studien für Rudolf Bultmann zu seinem 70. Geburtstag am 20. August 1954*, ed. Walther Eltester, BZNW 21 (Berlin: Alfred Töpelmann, 1954), 165–86.

2. See Henry J. Cadbury, *The Making of Luke-Acts*, 2d ed. (London: SPCK, 1958), 11.

3. See Robert C. Tannehill, *The Narrative Unity of Luke-Acts: A Literary Interpretation*, 2 vols., FF (Philadelphia: Fortress Press, 1986, 1990).

4. The only exception is the probable use of Mark 16:1–8 in Luke 24:1–11. But, as we suggested in chapter four, Luke has significantly reworked this section. See pp. 102–3, above.

5. See Christopher Mount, *Pauline Christianity: Luke-Acts and the Legacy of Paul*, NovTSup 104 (Leiden: Brill, 2002).

6. Mount, *Pauline Christianity*, 15.

7. Mount, *Pauline Christianity*, 16.

8. Mount, *Pauline Christianity*, 23.

9. See John Knox, *Marcion and the New Testament: An Essay in the Early History of the Canon* (Chicago: University of Chicago Press, 1942), 158–67.

10. Knox, *Marcion*, 158.

11. Knox, *Marcion*, 159.

12. Knox, *Marcion*, 159.

13. Knox, *Marcion*, 159.

14. Knox, *Marcion*, 160. Here Knox does not include the Revelation to John in this group, but earlier (p. 118) he had mentioned it, along with the Apocalypse of Peter, as part of the "apostle" section.

15. Knox, *Marcion*, 162–63, emphasis in original.

16. See Bart D. Ehrman, *Lost Christianities: The Battles for Scripture and the Faiths We Never Knew* (Oxford: Oxford University Press, 2003).

17. Ehrman, *Lost Christianities*, 111.

18. Ehrman, *Lost Christianities*, 111.

19. See Tertullian, *Adversus Marcionem* 2, 21:2; 3, 5:4; 3, 12:1.

20. See Tertullian, *Adv. Marc.* 3, 6:3; 3, 7:1–8; 3, 8:1–2; 3, 21:1.

21. This is not to say, of course, that Jewish interpretation was exclusively literal. Jewish writings of the protorabbinical period were quite varied, and many make abundant use of nonliteral methods of interpretation. Nevertheless the writings of Tertullian and others led Christians to avoid literal interpretation of the Hebrew Scriptures on the grounds that it would support Jewish and Marcionite beliefs.

22. Our emphasis on Luke-Acts is not intended to minimize the significance of other early Christian literature. Writing from within a different context, the author of the Gospel of Matthew, for example, surely played a role here as well.

23. For a fuller analysis of the treatment of Jews and Judaism in Luke-Acts, see my *Images of Judaism in Luke-Acts* (Columbia: University of South Carolina Press, 1992).

24. See further on the speech of Stephen, pp. 56–57, above.

25. Justin, *Dialogue with Trypho* 93 (Stephen B. Falls, *Saint Justin Martyr*, FC [New York: Christian Heritage, 1949]).

26. See Justin, *Dialogue* 9, 16, 92.

27. See Justin, *Dialogue* 18, 27, 46.

28. Justin, *Dialogue* 14.

29. See Justin, *Dialogue* 40.

30. See Justin, *Dialogue* 41.

31. See Justin, *Dialogue* 41.

32. See Justin, *Dialogue* 42.

33. Tertullian, *Adv. Marc.* 3, 5:2 (Ernest Evans, *Adversus Marcionem*, 2 vols., OECT [Oxford: Clarendon Press, 1972]).

34. Tertullian, *Adv. Marc.* 3, 5:3.

35. Tertullian, *Adv. Marc.* 3, 5:4.

36. It bears repeating that Jewish interpretations were not exclusively literal, despite Tertullian's judgment about them. See n. 21 above.

37. It was not inevitable that later Christians would employ nonliteral interpretive strategies. The Antiochenes of the third and fourth centuries were known to have emphasized the historical value and literal meaning of the Hebrew Scriptures, and even Origen, best known for his use of allegorical interpretation, did not deny that some biblical passages had literal meanings.

38. See Heikki Räisänen, "Marcion and the Origins of Christian Anti-Judaism: A Reappraisal," in *Challenges to Biblical Interpretation: Collected Essays 1991–2000*, BibInt 59 (Leiden: Brill, 2001), 191–205. Räisänen wrote: "Catholic Christianity wrenched the Scripture from the Jews, reinterpreting it to fit its own experience. Covenantal symbols were appropriated by way of spiritualizing interpretation: actual circumcision was replaced with the circumcision of the heart, observance of the law with obedience to moral commands. Precisely because it was asserted that the Old Testament had already spoken of Jesus, the continuing existence of Judaism as a religion with rival claims to Scripture was felt to be a threat" (p. 200).

BIBLIOGRAPHY

Primary Sources

The Ante-Nicene Fathers, 10 vols. Edited by Alexander Roberts and James Donaldson. 1885–1887. Reprint, Peabody, Mass.: Hendrickson, 1994.

Bettenson, Henry, editor. *Documents of the Christian Church.* 3rd ed. Edited by Chris Maunder. Oxford: Oxford University Press, 1999.

Blanchard, Monica J., and Robin Darling Young. *A Treatise on God Written in Armenian by Eznik of Kolb.* Leuven: Peeters, 1998.

1 Clement. *The First Epistle of Clement to the Corinthians.* Translated by Kirsopp Lake. LCL. Cambridge: Harvard University Press, 1912.

Clement of Alexandria. *Stromateis.* Books One to Three. Translated by John Ferguson. FC. Washington: Catholic University of America Press, 1991.

Epiphanius. *The Panarion of Epiphanius of Salamis,* 2 vols. Translated by Frank Williams. NHS 35. Leiden: Brill, 1987.

Irenaeus. *St. Irenaeus of Lyons Against the Heresies.* Translated by Dominic J. Unger and John J. Dillon. ACW 55. New York: Paulist Press, 1991.

Josephus. Translated by H. St. J. Thackeray et al., 10 vols. LCL. Cambridge: Harvard University Press, 1926–1965.

Justin Martyr. *The Dialogue with Trypho.* In *Saint Justin Martyr.* Translated by Stephen B. Falls. FC. New York: Christian Heritage, 1949.

———. *The First Apology.* In *Early Christian Fathers.* Translated by Edward Rochie Hardy, 242–89. LCC 1. Philadelphia: Westminster Press, 1953.

Polycarp. *The Epistle of Polycarp to the Philippians.* Translated by Kirsopp Lake. LCL. Cambridge: Harvard University Press, 1912.

Tertullian. *Adversus Marcionem,* 2 vols. Edited and translated by Ernest Evans. OECT. Oxford: Clarendon Press, 1972.

Secondary Sources

Aejmelaeus, Lars. *Die Rezeption der Paulusbriefe in der Miletrede (Apg 20:18–35).* Helsinki: Suomalainen Tiedeakatemia, 1987.

Aland, Barbara. "Marcion—Marcionites—Marcionism." In *Encyclopedia of the Early Church,* vol. 1, 523–24. Edited by Angelo Di Berardino. Translated by Adrian Walford. Cambridge and New York: Oxford University Press, 1992.

Aland, Kurt. "Neue neutestamentliche Papyri III." *NTS* 22 (1976): 375–96.

Alexander, Loveday. "The Acts of the Apostles as an Apologetic Text." In *Apologetics in the Roman Empire: Pagans, Jews, and Christians*, 15–44. Edited by Mark Edwards, Martin Goodman, and Simon Price. Oxford: Oxford University Press, 1999.

———. "Formal Elements and Genre: Which Greco-Roman Prologues Most Closely Parallel the Lukan Prologues?" In *Luke and the Heritage of Israel: Luke's Narrative Claim upon Israel's Legacy*, 9–26. Edited by David P. Moessner. Luke the Interpreter of Israel 1. Harrisburg: Trinity Press International, 1999.

———. "Luke's Preface in the Context of Greek Preface-Writing." *NovT* 28 (1986): 48–74.

———. *The Preface to Luke's Gospel: Literary Convention and Social Context in Luke 1.1–4 and Acts 1.1*. SNTSMS 78. Cambridge: Cambridge University Press, 1993.

Balas, David L. "Marcion Revisited: A 'Post-Harnack' Perspective." In *Texts and Testaments: Critical Essays on the Bible and Early Church Fathers*, 95–108. Edited by W. Eugene March. San Antonio: Trinity University Press, 1980.

Barnikol, Ernst. *Die Entstehung der Kirche im zweiten Jahrhundert und die Zeit Marcions*. 2d ed. Forschungen zur Enstehung des Urchristentums, des Neuen Testaments und der Kirche 8. Kiel: Walter G. Mühlau, 1933.

———. *Der nichtpaulinische Ursprung des Parallelismus der Apostel Petrus und Paulus (Galater 2. 7–8)*. Forschungen zur Enstehung des Urchristentums, des Neuen Testaments und der Kirche 5. Kiel: Mühlau, 1931.

Barrett, C. K. "Acts and the Pauline Corpus." *ExpTim* 88 (1976–77): 2–5.

———. *A Critical and Exegetical Commentary on the Acts of the Apostles*, 2 vols. ICC. Edinburgh: T & T Clark, 1994, 1998.

———. "The Third Gospel as a Preface to Acts? Some Reflections." In *The Four Gospels 1992: Festschrift Frans Neirynck*, vol. 2, 1451–1466. Edited by F. van Segbroeck et al. 3 vols. Leuven: University Press, 1992.

Bauer, J. "Πολλοι Luk 1, 1." *NovT* 4 (1960): 263–66.

Bauer, Walter. *Orthodoxy and Heresy in Earliest Christianity*. Edited by Robert A. Kraft and Gerhard Krodel. Philadelphia: Fortress Press, 1971.

Bauernfeind, Otto. *Kommentar und Studien zur Apostelgeschichte*. Edited by Volker Metelmann. WUNT 22. Tübingen: J. C. B. Mohr (Paul Siebek), 1980.

Baur, Ferdinand Christian. *Historisch-Kritische Untersuchungen zum Neuen Testament*. Stuttgart: Friedrich Frommann, 1963.

———. *Kritische Untersuchungen über die kanonischen Evangelien, ihr Verhältnisz zu einander, ihren Charakter und Ursprung*. Tübingen: L. F. Fues, 1847.

———. *Paul, the Apostle of Jesus Christ, His Life and Work, His Epistles and His Doctine: A Contribution to the Critical History of Primitive Christianity*, 2 vols. Edited by Eduard Zeller. Translated by A. Menzies. 2nd ed. London: Williams & Norgate, 1876.

Bellinzoni, Arthur J. "The Gospel of Luke in the Second Century CE." In *Literary Studies in Luke-Acts: Essays in Honor of Joseph B. Tyson*, 59–76. Edited by Richard P. Thompson and Thomas E. Phillips. Macon, Ga: Mercer University Press, 1998.

Blackman, E. C. *Marcion and His Influence*. London: SPCK, 1948.

Bock, Darrell L. *Proclamation from Prophecy and Pattern: Lucan Old Testament Christology*. JSNTSup 12. Sheffield: Sheffield Academic Press, 1987.

Boismard, M. E. *Les Actes des Deux Apôtres*, 3 vols. EBib 12 (n. s.). Paris: J. Gabalda, 1990.

Bonz, Marianne Palmer. *The Past as Legacy: Luke-Acts and Ancient Epic.* Minneapolis: Fortress Press, 2000.

Booth, Wayne. *The Rhetoric of Fiction.* 2d ed. Chicago: University of Chicago Press, 1983.

Bovon, François. *Das Evangelium nach Lukas.* Evangelisch-Katholischer Kommentar zum Neuen Testament. Zurich: Benziger Verlag, 1989.

―――. "Studies in Luke-Acts: Retrospect and Prospect." *HTR* 85 (1992): 175–96.

―――. "Tradition et redaction en Actes 10,1–11, 18." *TZ* 36 (1970): 22–45.

Brawley, Robert L. *Luke-Acts and the Jews: Conflict, Apology, and Conciliation.* SBLMS 33. Atlanta: Scholars Press, 1987.

Brodie, Thomas L. "A New Temple and a New Law: The Unity and Chronicler-based Nature of Luke 1:1–4:22a." *JSNT* 5 (1979): 21–45.

―――. "The Unity of Proto-Luke." In *The Unity of Luke-Acts,* 627–38. Edited by J. Verheyden. BETL 142. Leuven: University Press, 1999.

Brown, Raymond E. *The Birth of the Messiah: A Commentary on the Infancy Narratives in Matthew and Luke.* Garden City, N.Y.: Doubleday, 1977.

―――. *The Gospel According to John (XIII–XXI): Introduction, Translation, and Notes.* AB 29a. Garden City, N. Y.: Doubleday, 1970.

Bruce, F. F. *The Acts of the Apostles.* Grand Rapids: Wm. B. Eerdmans, 1951.

Busse, Ulrich. "Die Engelrede Lk 1, 13–17 und ihre Vorgeschichte." In *Nach den Anfängen Fragen,* 163–77. Edited by Cornelius Mayer, Karlheinz Müller, and Gerhard Schmalenberg. Giessen: University Press, 1994.

―――. "Das 'Evangelium' des Lukas: Die Funktion der Vorgeschichte im lukanischen Doppelwerk." In *Der Treue Gottes Trauen: Beiträge zum Werk des Lukas für Gerhard Schneider,* 161–77. Edited by Claus Bussmann and Walter Radl. Freiburg, Basel, Wien: Herder, 1991.

Cadbury, Henry J. *The Book of Acts in History.* London: Adam and Charles Black, 1955.

―――. "Commentary on the Preface of Luke." In *The Beginnings of Christianty,* vol. 2, 489–510. Edited by F. J. Foakes Jackson and Kirsopp Lake. London: Macmillan, 1920–1933. Reprint, Grand Rapids: Baker Book House, 1979.

―――. *The Making of Luke-Acts.* 2d ed. London: SPCK, 1958.

―――. *The Style and Literary Method of Luke.* Cambridge: Harvard University Press, 1920.

―――. "Subsidiary Points." In *The Beginnings of Christianity,* vol. 2, 349–59. Edited by F. J. Foakes Jackson and Kirsopp Lake. London: Macmillan, 1920–1933. Reprint, Grand Rapids: Baker Book House, 1979.

―――. "The Summaries in Acts." In *The Beginnings of Christianity,* vol. 5, 392–402. Edited by F. J. Foakes Jackson and Kirsopp Lake. London: Macmillan 1920–1933. Reprint, Grand Rapids: Baker Book House, 1979.

―――. "The Tradition." In *The Beginnings of Christianity,* vol. 2, 209–64. Edited by F. J. Foakes Jackson and Kirsopp Lake. London: Macmillan, 1920–1933. Reprint, Grand Rapids: Baker Book House, 1979.

Catchpole, David R. "Paul, James and the Apostolic Decree." *NTS* 23 (1977): 428–44.

Clabeaux, John J. "Abraham in Marcion's Gospel and Epistles." In *When Judaism and Christianity Began: Essays in Memory of Anthony J. Saldarini,* vol. 1, 69–92. Edited by Alan J. Avery-Peck, Daniel Harrington, and Jacob Neusner. Supplements to the Journal for the Study of Judaism 85. Leiden: Brill, 2004.

———. *A Lost Edition of the Letters of Paul: A Reassessment of the Text of the Pauline Corpus Attested by Marcion.* Washington, D.C.: Catholic Biblical Association of America, 1989.

Clark, Andrew C. *Parallel Lives: The Relation of Paul to the Apostles in the Lucan Perspective.* Carlisle, U.K.: Paternoster Press, 2001.

———. "The Role of the Apostles." In *Witness to the Gospel: The Theology of Acts,* 169–90. Edited by I. Howard Marshall and David Peterson. Grand Rapids: Wm. B. Eerdmans, 1998.

Conybeare, Fred C. "Ein Zeugnis Ephräms über das Fehlen von c. 1 und 2 im Texte des Lucas." *ZNW* 3 (1902): 192–97.

Conzelmann, Hans. *The Acts of the Apostles: A Commentary on the Acts of the Apostles.* Translated by James Limburg, A. Thomas Kraabel, and Donald H. Juel. Hermeneia Commentaries. Philadelphia: Fortress Press, 1987.

———. "Luke's Place in the Development of Early Christianity." In *Studies in Luke-Acts: Essays Presented in Honor of Paul Schubert,* 298–316. Edited by Leander E. Keck and J. Louis Martyn. Nashville: Abingdon Press, 1966.

———. *The Theology of St. Luke.* Translated by Geoffrey Buswell. New York: Harper & Brothers, 1960.

Couchoud, Paul-Louis. "Is Marcion's Gospel One of the Synoptics?" *HibJ* 34 (1936): 265–77.

Creed, J. M. *The Gospel According to St. Luke.* London: Macmillan, 1950.

Darr, John. *On Character Building: The Reader and the Rhetoric of Characterization in Luke-Acts.* Literary Currents in Biblical Interpretation. Louisville, Ky.: Westminster / John Knox, 1992.

Dauer, Anton. "Lk 24,12—Ein Produkt Lukanischer Redaktion?" In *The Four Gospels 1992: Festschrift Frans Neirynck,* vol. 2, 1697–1716. Edited by F. van Segbroeck et al. Leuven: University Press, 1992.

Davies, J. H. "The Lucan Prologue (1–3): An Attempt at Objective Redaction Criticism." In *Studia Evangelica,* vol. 6, 78–85. Edited by Elizabeth A. Livingstone. TU 112. Berlin: Akademie-Verlag, 1973.

Dawsey, James M. "The Literary Unity of Luke-Acts: Questions of Style—A Task for Literary Critics." *NTS* 35 (1989): 48–66.

De Boer, Martinus. "Comment: Which Paul?" In *Paul and the Legacies of Paul,* 45–54. Edited by William S. Babcock. Dallas: Southern Methodist University Press, 1990.

Decock, Paul B. "The Breaking of Bread in Luke 24." *Neot* 36 (2002): 39–56.

Denova, Rebecca I. *The Things Accomplished Among Us: Prophetic Tradition in the Structural Pattern of Luke-Acts.* JSNTSup 141. Sheffield: Sheffield Academic Press, 1997.

Dibelius, Martin. *Studies in the Acts of the Apostles.* Edited by Heinrich Greeven. Translated by Mary Ling. New York: Charles Scribner's Sons, 1956.

———, and Hans Conzelmann. *The Pastoral Epistles.* Translated by Philip Buttolph and Adela Yarbro. Hermeneia Commentaries. Philadelphia: Fortress Press, 1972.

Dillon, Richard J. "Previewing Luke's Project from His Prologue (Luke 1:1–4)." *CBQ* 43 (1981): 205–27.

Dodd, C. H. "The Fall of Jerusalem and the 'Abomination of Desolation.'" *JRS* 37 (1947): 47–54.

Drijvers, Hans J. W. "Marcionism in Syria: Principles, Problems, Polemics." *SecCent* 6 (1987–1988): 153–72.

Dunn, James D. G. *The Acts of the Apostles.* Narrative Commentaries. Valley Forge, Pa.: Trinity Press International, 1996.

Dupont, Jacques. *The Salvation of the Gentiles: Essays on the Acts of the Apostles.* Translated by John R. Keating. New York: Paulist Press, 1979.

Efroymson, David P. "The Patristic Connection." In *Antisemitism and the Foundations of Christianity,* 98–117. Edited by Alan Davies. New York: Paulist Press, 1979.

Ehrman, Bart D. *Lost Christianities: The Battles for Scripture and the Faiths We Never Knew.* Oxford: Oxford University Press, 2003.

———. *The Orthodox Corruption of Scripture: The Effect of Early Christological Controversies on the Text of the New Testament.* New York and Oxford: Oxford University Press, 1993.

Elliott, J. K. "Does Luke 2:41–52 Anticipate the Resurrection?" *ExpTim* 83 (1971–1972): 87–89.

Ellis, John M. *The Theory of Literary Criticism.* Berkeley: University of California Press, 1974.

Enslin, Morton S. "'Luke' and Paul." *JAOS* 58 (1938): 81–91.

———. "Once Again, Luke and Paul." *ZNW* 61 (1970): 253–71.

Epp, Eldon J. *The Theological Tendency of Codex Bezae Cantabrigiensis in Acts.* SNTSMS 3. Cambridge: Cambridge University Press, 1966.

Esler, Philip F. *Community and Gospel in Luke-Acts: The Social and Political Motivations of Lucan Theology.* SNTSMS 57. Cambridge: Cambridge University Press, 1987.

Evans, Craig A, and James A. Sanders. *Luke and Scripture: The Function of Sacred Tradition in Luke-Acts.* Minneapolis: Fortress Press, 1993.

Farmer, William R. *The Synoptic Problem: A Critical Analysis.* New York: Macmillan, 1964.

Fearghail, Fearghus Ó. *The Introduction to Luke-Acts: A Study of the Role of Lk1,1–4,44 in the Composition of Luke's Two-Volume Work.* AnBib 126. Rome: Editrice Pontificio Instituto Biblico, 1991.

Fitzmyer, Joseph A. *The Acts of the Apostles: A New Translation with Introduction and Commentary.* AB 31. New York: Doubleday, 1998.

———. *The Gospel According to Luke (I–IX): Introduction, Translation, and Notes.* AB 28. Garden City, N.Y.: Doubleday, 1981.

———. *The Gospel According to Luke (X–XXIV): Introduction, Translation, and Notes.* AB 28A. Garden City, N.Y.: Doubleday, 1985.

Foakes Jackson, F. J., and Kirsopp Lake, editors. *The Beginnings of Christianity. Part 1. The Acts of the Apostles,* 5 vols. London: Macmillan, 1920–1933. Reprint, Grand Rapids: Baker Book House, 1979.

Forbes, Greg W. *The God of Old: The Role of the Lukan Parables in the Purpose of Luke's Gospel.* JSNTSup198. Sheffield: Sheffield Academic Press, 2000.

Franklin, Eric. *Luke: Interpreter of Paul, Critic of Matthew.* JSNTSup 92. Sheffield: Journal for the Study of the Old Testament Press, 1994.

Freedman, David N., editor. *Anchor Bible Dictionary,* 6 vols. New York: Doubleday, 1992.

Gaston, Lloyd. *Horae Synopticae Electronicae: Word Statistics of the Synoptic Gospels.* SBLSBS 3. Missoula, Mont.: SBL, 1973.

Gibbs, J. M. "Mark 1, 1–15, Matthew 1, 1–4, 16, Luke 1, 1–4,30, John 1, 1–51: The Gospel Prologues and their Function." In *Studia Evangelica,* vol. 6, 154–88. Edited by Elizabeth A. Livingstone. TU 112. Berlin: Akademie-Verlag, 1973.

Goodspeed, Edgar J. *An Introduction to the New Testament.* Chicago: University of Chicago Press, 1937.

Goulder, Michael D. "Did Luke Know Any of the Pauline Letters?" *PRSt* 13 (1986): 97–112.

———. *St. Paul versus St. Peter: A Tale of Two Missions.* Louisville: Westminster / John Knox, 1995.

———, and M. L. Sanderson. "St. Luke's Genesis," *JTS* 8 (1957): 12–30.

Green, Joel B. *The Gospel of Luke.* NICNT. Grand Rapids: Wm. B. Eerdmans, 1997.

Gregory, Andrew. *The Reception of Luke and Acts in the Period before Irenaeus: Looking for Luke in the Second Century.* WUNT 2:169. Tübingen: Mohr Siebeck, 2003.

Haacker, Klaus. "Dibelius und Cornelius: Ein Beispiel formgeschichtlicher Überlieferungskritik." *BZ* 24 (1980): 234–51.

Haenchen, Ernst. *The Acts of the Apostles: A Commentary.* Translated by Bernard Noble and Gerald Shinn. Oxford: Basil Blackwell, 1971.

———. "Judentum und Christentum in der Apostelgeschichte." *ZNW* 54 (1963): 155–87.

———. "Tradition und Komposition in der Apostelgeschichte." *ZTK* 52 (1955): 205–25.

Harnack, Adolf von. *The Acts of the Apostles.* Translated by J. R. Wilkinson. New Testament Studies 3. London: Williams & Norgate / New York: G. P. Putnam's, 1909.

———. *Die Chronologie der Altchristlichen Litteratur bis Eusebius,* 2 vols. Leipzig: J. C. Hinrichs, 1897.

———. *The Date of Acts and of the Synoptic Gospels.* Translated by J. R. Wilkinson. New Testament Studies 4. London: Williams & Norgate / New York: G. P. Putnam's, 1911.

———. *Luke the Physician: The Author of the Third Gospel and the Acts of the Apostles.* Translated by J. R. Wilkinson. New Testament Studies 1. London: Williams & Norgate / New York: G. P. Putnam's, 1908.

———. *Marcion: Das Evangelium vom Fremden Gott: Eine Monographie zur Geschichte der Grundlegung der Katholischen Kirche.* TU 45. Leipzig: J. C. Hinrichs, 1921. Published in English as *Marcion: The Gospel of the Alien God.* Translated by John E. Steely and Lyle D. Bierma. Durham, N. C.: Labyrinth Press, 1990.

Harrison, P. N. *Polycarp's Two Epistles to the Philippians.* Cambridge: Cambridge University Press, 1936.

Hawkins, John C. *Horae Synopticae: Contributions to the Study of the Synoptic Problem.* 2d ed. Oxford: Clarendon Press, 1909.

Head, Peter M. "The Foreign God and the Sudden Christ: Theology and Christology in Marcion's Gospel Redaction." *TynBul* 44 (1993): 307–21.

Hemer, Colin J. *The Book of Acts in the Setting of Hellenistic History.* Edited by Conrad H. Gempf. Winona Lake, Ind.: Eisenbrauns, 1990.

Hengel, Martin. *Acts and the History of Earliest Christianity.* Translated by John Bowden. Philadelphia: Fortress Press, 1979.

————. *The Four Gospels and the One Gospel of Jesus Christ: An Investigation of the Collection and Origin of the Canonical Gospels.* Harrisburg: Trinity Press International, 2000.

Hilgenfeld, Adolf. *Kritische Untersuchungen über die Evangelien Justin's, der clementinischen Homilien und Marcion's.* Halle: Schwentschke & Sohn, 1850.

Hoffmann, R. Joseph. *Marcion: On the Restitution of Christianity: An Essay on the Development of Radical Paulinist Theology in the Second Century.* American Academy of Religion Academy Series 46. Chico, Calif.: Scholars Press, 1984.

Holladay, Carl R. "Acts and the Fragments of Hellenistic Jewish Historians." In *Jesus and the Heritage of Israel: Luke's Narrative Claim upon Israel's Legacy,* 171–98. Edited by David P. Moessner. Luke the Interpreter of Israel 1. Harrisburg: Trinity Press International, 1999.

Houlden, J. L. "The Purpose of Luke." *JSNT* 21 (1984): 53–65.

Iser, Wolfgang. *The Implied Reader: Patterns of Communication in Prose Fiction from Bunyan to Beckett.* Baltimore: Johns Hopkins University Press, 1974.

Jervell, Jacob. "Das Aposteldekret in der lukanischen Theologie." In *Texts and Contexts: Biblical Texts in their Textual and Situational Contexts: Essays in Honor of Lars Hartman,* 227–43. Edited by Todd Fornberg and David Hellholm. Oslo: Scandinavian University Press, 1995.

————. *Die Apostelgeschichte.* 17th ed. KEK 3. Göttingen: Vandenhoeck & Ruprecht, 1998.

————. *Luke and the People of God: A New Look at Luke-Acts.* Minneapolis: Augsburg, 1972.

————. "Paulus in der Apostelgeschichte und die Geschichte des Urchristentums." *NTS* 32 (1986): 378–92.

————. *The Theology of the Acts of the Apostles.* New Testament Theology. Cambridge: Cambridge University Press, 1996.

————. *The Unknown Paul: Essays on Luke-Acts and Early Christian History.* Minneapolis: Augsburg, 1984.

Johnson, Luke Timothy. *The Acts of the Apostles.* SP 5. Collegeville, Minn.: Liturgical Press, 1992.

————. *The Gospel of Luke.* SP 3. Collegeville, Minn.: Liturgical Press, 1991.

————. "Luke-Acts, Book of." In *ABD,* vol. 4, 403–20. Edited by David Noel Freedman. New York: Doubleday, 1992.

Johnson, Marshall D. *The Purpose of the Biblical Genealogies with Special Reference to the Setting of the Genealogies of Jesus.* SNTSMS 8. Cambridge: Cambridge University Press, 1969.

Jones, Douglas R. "The Background and Character of the Lukan Psalms." *JTS* 19 (1968): 19–50.

Karris, Robert J. *Luke: Artist and Theologian: Luke's Passion Account as Literature.* Theological Inquiries: Studies in Contemporary Biblical and Theological Problems. New York, Mahwah, N.J., and Toronto: Paulist Press, 1985.

Keck, Leander E., and J. Louis Martyn, editors. *Studies in Luke-Acts: Essays Presented in Honor of Paul Schubert.* Nashville and New York: Abingdon Press, 1966.

Klein, Günter. "Lukas 1,1–4 als Theologisches Programm." In *Zeit und Geschichte: Dankesgabe an Rudolf Bultmann zum 80. Geburtstag,* 193–216. Edited by Erich Dinkler. Tübingen: J. C. B. Mohr (Paul Siebeck), 1964.

———. *Die Zwölf Apostel: Ursprung und Gehalt einer Idee.* Göttingen: Vandenhoeck & Ruprecht, 1961.

Klinghardt, Matthias. *Gesetz und Volk Gottes: Das lukanische Verständnis des Gesetzes nach Herkunft, Funktion und seinem Ort in der Geschichte des Urchristentums.* WUNT 32. Tübingen: J. C. B. Mohr (Paul Siebeck), 1988.

Knox, John. "Acts and the Pauline Letter Corpus." In *Studies in Luke-Acts: Essays Presented in Honor of Paul Schubert,* 279–87. Edited by Leander E. Keck and J. Louis Martyn. Nashville: Abingdon Press, 1966,

———. "J. A. T. Robinson and the Meaning of New Testament Scholarship." *Theology* 92 (1989): 251–68.

———. *Marcion and the New Testament: An Essay in the Early History of the Canon.* Chicago: University of Chicago Press, 1942.

———. "Marcion's Gospel and the Synoptic Problem." In *Jesus, the Gospels, and the Church,* 25-31. Edited by E. P. Sanders. Macon, Ga.: Mercer University Press, 1987.

Koester, Helmut. "From the Kerygma-Gospel to Written Gospels." *NTS* 35 (1989): 361–81.

Leppä, Heikki. "Luke's Critical Use of Galatians." Ph.D. diss., University of Helsinki, 2002.

Lightfoot, J. B. *The Apostolic Fathers,* Part 2, 3 vols. London: Macmillan, 1885.

———. *St. Paul's Epistle to the Galatians.* London: Macmillan, 1890. Reprint, Grand Rapids: Zondervan, 1957.

Lindemann, Andreas. "Paul in the Writings of the Apostolic Fathers." In *Paul and the Legacies of Paul,* 25–45. Edited by William S. Babcock. Dallas: Southern Methodist University Press, 1990.

Lohfink, Gerhard. *Die Sammlung Israels: Eine Untersuchung zur lukanischen Ekklesiologie.* SANT 39. Munich: Kösel, 1975.

Löhr, Winrich Alfried. *Basilides und seine Schule: Eine Studie zur Theologie- und Kirchengeschichte des zweiten Jahrhunderts.* Tübingen: J. C. B. Mohr (Paul Siebeck), 1996.

Loisy, Alfred. "Marcion's Gospel: A Reply." *HibJ* 34 (1936): 378–87.

Lüdemann, Gerd. *The Acts of the Apostles: What Really Happened in the Earliest Days of the Church.* Amherst, N.Y.: Prometheus Books, 2005.

———. *Early Christianity According to the Traditions in Acts: A Commentary.* Translated by John Bowden. Minneapolis: Fortress Press, 1989.

———. *Heretics: The Other Side of Early Christianity.* Translated by John Bowden. Louisville: Westminster / John Knox, 1996.

———. *Opposition to Paul in Jewish Christianity.* Translated by M. Eugene Boring. Minneapolis: Fortress Press, 1989).

———. *The Resurrection of Jesus: History, Experience, Theology.* Translated by John Bowden. London: SCM Press, 1994.

Maddox, Robert. *The Purpose of Luke-Acts.* Edited by John Riches. Edinburgh: T & T Clark, 1982.

Mainville, Odette. "De Jésus à l'Église: Étude rédactionnelle de Luc 24." *NTS* 51 (2005): 192–211.

Marguerat, Daniel. "The Enigma of the Silent Closing of Acts (28:16–31)." In *Jesus and the Heritage of Israel: Luke's Narrative Claim upon Israel's Legacy,* 284–304. Edited by

David P. Moessner. Luke the Interpreter of Israel 1. Harrisburg: Trinity Press International, 1999.

———. *The First Christian Historian: Writing the "Acts of the Apostle"* SNTSMS 121. Cambridge: Cambridge University Press, 2002.

Marshall, I. Howard. *The Gospel of Luke: A Commentary on the Greek Text.* NIGTC. Grand Rapids: Wm. B. Eerdmans, 1978.

Martin, Michael Wade. "Defending the 'Western Non-Interpolations': The Case for an Anti-Separationist *Tendenz* in the Longer Alexandrian Readings." *JBL* 124 (2005): 269–94.

Matson, Mark A. *In Dialogue with Another Gospel? The Influence of the Fourth Gospel on the Passion Narrative of the Gospel of Luke.* SBLDS 178. Atlanta: SBL, 2001.

Mattill, A. J., Jr. "The Purpose of Acts: Schneckenburger Reconsidered." In *Apostolic History and the Gospel: Biblical and Historical Essays Presented to F. F. Bruce on His 60th Birthday,* 108–22. Edited by W. Ward Gasque and Ralph P. Martin. Grand Rapids: Wm. B. Eerdmans, 1970.

———. "The Value of Acts as a Source for the Study of Paul." In *Perspectives on Luke-Acts,* 76–98 Edited by Charles H. Talbert. Edinburgh: T & T Clark, 1978.

May, Gerhard. "Ein neues Markionbild?" *TRu* 51 (1986): 404–13.

———. "Marcion ohne Harnack." In *Marcion und seine kirchengeschichtliche Wirkung: Vorträge der Internationalen Fachkonferenz zu Marcion, gehalten vom 15.–18. August 2001 in Mainz,* 1–7. Edited by May and Katharina Greschat. TUGAL 150. Berlin and New York: Walter de Gruyter, 2002.

———, and Katharina Greschat, editors. *Marcion und seine kirchengeschichtliche Wirkung: Vorträge der Internationalen Fachkonferenz zu Marcion, gehalten vom 15.–18. August 2001 in Mainz.* TUGAL150. Berlin and New York: Walter de Gruyter, 2002.

Metzger, Bruce M. "The Bodmer Papyrus of Luke and John." *ExpTim* 73 (1962): 201–3.

———. *A Textual Commentary on the Greek New Testament.* London and New York: United Bible Societies, 1971.

Minear, Paul S. "Luke's Use of the Birth Stories." In *Studies in Luke-Acts: Essays Presented in Honor of Paul Schubert,* 111–30. Edited by Leander E. Keck and J. Louis Martyn. Nashville and New York: Abingdon Press, 1966.

Moessner, David P. "The Meaning of ΚΑΘΕΞΗΣ in the Lukan Prologue as a Key to the Distinctive Contribution of Luke's Narrative among the 'Many.'" In *The Four Gospels 1992: Festschrift Frans Neirynck,* vol. 2, 1513–1528. Edited by F. van Segbroeck et al. Leuven: University Press, 1992.

Mount, Christopher. *Pauline Christianity: Luke-Acts and the Legacy of Paul.* NovTSup104. Leiden: Brill, 2002.

Nanos, Mark D., editor. *The Galatians Debate: Contemporary Issues in Rhetorical and Historical Interpretation.* Peabody, Mass.: Hendrickson, 2002.

———. *The Irony of Galatians: Paul's Letter in First-Century Context.* Minneapolis: Fortress Press, 2002.

Neagoe, Alexander. *The Trial of the Gospel: An Apologetic Reading of Luke's Trial Narratives.* SNTSMS 116. Cambridge: Cambridge University Press, 2002.

Neirynck, Frans. "John and the Synoptics: The Empty Tomb Stories." *NTS* 30 (1984): 161–87.

————. "Luke 4,16–30 and the Unity of Luke-Acts." In *The Unity of Luke-Acts*, 357–95. Edited by J. Verheyden. BETL 142. Leuven: University Press, 1999.

————. "The Uncorrected Historic Present in Lk. xxiv. 12." *ETL* 48 (1972): 548–53.

Neusner, Jacob. "Vow-Taking, the Nazirites, and the Law: Does James' Advice to Paul Accord with Halakhah?" In *James the Just and Christian Origins*, 59–82. Edited by Bruce Chilton and Craig Evans. Leiden: Brill, 1999.

Oliver, H. H. "The Lucan Birth Stories and the Purpose of Luke-Acts." *NTS* 10 (1964): 202–26.

O'Neill, John C. *The Theology of Acts in its Historical Setting*. London: SPCK, 1961.

Parker, Pierson. "The 'Former Treatise' and the Date of Acts." *JBL* 84 (1965): 52–58.

Parsons, Mikeal C. "A Christological Tendency in P75." *JBL* 105 (1986): 463–79.

————, and Richard I. Pervo. *Rethinking the Unity of Luke and Acts*. Minneapolis: Fortress Press, 1993.

————, and Joseph B. Tyson, editors. *Cadbury, Knox, and Talbert: American Contributions to the Study of Acts*. SBLCP. Atlanta: Scholars Press, 1992.

Penner, Todd, and Caroline Vander Stichele, editors. *Contextualizing Acts: Lukan Narrative and Greco-Roman Discourse*. SBLSymS 20. Atlanta: SBL, 2003.

Pervo, Richard I. *Dating Acts: Between the Evangelists and the Apologists*. Santa Rosa, Calif.: Polebridge Press, 2006.

————. *Profit with Delight: The Literary Genre of the Acts of the Apostles*. Philadelphia: Fortress Press, 1987.

Pesch, Rudolf. *Die Apostelgeschichte*, 2 vols. Evangelisch-Katholischer Kommentar zum Neuen Testament. Zurich: Benziger Verlag, 1986.

Plümacher, Eckhard. *Lukas als hellenistischer Schriftsteller: Studien zur Apostelgeschichte*. Göttingen: Vandenhoeck & Ruprecht, 1972.

Plummer, Alfred. *A Critical and Exegetical Commentary on the Gospel According to S. Luke*. 5th ed. ICC. Edinburgh: T & T Clark, 1922.

Porter, Stanley E. *The Paul of Acts*. WUNT 115. Tübingen: Mohr Siebeck, 1999.

————, and Dennis L. Stamps, editors. *The Rhetorical Interpretation of Scripture: Essays from the 1996 Malibu Conference*. JSNTSup180. Sheffield: Journal for the Study of the New Testament, 1999.

Price, Robert M. "The Evolution of the Pauline Canon." *Hervormde Teologiese Studies* 53 (1997): 36–67.

Rackham, R. B. *The Acts of the Apostles*. WC. London: Methuen, 1901.

Räisänen, Heikki. "Marcion and the Origins of Christian Anti-Judaism: A Reappraisal." In *Challenges to Biblical Interpretation: Collected Essays 1991–2000*, 191–205. BibInt 59. Leiden: Brill, 2001.

————. "The Redemption of Israel: A Salvation-Historical Problem in Luke-Acts." In *Luke-Acts: Scandinavian Perspectives*, 94–114. Edited by Petri Luomanen. Suomen Eksegeettisen Seuran julkaisuja 54. Göttingen: Vandenhoeck & Ruprecht, 1991.

Ravens, David. *Luke and the Restoration of Israel*. JSNTSup119. Sheffield: Sheffield Academic Press, 1995.

Refoulé, François "Le Discours de Pierre à l'Assemblée de Jérusalem." *RB* 100 (1993): 239–51.

Rice, George. "Western Non-Interpolations: A Defense of the Apostolate." In *Luke-Acts: New Perspectives from the Society of Biblical Literature Seminar*, 1–16. Edited by Charles H. Talbert. New York: Crossroad, 1984.

Ritschl, Albrecht. *Die Entstehung der altkatholischen Kirche: Eine kirchen- und dogmengeschichtliche Monographie*. 2d ed. Bonn: Adolph Marcus, 1857.

———. *Das Evangelium Marcions und das kanonische Evangelium des Lukas*. Tübingen: Osiander, 1846.

———. "Über den gegenwärtigen Stand der Kritik der synoptischen Evangelien." *Theologische Jahrbücher* 10 (1851): 480–538.

Robbins, Vernon K. *Exploring the Texture of Texts: A Guide to Socio-Rhetorical Interpretation*. Valley Forge, Pa.: Trinity Press International, 1996.

———. *The Tapestry of Early Christian Discourse: Rhetoric, Society, and Ideology*. New York: Routledge, 1996.

Roberts, Deborah H., Francis M. Dunn, and Don Fowler, editors. *Classical Closure: Reading the End in Greek and Latin Literature*. Princeton: Princeton University Press, 1997.

Robinson, John A. T. *Redating the New Testament*. Philadelphia: Westminster Press, 1976.

Roetzel, Calvin J. "Paul in the Second Century." In *The Cambridge Companion to St. Paul*, 227–41. Edited by James D. G. Dunn. Cambridge: Cambridge University Press, 2003.

Roukema, Riemer. "The Good Samaritan in Ancient Christianity." *VC* 58 (2004): 56–74.

Russell, Henry G. "Which Was Written First, Luke or Acts?" *HTR* 48 (1955): 167–74.

Sahlin, Harald. *Der Messias und Das Gottesvolk: Studien zur Protolukanischen Theologie*. Uppsala: Almquist & Wiksells, 1945.

Sanday, William. *The Gospels in the Second Century: An Examination of the Critical Part of a Work Entitled "Supernatural Religion."* London: Macmillan, 1876.

Sanders, E. P. *Paul and Palestinian Judaism: A Comparison of Patterns of Religion*. Philadelphia: Fortress Press, 1977.

Schmid, Ulrich. "How Can We Access Second Century Gospel Texts? The Cases of Marcion and Tatian." In *The New Testament Text in Early Christianity: Proceedings of the Lille Colloquium, July 2000*, 139–50. Edited by Christian-B. Amphoux and J. Keith Elliott. HTB. Lausanne: Editions du Zebre, 2003.

Schmidt, Daryl D. "Remembering Jesus: Assessing the Oral Evidence." Paper presented at the annual meeting of the Southwest Region of the SBL, Irving, Tex., March 13, 2005.

———. "Rhetorical Influences and Genre: Luke's Preface and the Rhetoric of Hellenistic Historiography." In *Luke and the Heritage of Israel: Luke's Narrative Claim upon Israel's Legacy*, 27–60. Edited by David P. Moessner. Luke the Interpreter of Israel 1. Harrisburg: Trinity Press International, 1999.

Schmithals, Walter. *The Theology of the First Christians*. Translated by O.C. Dean, Jr. Louisville: Westminster / John Knox, 1997.

Schneckenburger, Matthias. *Über den Zweck der Apostelgeschichte*. Bern: Fischer, 1841.

Schneider, Gerhard. *Die Apostelgeschichte. I. Teil*. HTKNT. Freiburg, Basel, Wien: Herder, 1980.

———. *Die Apostelgeschichte. II. Teil*. HTKNT. Freiburg, Basel, Wien: Herder, 1982.

Schoedel, William R. *Ignatius of Antioch: A Commentary on the Letters of Ignatius of Antioch.* Edited by Helmut Koester. Hermeneia Commentaries. Philadelphia: Fortress Press, 1985.

Schubert, Paul. "The Structure and Significance of Luke 24." In *Neutestamentliche Studien für Rudolf Bultmann zu seinem 70. Geburtstag am 20. August 1954*, 165–86. Edited by Walther Eltester. Berlin: Alfred Töpelmann, 1954.

Shellard, Barbara. *New Light on Luke: Its Purpose, Sources and Literary Context.* JSNTSup 215. London: Sheffield Academic Press, 2002.

Simon, Marcel. "The Apostolic Decree and Its Setting in the Ancient Church." *BJRL* 52 (1969): 437–60.

Soards, Marion L. *The Speeches in Acts: Their Content, Context, and Concerns.* Louisville: Westminster / John Knox, 1994.

Spencer, F. Scott. *Acts.* Sheffield: Sheffield Academic Press, 1997.

Squires, John T. *The Plan of God in Luke-Acts.* SNTSMS 76. Cambridge: Cambridge University Press, 1993.

Sterling, Gregory E. *Historiography and Self-Definition: Josephos, Luke-Acts and Apologetic Historiography.* NovTSup 64. Leiden: Brill, 1992.

———. "'Opening the Scriptures' The Legitimation of the Jewish Diaspora and the Early Christian Mission." In *Jesus and the Heritage of Israel: Luke's Narrative Claim upon Israel's Legacy*, 199–225. Edited by David P. Moessner. Luke the Interpreter of Israel 1. Harrisburg: Trinity Press International, 1999.

Steward-Sykes, Alistair. "Bread and Fish, Water and Wine: The Marcionite Menu and the Maintenance of Purity." In *Marcion und seine kirchengeschichtliche Wirkung: Vorträge der Internationalen Fachkonferenz zu Marcion, gehalten vom 15.–18. August 2001 in Mainz*, 207–20. Edited by Gerhard May and Katharina Greschat. TUGAL 150. Berlin and New York: Walter de Gruyter, 2002.

Streeter, B. H. *The Four Gospels: A Study of Origins.* London: Macmillan, 1924.

Talbert, Charles H. "An Anti-Gnostic Tendency in Lucan Christology." *NTS* 14 (1968): 259–71.

———. *Literary Patterns, Theological Themes and the Genre of Luke-Acts.* SBLMS 20. Missoula, Mont.: Scholars Press, 1974.

———. *Luke and the Gnostics.* Nashville: Abingdon Press, 1966.

———. "Once Again: The Gentile Mission in Luke-Acts." In *Der Treue Gottes Trauen: Beiträge zum Werk des Lukas für Gerhard Schneider*, 99–109. Edited by Claus Bussmann and Walter Radl. Freiburg, Basel, Wien: Herder, 1991.

———. "Promise and Fulfillment in Lucan Theology." In *Luke-Acts: New Perspectives from the Society of Biblical Literature Seminar*, 91–103. Edited by Charles H. Talbert. New York: Crossroad, 1984.

———. "Prophecies of Future Greatness: The Contribution of Greco-Roman Biographies to an Understanding of Luke 1:5–4:15." In *The Divine Helmsman: Studies on God's Control of Human Events, Presented to Lou H. Silberman*, 129–41. Edited by James L. Crenshaw and Samuel Sandmel. New York: KTAV Publishing House, 1980.

———. "The Redaction Critical Quest for Luke the Theologian." In *Jesus and Man's Hope*, vol. 1, 171–222. Edited by D. G. Buttrick. Pittsburgh: Pittsburgh Theological Seminary, 1970.

Tannehill, Robert C. "The Mission of Jesus According to Luke IV: 16–30." In *Jesus in Nazareth,* 51–75. Edited by Walther Eltester. Berlin: Walter de Gruyter, 1972.

———. *The Narrative Unity of Luke-Acts: A Literary Interpretation.* 2 vols. FF. Minneapolis: Fortress Press, 1986, 1990.

Taylor, Vincent. *Behind the Third Gospel: A Study of the Proto-Luke Hypothesis.* Oxford: Clarendon Press, 1926.

———. "Is the Proto-Luke Hypothesis Sound?" *JTS* 29 (1927–1928): 147–55.

Thompson, Richard P., and Thomas E. Phillips, editors. *Literary Studies in Luke-Acts: Essays in Honor of Joseph B. Tyson.* Macon, Ga.: Mercer University Press, 1998.

Tiede, David L. "'Glory to Thy People Israel': Luke-Acts and the Jews." In *Luke-Acts and the Jewish People: Eight Critical Perspectives,* 21–34. Edited by Joseph B. Tyson. Minneapolis: Augsburg, 1988.

Townsend, John T. "The Date of Luke-Acts." In *Luke-Acts: New Perspectives from the Society of Biblical Literature Seminar,* 47–62. Edited by Charles H. Talbert. New York: Crossroad, 1984.

Tyson, Joseph B. "Acts 6:1–7 and Dietary Regulations in Early Christianity." *PRSt* 10 (1983): 145–61.

———. "Conflict as a Literary Theme in the Gospel of Luke." In *New Synoptic Studies,* 303–27. Edited by William R. Farmer. Macon, Ga.: Mercer University Press, 1983.

———. *The Death of Jesus in Luke-Acts.* Columbia: University of South Carolina Press, 1986.

———. "The Gentile Mission and the Authority of Scripture in Acts." *NTS* 33 (1987): 619–31.

———. *Images of Judaism in Luke-Acts.* Columbia: University of South Carolina Press, 1992.

———, and Thomas R. W. Longstaff. *Synoptic Abstract.* Computer Bible 15. Wooster, Ohio: Biblical Research Associates, 1978.

Van Unnik, W. C. "Once More St. Luke's Prologue." *Neot* 7 (1973): 7–26.

Verheyden, Jozéf, editor. *The Unity of Luke-Acts.* BETL 142. Leuven: University Press, 1999.

Vielhauer, Philip. "Zum 'Paulinismus' der Apostelgeschichte." *EvT* 10 (1950–51): 1–15. Translated as "On the 'Paulinism' of Acts." In *Studies in Luke-Acts: Essays Presented in Honor of Paul Schubert,* 33–50. Edited by Leander E. Keck and J. Louis Martyn. Translated by William C. Robinson, Jr., and Victor P. Furnish. Nashville and New York: Abingdon Press, 1966.

Vinzent, Markus. "Der Schluss des Lukasevangelium bei Marcion." In *Marcion und seine kirchengeschichtliche Wirkung: Vorträge der Internationalen Fachkonferenz zu Marcion, gehalten vom 15.–18. August 2001 in Mainz,* 79–94. Edited by Gerhard May and Katharina Greschet. TUGAL 150. Berlin and New York: Walter de Gruyter, 2002.

Volckmar, Gustav. "Über das Lukas-Evangelium nach seinem Verhältniss zu Marcion und seinem dogmatischen Character, mit besonderer Beziehung auf die kritischen Untersuchungen F. Ch. Baur's und A. Ritschl's." *Theologische Jahrbücher* 9 (1850): 110–38; 185–235.

Volter, D. "Das angebliche Zeugnis Ephräms über das Fehlen von c. 1 und 2 im Texte des Lucas." *ZNW* 10 (1909): 177–80.

Walker, William O., Jr. "Acts and the Pauline Corpus Reconsidered." *JSNT* 24 (1985): 3–23.

———. "Acts and the Pauline Corpus Revisited: Peter's Speech at the Jerusalem Conference." In *Literary Studies in Luke-Acts: Essays in Honor of Joseph B. Tyson,* 77–86. Edited by Richard P. Thompson and Thomas E. Phillips. Macon, Ga.: Mercer University Press, 1998.

———. "Galatians 2:7b–8 as a Non-Pauline Interpolation." *CBQ* 65 (2003): 568–87.

Wasserberg, Günter. "Lk-Apg als Paulusapologie." In *The Unity of Luke-Acts,* 723–29. Edited by J. Verheyden. BETL 142. Leuven: Leuven University Press, 1999.

West, H. Philip, Jr. "A Primitive Version of Luke in the Composition of Matthew." *NTS* 14 (1967): 75–95.

Westcott, B. F., and F. J. A. Hort. *The New Testament in the Original Greek.* New York: Macmillan, 1957.

Wiefel, Wolfgang. *Das Evangelium nach Lukas.* THKNT 3. Berlin: Evangelische Verlagsanstalt, 1988.

Wilcox, Max. "Luke 2, 36-38: 'Anna Bat Phanuel, of the Tribe of Asher, a Prophetess ' A Study in Midrash in Material Special to Luke." In *The Four Gospels 1992: Festschrift Frans Neirynck,* vol. 2, 1571–1579. Edited by F. van Segbroeck et al. Leuven: University Press, 1992.

Williams, C. S. C. "The Date of Luke-Acts." *ExpTim* 64 (1952–1953): 283–84.

Williams, David S. "Reconsidering Marcion's Gospel." *JBL* 108 (1989): 477–96.

Wilshire, Leland E. "Was Canonical Luke Written in the Second Century?—A Continuing Discussion." *NTS* 20 (1974): 246–53.

Wilson, Stephen G. *The Gentiles and the Gentile Mission in Luke-Acts.* SNTSMS 23. Cambridge: Cambridge University Press, 1973.

———. *Luke and the Law.* SNTSMS 50. Cambridge: Cambridge University Press, 1983.

———. *Luke and the Pastoral Epistles.* London: SPCK, 1979.

———. "Marcion and the Jews." In *Anti-Judaism in Early Christianity,* vol. 2, 45–58. Edited by Peter Richardson, David Granskou, and Stephen G. Wilson. Studies in Christianity and Judaism 2. Waterloo, Ontario: Wilfred Laurier University Press, 1986.

Wilson, Walter T. "Urban Legends: Acts 10:1–11:18 and the Strategies of Greco-Roman Foundation Narratives." *JBL* 120 (2001): 77–99.

Windisch, Hans. "The Case Against the Tradition." In *The Beginnings of Christianity,* vol. 2, 298–348. Edited by F. J. Foakes Jackson and Kirsopp Lake. London: Macmillan, 1920–1933. Repr., Grand Rapids, Mich.: Baker Book House, 1979.

———. "Das Evangelium des Basilides." *ZNW* 7 (1906): 236–46.

Winter, Bruce W., editor. *The Book of Acts in its First Century Setting.* 5 vols. Grand Rapids: Wm. B. Eerdmans, 1993–1996.

Winter, Paul. "The Treatment of His Sources by the Third Evangelist in Luke XXI–XXIV." *ST* 8 (1954): 138–72.

Witherington, Ben, III. *The Acts of the Apostles: A Socio-Rhetorical Commentary.* Grand Rapids: Wm. B. Eerdmans, 1998.

Zwiep, A. W. "The Text of the Ascension Narratives (Luke 24:50–53; Acts 1:1–2, 9–11)." *NTS* 42 (1996): 219–44.

INDEX OF BIBLICAL AND
EARLY CHRISTIAN LITERATURE

INDEX OF MODERN AUTHORS

Martyn, J. Louis, 140n. 46, 150n. 38, 158n. 72, 170, 173–75, 179

Matson, Mark A., 175

Mattill, A. J., Jr., 3, 138n. 13, 175

May, Gerhard, 26, 143nn. 10–11, 145nn. 72, 74, 175, 178–79

Metzger, Bruce M., 107, 141n. 79, 149n. 23, 151n. 64, 160n. 103, 161n. 117, 162n. 128, 175

Minear, Paul S., 93, 158nn. 72–74, 175

Moessner, David P., 114, 163nn. 158–62, 168, 173, 175, 177–78

Mount, Christopher, 123–24, 147n. 5, 164nn. 5–8, 175

Nanos, Mark D., 67–68, 151nn. 58–59, 175

Neagoe, Alexander, 175

Neirynck, Frans, 161n. 117, 168, 170, 175–76, 180

Neusner, Jacob, 153n. 76, 169, 176

Oliver, H. H., 158n. 74, 176

O'Neill, J. C., 16, 141nn. 73–75, 176

Parker, Pierson, 176

Parsons, Mikeal C., 103–4, 108, 160n. 111, 161n. 112, 162n. 131, 176

Penner, Todd, 139n. 43, 149n. 19, 176

Pervo, Richard I., 14–15, 20–22, 137n. 1, 140nn. 62–66, 142nn. 100–101, 103–4, 106, 148n. 9, 176

Pesch, Rudolf, 176

Phillips, Thomas E., 142n. 89, 153n. 5, 168, 179–80

Plümacher, Eckhard, 176

Plummer, Alfred, 107–8, 157n. 49, 162nn. 129–30, 176

Porter, Stanley E., 66–67, 150nn. 53, 55–56, 176

Price, Robert M., 141n. 67, 176

Rackham, R. B., 149n. 20, 176

Räisänen, Heikki, 165n. 38, 176

Ravens, David, 176

Refoulé, François, 176

Rice, George, 161n. 117, 177

Ritschl, Albrecht, 5–6, 83–85, 138n. 20, 154nn. 26–27, 155n. 31, 177, 179

Robbins, Vernon K., 139n. 43, 177

Roberts, Deborah H., 140n. 61, 177

Robinson, John A. T., 1–3, 9, 11–14, 137n.1, 140nn. 54, 56, 177

Roetzel, Calvin J., 177

Roukema, Riemer, 156n. 48, 177

Russell, Henry G., 177

Sahlin, Harald, 158n. 62, 159n. 82, 177

Sanday, William, 177

Sanders, E. P., 67, 151n. 57, 177

Sanders, James A., 171

Sanderson, M. L., 172

Schmid, Ulrich, 163n. 175, 177

Schmidt, Daryl D., 160n. 107, 177

Schmithals, Walter, 177

Schneckenburger, Matthias, 3, 4, 62, 138n. 13, 142n. 90, 175, 177

Schneider, Gerhard, 169, 177, 178

Schoedel, William R., 82, 154n. 22, 178

Schubert, Paul, 16–17, 105–6, 108, 122, 140n. 46, 150n. 38, 158n. 72, 161nn. 119, 124, 162n. 133, 164n. 1, 170, 173–75, 178–79

Shellard, Barbara, 154n. 25, 161n. 115, 178

Simon, Marcel, 178

Soards, Marion L., 178

Spencer, F. Scott, 1, 137n. 5, 178

Squires, John T., 178

Stamps, Dennis L., 176

Sterling, Gregory E., 147n. 8, 148n. 11, 178

Steward-Sykes, Alistair, 35, 145nn. 74–75, 178

Streeter, Burnett Hillman, 91, 145n. 90, 157nn. 57–58, 178

Talbert, Charles H., 140n. 49, 149n. 25, 154n. 25, 158n. 62, 175–79

Tannehill, Robert C., 92, 122, 149n. 18, 153n. 74, 158nn. 64–65, 164n. 3, 179

Taylor, Vincent, 91, 157nn. 57, 59–60, 179

Thompson, Richard P., 142n. 89, 153n. 5, 168, 179, 180

Tiede, David L., 156n. 76, 179

Townsend, John T., 11, 140nn. 49–52, 154n. 25, 179

Tyson, Joseph B., 141n. 89, 153n. 5, 155nn. 40–41, 158nn. 67, 75–76, 159nn. 88–89, 168, 176, 179–80

www.ingramcontent.com/pod-product-compliance
Lightning Source LLC
Chambersburg PA
CBHW030306100426

42812CB00002B/589